VISION

Contributors: **Melvyn Bragg** • **Michael Craig-Martin** • **Christopher Frayling** • **Martin Harrison**

David Hockney • **Nicholas Serota** • **David Sylvester**

Introduction and commentaries by **Michael Raeburn**

VISION 50 years of British creativity

with 270 illustrations

 Thames & Hudson

ACKNOWLEDGMENTS

I am indebted for advice and information
to *Simonetta Fraquelli, Helen Hamlyn,
John Latham, Marilyn McCully,
Isabella McIntyre, Frank Newby,
Henry Newton Dunn, Cedric Price,
Sam Raeburn, Alan Sekers, Sue Timney.*

M.R.

First published in the United Kingdom in 1999 by
Thames & Hudson Ltd, 181A High Holborn,
London WC1V 7QX

British Library Cataloguing-in-Publication Data
A catalogue record for this book is available from
the British Library

ISBN 0-500-01906-1 (hardback)
ISBN 0-500-28166-1 (paperback)

Typeset in Scala Sans and Futura Bold

Printed and bound in the United Kingdom by
Jarrold Book Printing

CONTENTS

FOREWORD

IN THE 1980S, IT WAS FASHIONABLE TO ARGUE THAT one of the most distinctive features of British cultural history from the era of the Great Exhibition to the present day was its reaction *against* the twin traumas of industrialization and new technologies: Britain may have been the first to industrialize, the argument went, but we never really industrialized culturally. Sure, Mr Toad flirted with the new technologies of his day, but there was always a small army of Ratties, Moles and Badgers to bring him back to his senses. A French study of the 'Made in England' phenomenon, published in 1988, revealed that this tweedy image was if anything even stronger abroad: the list of the most significant British designs of the late twentieth century included Les Chaussures Church's, Le Burberry and of course Les Petites Culottes de Marks & Spencer.

Only two of the designs from that book appear in *Vision: 50 Years of British Creativity* – La Jaguar Type E and L'Austin Mini. For *Vision* tells a very different story, and a very timely one. Starting with the 1951 Festival of Britain, which popularized modern architecture and provided a 'tonic to the nation', and ending with Richard Rogers's Millennium Dome, it explores the interconnections between fine art, applied art (or 'craft' as it used to be called), design and communications during a half century which most certainly *has* adjusted to – and been highly stimulated by – the imagery and culture of the postmodern world. Cecil Beaton's coronation portrait of 1953 sits side by side with Francis Bacon's screaming pope; the 1977 Jubilee was also the year of the Sex Pistols' *Never Mind the Bollocks*. Some commentators have pinpointed the turning-point as being in the late 1970s, with the rise of the style press, industrial design in the post-black-box era and street fashion on the catwalk. But in fact it started over twenty years earlier, with the student magazine *Ark*, the discovery of Pop and the shift in the centre of gravity from Paris to New York. 'Don't do a still life with a bottle of wine and an apple', Peter Blake famously suggested, 'paint something that means something to *you*.'

These cultural explosions happened – almost simultaneously – at the Royal College of Art, where postgraduate art students worked in a design environment and postgraduate design students worked in an art environment. They still do. One of the themes of *Vision* is the key role that RCA staff and graduates have played, and continue to play, in the cultural history of Britain, from Lucienne Day's 'Calyx' fabrics and the Lion and Unicorn Pavilion of 1951 to Ron Arad's chairs, James Dyson's cyclonic vacuum cleaner and the Chapman brothers' bizarre mannequins of the late 1990s. Even the phrase 'Cool Britannia' originated thirty years ago (I'm slightly ashamed to admit) with a group of Royal College of Art graduates who formed themselves into the Bonzo Dog Doo-Dah Band. First time round, though, it was intended as a joke. The subjects covered in *Vision: 50 Years of British Creativity* are much more grown-up than transient labels like this. They amount to a fascinating and important cultural mosaic, full of surprising cross-references. Some analysts reckon that Britain's future, in the post-industrial world, may depend on our creativity and visual flair. Here's where it came from.

CHRISTOPHER FRAYLING

Rector, Royal College of Art

INTRODUCTION

ART, DESIGN, TASTE, FASHION, STYLE. Their cross-currents, mutual influences, conflicts and contradictions go to make up the vision of any society. In Britain the second half of the twentieth century has seen an unprecedentedly close relationship between these quite distinct concepts, as well as a profound questioning of the very definition of a 'work of art' and of the role of the 'artist'. However, while any attempt to establish a hierarchy of forms or media would be to misunderstand the ties between them, it could be argued that it is the role of the artist to respond to all the components of the visual environment, and that the quality of art in a community is a measure of its aesthetic health. It is with this in mind that the connecting threads between the work of artists, designers and architects are traced in these pages.

The appearance of Britain has undergone real changes in the past fifty years. Tall buildings, motor traffic and the roads to accommodate it have transformed cities and the means of communication between them; television has changed the way we see our surroundings and has introduced a visual awareness of the rest of the world, so that the exotic has become commonplace; information technology has affected every aspect of life, so that ways of working, tasks and functions in office and factory have little in common with those in the years just after World War II; while the culture of Britain has been greatly enriched by immigrants from all over the world. When looking at the work in art and design of earlier decades it is important to remember how much smaller the world was, how much more limited the technical resources, how much narrower the concept of British culture.

The works reproduced in this book can be identified as characteristically British, but the task of defining this Britishness is not a simple one. In 1955 Nikolaus Pevsner gave the Reith Lectures on a subject that had interested him since his student days in Germany in the 1920s, 'The Englishness of English Art'. The taste for pattern found in Anglo-Saxon art or the vaulting of English cathedrals, the feeling for landscape found in the English tradition of garden design as well as in Constable, Turner and Palmer, the unidealized treatment of scenes of everyday life of which Hogarth was a master, all these characteristics found some resonance during the 1950s, but it is harder to relate them to more recent developments; indeed, to define a national character on the basis of climate or other environmental or innate factors seems hardly respectable today. George Orwell in his essay on 'The English People' (1947) had suggested that a foreigner, 'new to England, but unprejudiced ... would find the salient characteristics of the English common people to be artistic insensibility, gentleness, respect for legality, suspicion of foreigners, sentimentality about animals, hypocrisy, exaggerated class distinctions, and an obsession with sport,' and he went on to point out that 'artists like supporters of extreme political parties were almost exclusively from the middle classes.' One of the underlying themes in the history of British art and design since that time has been a determination to break the middle-class monopoly on artistic activity and to create a visual culture to which ordinary people would not be insensible. However, Britishness in art during this period seems to consist of a collection of specific responses to political, social and cultural developments rather than the persistence of age-old national traits.

Taste was the weapon with which middle-class culture defended its artistic citadel. To destroy the accepted canons – which embraced art, architecture, decoration, and every aspect of design – offered the hope of opening the eyes of a far greater public to the visual world. Pop, Punk and postmodernism in their British incarnations all attacked the narrow 'highbrow' notion of good taste and did their best to undermine the institutions that supported it. The invigorating influence of popular culture on British art during this period is one of its most notable features. Another constant target was the 'artworld', a protean grouping of critics, administrators, educators, dealers, patrons and favoured artists, which seemed – at least to those who felt excluded from it – bent on promoting themselves and each other and preventing outsiders straying on to their territory. Today, looking back twenty or thirty years, this artworld seems then to have been astonishingly broadly based and open-minded, but suspicions of conspiracy gave powerful motivation to some of the more extreme forms of artistic activity which have had a clear influence on the work of artists today.

Art education has certainly been one of the conditioning factors of British art and design. Art schools in Britain have been organized very differently from those in continental Europe or in America. Even at the beginning of our period the curriculum was much less rigid than the traditional academy, and the teachers have always been, for the most part, practising artists and designers. Many of the most significant groups or movements have been associated with particular art schools: the Architectural Association, the Royal College of Art, St Martin's and Goldsmiths Colleges in London, and Corsham (Bath Academy of Art), Leeds, Newcastle and Glasgow Art Schools are among the many that, at different times, have had a defining effect on the course of British art, design and fashion. In particular, a series of initiatives, since the early fifties, has tried to bridge the gap between art and design, fine and applied art, leading in many instances to an artistic practice that makes such distinctions meaningless. Not that the system has met with universal approval. Many artists felt that they learned more from their fellow-pupils than from their teachers, and instruction from mediocre artists could have a stultifying effect. Nonetheless, the fact that art and design students could work with experienced artists did much to consolidate the developing characteristics of a specifically British visual culture.

A crisis of cultural identity went hand in hand with the crisis of national identity that followed World War II. In that war the USA, it seemed, had been the only ally for the British Empire against both fascism and communism, but once the war was over envy had intensified the disdain British intellectuals felt for American culture, and Paris appeared to be re-established as the artistic capital of a new Europe of which Britain, with its Empire falling away, needed to be a member. The opposing poles of Europe and America have continued to affect British culture just as they have Britain's political position, while the contribution made by ethnic artists from the Commonwealth has become increasingly significant in the past two decades. The wide range of British style has reflected the unique nature of Britain's role in the modern world.

Art outside the mainstream is a fascinating phenomenon, and studies devoted to other countries suggest that there are common features to cultures that might be called 'provincial' – though without any of the negative connotations so often attached to that term. While artists in such cultures are affected by new movements and tendencies occurring at the cutting edge, local tradition continues to play a much stronger role. The outstanding individuals who emerge cannot easily be classified into the familiar schools of western art — one could cite Henry Moore, Anthony Caro, Francis Bacon or Lucian Freud — and local variants of international movements, British Pop for example, retain a clearly distinct character. However, perhaps the most notable characteristic is a sense of aesthetic purpose which extends across the boundaries of forms and media, so that the same impulse can be found in music and performance, in the theatre and film, in photography and fashion, in architecture, industrial design and studio craft as in sculpture and painting.

This is not to suggest that everything can brought together in a single tendency — but that all the differences, often quite fierce, have a local point of reference. Throughout the period attempts have been made by both artists and official bodies to broaden the appreciation of art and design. The Arts Council, Council for Industrial Design and Crafts Council (each of which underwent some changes of name and function during the period) were public bodies set up both to improve standards and to offer support to artists and designers, while in the postwar years many local bodies were important patrons of public art. The development of local authority housing and the mass-production of furniture and cheap and stylish clothing also narrowed class differences and encouraged a far wider visual awareness of our environment. The Institute for Contemporary Arts (ICA) has been an indefatigable supporter of new ventures, while many commercial galleries have given indispensable support to a succession of artistic groups — from Helen Lessore's Beaux Arts Gallery and Victor Musgrave's Gallery One, through John Kasmin, Robert Fraser and Nigel Greenwood, to Angela Flowers, Robin Klassnik, and Nicholas Logsdail's Lisson Gallery.

Increasingly, however, the worlds of popular music, fashion and advertising attracted visual artists, who were concerned to avoid the charge of elitism that so often attached to the fine arts. There were also more radical attempts to produce work that would attack the values of the establishment and undermine the commercial structure of the artworld, whether in the 'anti-art' of Gustav Metzger and John Latham, the conceptual art of Victor Burgin and Art & Language, or the early environmental works of Richard Long and Barry Flanagan.

Each generation views the work of its predecessors in a fresh light. In 1956 Robyn Denny and Dick Smith wrote a polemical open letter to their RCA tutor John Minton: 'To your generation the thirties meant the Spanish Civil War; to us it means Astaire and Rogers. For you "today" suggests angry young men, rebels without causes; we believe in the dynamism of the times, where painting being inseparable from the whole is an exciting problem linked now more than ever with the whole world problem of communication and makes its essential contribution to the total which is knowledge.' The nineties view of the sixties is equally selective and nostalgic, although the postmodern era, with its delight in appropriation, may look with greater tolerance and sympathy on the art of the past than was the case with the more dogmatic age of modernism.

Vision is often at its most challenging in the creativity of young artists, and a high proportion of the works illustrated in this book were made or designed by artists under the age of forty. This should not be interpreted as a suggestion that British artists during these fifty years blazed briefly and then burned out; several artists whose work spans the whole period are today producing some of their finest work, but the spirit of the moment is often best captured with what is new. The commentaries written for the publishers' bold and imaginative selection of works are intended to give a thread of continuity by providing an account of the cultural context in which these works were made, rather than to make critical evaluations. Over the period social and economic conditions for artists have been extremely varied, but neither neglect and destitution nor affluence and approval are necessarily going to foster or inhibit good art. Final judgments must be left to later generations, but what is certain is that the works shown here can stand as representatives for the great wave of creative effort that has affected our vision in Britain, the way we perceive our world.

Immediately after the war Graham Sutherland was undoubtedly the British painter with the widest international reputation. As is so often the case with cultures outside the mainstream, landscape – representing the homeland – was the most consciously British art movement, and since artists in Britain looked back to Samuel Palmer and the English watercolour school for their models, they were known as the Neo-Romantics. In addition to Sutherland, they included John Piper, John Minton, Michael Ayrton, John Craxton, and others whose work appears in this book. Certainly the mood of their work was coloured by the pain generated by wartime experiences; in Sutherland's case the anguish was emphasized in the thorny angularity that characterized the natural forms in his drawings and paintings of landscape. It was also reflected in his religious paintings and, to some extent, in the remarkable series of portraits he began to paint in 1949. It was, in fact, an encounter with Somerset Maugham in the south of France (which Sutherland first visited in 1947, meeting Picasso and Matisse), that gave him the idea of applying his style to portraiture, and his sitters over the next thirty years included statesmen such as Konrad Adenauer and Winston Churchill and luminaries of the international world of culture, from Kenneth Clark and Douglas Cooper to Baron Elie de Rothschild and Prince Max Egon von Fürstenberg.

The Welsh painter Ceri Richards was also associated with the Neo-Romantics, especially in his wartime drawings of tin-plate workers, but he was strongly affected by the work of Picasso, which was exhibited in London (with that of Matisse) in 1945. The dionysiac quality of *Saudade* – one of a series of paintings on the theme of the rape of the Sabine women – also reflects a variety of other sources of inspiration, from the poetry of Dylan Thomas to the nostalgia of Darius Milhaud's orchestral suite *Saudades do Brasil*, from which the title is taken.

GRAHAM SUTHERLAND
Somerset Maugham, 1949

Opposite: **CERI RICHARDS**
Saudade, 1949

THE LATE 1940S HAD BEEN YEARS OF AUSTERITY – food and clothing were strictly rationed (so that the black-market 'spiv' was a stock figure of comedy), while the 'Utility' mark on furniture, clothes and other consumer goods was a joyless sign of practical 'good design'. Nevertheless, the welfare state, introduced by the postwar Labour government and carried on by its Conservative successor, brought about a real social revolution. The shared experiences of war had broken down many class distinctions, and novels such as John Braine's *Room at the Top* (1957) were shocking in their realistic depiction of working-class ambition as well as of sex. The decisive intervention of the United States in the war had aroused more resentment than gratitude, and middle-class Britain, unwilling to admit its economic and political dependence on the USA, envied American prosperity while deploring the corrupting influence of American popular culture.

Neo-Romanticism – described by the painter William Scott as 'the wave of the English watercolour nationalist romantic patriotic isolationist self-preservationist movement' – was evidently not the path to the long-term future, and during the 1950s British artists still looked principally to Europe for leadership. Familiar values were preserved by Matisse, Bonnard, Giacometti, Picasso (though there was much anxious Picasso-watching, to see what the artist would be up to next) and, among younger artists, Poliakoff and Richier: figuration underlay the abstract, formal qualities of their compositions, which were executed with a delight in the traditional materials of western painting and sculpture. Surrealism, which had touched Neo-Romanticism in the work of Moore and Hepworth, Sutherland, Trevelyan and Paul Nash (who had died in 1946), was renewed in the outsider art – *art brut* – of Jean Dubuffet and the quasi-automatic art of *tachisme*. The group of British painters who gathered at St Ives in Cornwall and the sculptors whose work the critic Herbert Read associated with the 'Geometry of Fear' strove to resolve the conflicts between abstraction and figuration, expression and formalism.

However, from 1952 a group of younger artists and critics began to meet informally at the new Institute for Contemporary Arts for lectures and discussions, which focused on the possibilities offered by American popular culture for the future of art and architecture. Eduardo Paolozzi showed the collages he had been making from American pulp magazines and comics there, and Reyner Banham discussed the urban culture of automobiles and consumption. The meetings of this Independent

Group led to an exhibition at the Whitechapel Art Gallery in 1956, entitled 'This is Tomorrow', opened by Robby the robot from *Forbidden Planet*. The exhibition, co-ordinated by the designer Theo Crosby, consisted of twelve different sections, each put together by artists, designers and architects in collaboration. Although Lawrence Alloway, the critic who represented this pro-American view, was to trace the origin of British Pop Art to the Independent Group and the 'TIT' exhibition, the impact on architecture was at least as important: contributors to the show included John Voelcker, the Smithsons (whose remarkable section incorporated work by Paolozzi and the photographer Nigel Henderson), Ernö Goldfinger (with Victor Pasmore and Helen Phillips), James Stirling and Colin St John Wilson (with Peter Carter, Robert Adams and Frank Newby).

The same year saw the first exhibition of American Abstract Expressionist art in London, although even as percipient a critic as David Sylvester remained unimpressed until the Tate showed a touring show of recent American art in 1959. A different ideal was proposed by the Marxist critic John Berger, who supported the 'New Realists' – although their leader, John Bratby, denied that their work had any social or political dimension. It was Sylvester, launching an assault on Berger, who named them the 'Kitchen Sink School'. Nevertheless, in the second half of the fifties many young artists saw their salvation in America: in 1956, at the time of the Suez crisis, when the political impotence of Britain became painfully clear, Robyn Denny, William Green and Richard Smith led a group of defiant students at the Royal College of Art, claiming the boxer Floyd Patterson and supersonic pilot Col. Peter Everest as their cultural heroes, rather than the 'Angry Young Men' of English literature Colin Wilson and John Osborne.

The American–European dialectic was mirrored in popular culture in the conflict between the Rockers, with their leather jackets and motorcycles, and the Mods, who favoured dandified Italian styles – Cecil Gee introduced flared trousers, bum-freezer jackets, striped shirts and pointed shoes in 1956 – and rode motor-scooters. The 'good' design promoted by the Council of Industrial Design had at first, like the new architecture, been founded on Bauhaus principles, but just as Le Corbusier became the presiding genius for progressive British architects, so Italian design – from Olivetti typewriters to Gio Ponti furniture – and Italian cinema set new standards, and the espresso coffee bar became a new style-symbol for youth.

A NEW-FOUND LAND

David Sylvester

IN THE FIRST HALF OF THE CENTURY BRITISH artists seeking guidance or example in work currently being done abroad expected to find it in Paris. And they constantly did so, not only in the art of Frenchmen such as Matisse, Braque, Bonnard, Derain and Léger, but also in that of immigrants such as Picasso, Miró, Mondrian, Ernst and Brancusi. They paid little attention to what was being done in other European centres and none at all to what went on in other continents. In their moments of revulsion against Paris they tended to withdraw into their native traditions, often unearthing forgotten aspects of them: hence, say, the cult of Samuel Palmer around the time of World War II.

In the years just after the war French art was still almost in full flow. Among the old masters, Matisse and Braque were achieving some of their best work ever; Picasso was relaxing between periods of doing the same. And there were three new stars: Giacometti in his second incarnation, Dubuffet and, for a time, de Staël. All three had some influence on British artists, de Staël most conspicuously, though this was an influence that mostly produced mere imitation. A more interesting kind of inspiration was that of Giacometti for William Turnbull and Eduardo Paolozzi, and later that of Dubuffet for Paolozzi. These two Scots sculptors born in the early 1920s were actually working in Paris in the late 1940s and were already showing their exceptional knack for sensing what was vibrant and relevant in the atmosphere of current art. And perhaps they were both back in London by 1950 because they were quick to sense that Paris was ceasing to generate its old excitement. (Yves Klein has been the only important French artist to appear thereafter: the genius that had once bred painters came to be channelled into cinema.) Paris as a city became increasingly touristic and with this lost its role as the capital of international bohemia.

Part of this transformation of Paris was the takeover of its culture by American culture: the history of the city over the second half of this century is epitomized by the steady replacement of bistrots by hamburger bars. That is to say, a wine culture has been ousted by the Coke culture. A wine culture has a slow tempo and cherishes things weathered by time; it accepts the presence of horseflies and bedbugs and likes its food to taste as if it had been grown, not made; it appreciates the unpredictable; it looks for the durable object and the unique object. The Coke culture has a serene confidence that, when you go into a drugstore or deli and order a tuna salad sandwich, you know exactly how it's going to taste; it doesn't care too much about the flavour that goes with its alcohol intake, provided there's plenty of ice; it accepts brand advertising everywhere and Muzak; it likes the expendable product and the standardized product.

Traditionally, cultivated Europeans, perhaps the English above all, looked down their noses at the country which bred this culture. The United States was seen as a country capable of building great bridges but not of painting great pictures. Even Marcel Duchamp, who escaped from Paris to settle in New York, may not have had his tongue entirely in his cheek when, writing as Richard Mutt, he said: 'The only works of art America has given are her plumbing and her bridges.' But that attitude was changing around the middle of the century. The European intelligentsia was ceasing to view the Coke culture as a subject for contempt and satire but as worthy of celebration – a somewhat amused, detached celebration at first, but increasingly meant.

It was Schwitters, working in England, who, a year or two before he died in 1948, became the first European to create art that delighted in the iconography of the Coke culture. Paolozzi, with his nose for the relevant, started doing the same thing two or three years later, also in collages (though he surely didn't yet know of those particular pieces by Schwitters). But with both of them this happened in marginal work, work done as comic relief. Richard Hamilton did it in his crucial work. True, his famous 1956 collage, *Just What is it that Makes Today's Homes so Different, so Appealing?*, was also marginal – it was designed as a poster – and has a good deal of jokey satire in it, but *Hommage à Chrysler Corp.* of 1957 and the similar paintings that followed it are a real celebration of the Coke culture. They remain amazing works in the way they combine a knowing but tender love of its advertising iconography, an eroticism which while sly also gets under our skin, and the aesthetic of a Cézanne watercolour.

So by the mid-fifties we were beginning to relish an American lifestyle but not yet its art styles. Except that Alan Davie had for some time been painting wild mythic canvases inspired by Pollock's art of the middle and late forties, paintings in which a splendid freedom and vehemence of gesture was allied to a Titianesque richness of colour. It was the old story for British artists: the integration of seasoned traditional qualities into the new.

Suddenly we were given a glimpse of current American painting at its highest level. A mixed show of gestural abstraction, American and European, called 'Opposing Forces', was held at the ICA, and it included Pollock's *One* of 1950: I say we had a glimpse in that the canvas was too big for the gallery and had to be hung partly rolled. In the meantime Lawrence Alloway's relentless and challenging advocacy of the glories of the New York School was mesmerizing us into a state of preparedness to cry out: 'O my America! my new-found land' (as John Donne put it in another context). We were well softened-up, then, to be K.O.'d by the exhibition of 'Modern Art in the United States' when it opened at the Tate in January 1956. All that was required was a straight left from Pollock's *Number One* of 1948, a right cross from Rothko's *Number 10* of 1950, and an uppercut from de Kooning's *Woman I* of 1950–52 – works, by the way, which were no more products of the Coke culture than of a wine culture. They came out of a whiskey culture.

Those pictures were hung in a room containing twenty-eight more-or-less Abstract Expressionist works by seventeen artists. It was the 'only section [of the exhibition] that is remembered today', says Margaret Garlake in her recent *New Art New World: British Art in Postwar Society*. She's right, but at the time something was communicated that is now taken for granted. This was the realization not only that American Abstract Expressionism was by far the most fertile movement in current art, but that it had not appeared from nowhere, that it had a background other than the wartime migration to the States of a number of European Surrealists. It had some good American art behind it. The surprise of the exhibition was the whole panorama of American art throughout the first half of the century. At the opening I ran into John Pope-Hennessy, deeply impressed by the Abstract Expressionist works but also impressed by the rest of the show. He said he thought it unlikely that an exhibition of British art covering the same period would be as good.

Looking back, the triumph of Abstract Expressionism was to be expected. The news was that a British mandarin could allow that the Americans might have been our betters for some time.

Although Hitchens was associated with the Neo-Romantics in the immediate prewar period, he moved to a remote woodland house in Sussex after his London house was bombed, developing his individual style in isolation. He was inspired by the effects of space and light produced by the tangled woodland, and his rich colours were applied with increasing freedom, while he worked almost always in a long narrow format, so as not to inhibit 'the natural flow of the horizontals'.

The English landscape tradition was also carried on in the work of many printmakers and book illustrators – woodcuts by Reynolds Stone and Blair Hughes-Stanton, lithographs by John Nash, John Piper, Edward Bawden and many other Neo-Romantics. Bawden's bold style was also well suited for large-scale compositions, and his prewar murals had included the display stand for the British pavilion at the Paris Exposition of 1937 (where Picasso's *Guernica* had been shown in the Spanish Republican pavilion designed by Mies van der Rohe). *The English Pub* was commissioned for the first-class lounge of the *SS Oronsay*, which sailed between Britain and Australia. Through an open screen of heraldic inn-signs it portrays a nostalgic view of old village England.

Carel Weight's meticulously painted views of suburban scenes with wintry trees and wide open skies are often disrupted by violence or, as here, by a sense of menace, as the man beneath the railway bridge stares at the two children. The feeling of anxiety, which would intensify as the grip of Cold War and the fear of the atom bomb intensified during the 1950s, was an underlying theme throughout the decade.

Left above: **IVON HITCHENS**
Woodland and Blue Distance, *c.* 1950

Above: **CAREL WEIGHT**
Going Home, 1950

Left: **EDWARD BAWDEN**
The English Pub, 1949–51

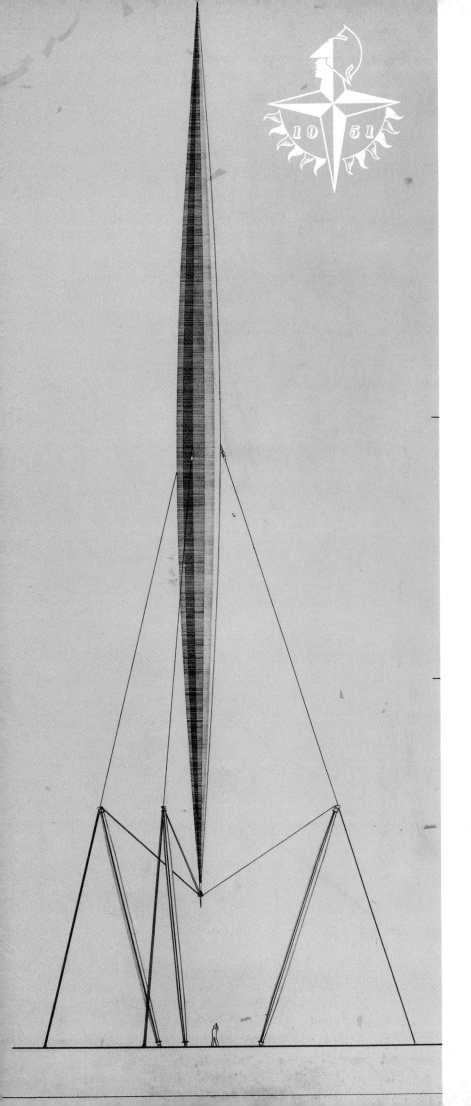

Left: **POWELL & MOYA WITH FELIX SAMUELY**
Skylon, 1951

Left (inset): **ABRAM GAMES**
Festival of Britain logo, 1951

Right: **BRIAN PEAKE**
Science Exhibition at the Science
Museum, London, 1951

The Festival of Britain on London's South Bank was intended to
celebrate the recovery of postwar Britain, and also to establish the
nation's place in the new world. Whereas the 'Great Exhibition of the
Industries of All Nations' in 1851 in the Crystal Palace had asserted
Britain's world leadership in manufacturing and the 'useful arts', the
new commemoration emphasized the civilizing role that the nation
could undertake in the world with a fusion of science, art and design.
Every artist and designer of note was called upon, from Henry Moore,
Ben Nicholson and Graham Sutherland to the *Punch* cartoonist
Rowland Emett, whose eccentric train was the centrepiece of the
Funfair in Battersea Park. The most memorable structures built for the
exhibition were Ralph Tubbs's Dome of Discovery, where the principal
exhibits were displayed, the symbolic Skylon, a collaboration between
the architects Powell & Moya and the engineer Felix Samuely, and the
one permanent building, the Royal Festival Hall, a new concert hall for
the capital designed by a team of London County Council architects,
of whom Leslie Martin and Peter Moro were the principal designers.
The overall design team for the Festival was led by Gerald Barry, Hugh
Casson, Misha Black and James Gardner.

Another part of the London exhibition, showing advances in
science, was installed in an annex to the Science Museum in South
Kensington. Models of atomic structures, cells as seen under
the microscope, and other natural forms offered inspiration to
designers in a wide variety of fields. At the same time, the utopian
vision of the better world that scientists could provide was poignantly
satirized in the Ealing Comedy *The Man in the White Suit*, in which
narrow business and labour interests, locked in traditional British
confrontation, were nonetheless allied in opposing scientific progress
– which, in any case, proved illusory.

ALEXANDER MACKENDRICK
The Man in the White Suit, 1951

Opposite left:
ERNEST RACE
Antelope chairs, 1951

Opposite right:
LUCIENNE DAY
Calyx, 1951
Textile design for Heal's

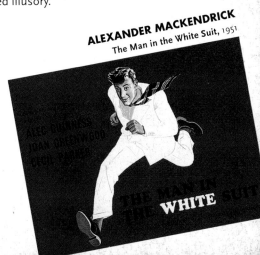

The organizers of the Festival of Britain wanted to celebrate British achievements in every field: not only did they commission '60 paintings for 51' from a wide range of artists, but many painters were also called on to provide decorations for the Festival's buildings. For the Regatta Restaurant, designed by Misha Black, Victor Pasmore executed a huge 'jazz' abstract ceramic mural (he is shown here painting the full-size maquette in the gymnasium of the Central School of Art), while there was a painting by John Tunnard in the interior and furnishings and tableware reflected the taste for atomic and crystalline structures.

Pasmore had been a co-founder of the prewar Euston Road School, a group of painters also including Coldstream and Gowing who used a quite conventional technique, in the tradition of Sickert, to paint pictures of unglamorous landscapes, nudes and scenes of ordinary life. However, in 1948 Pasmore experienced a conversion to abstraction, at first building patterns composed of geometric and linear elements like the Regatta Restaurant mural, then making constructions of flat planes, and later (into the 1980s) painting spare compositions of more organic forms. Pasmore also became an important educator, and his Basic Design course (merged with Richard Hamilton's similar plan) led to a revolution in the pattern of teaching in British art schools.

VICTOR PASMORE
At work on a mural for the Regatta Restaurant, South Bank, London, 1951

Stanley Spencer had evolved his individual hard-edged realism before the war, most notably in the religious scenes he painted acted out by ordinary people from his native village of Cookham. Visionary, if tinged with madness, his crowded paintings seem to prolong the narrative tradition of Victorian painting. As a war artist, Spencer was commissioned to do a series of works showing construction in the shipyards of Port Glasgow, and he later did a series of *Resurrection* paintings in the cemetery there. In this example the children doing acrobatics on the railings – about to be recorded by the artist with his portfolio – celebrate life after death.

Freud is the outstanding figure-painter of postwar Britain. Although in 1950 David Sylvester wrote that 'Lucian Freud has succeeded Dylan Thomas as the legendary figure of the younger generation', other critics in the same decade were uncomfortable with the obsessive realism with which he painted bodies: Pierre Rouve wrote of his 'progressive desertion from art to the unenviable position of a morbid Annigoni catering for the more sophisticated upper classes who have read Proust and have heard of Sade.' Herbert Read summed up the dilemma which his work presented for those who wanted their modernism clear-cut when he described Freud as 'the Ingres of existentialism'.

STANLEY SPENCER
The Glen, Port Glasgow, 1952

Opposite: **LUCIAN FREUD**
Girl With a White Dog, 1951–52

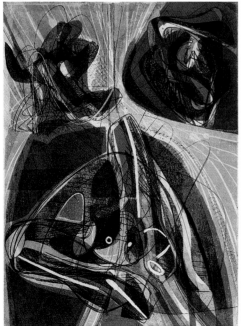

Above: **PETER LANYON**
Bojewyan Farms, 1951–52

Left:
STANLEY WILLIAM HAYTER
Night and Day, 1951–54

Opposite: **BERNARD MEADOWS**
Black Crab, 1952

The emergence of an outstanding group of younger British artists in the exhibition 'New Aspects of British Sculpture' at the Venice Biennale this year – Lynn Chadwick, Bernard Meadows, Kenneth Armitage, Reg Butler and Robert Adams, all in their thirties, and William Turnbull, Eduardo Paolozzi and Geoffrey Clarke, who were still in their twenties – signalled that the outstanding contributions made by Henry Moore and Barbara Hepworth were being carried on by the next generation. Meadows was one of those whose anguished forms led the critic Herbert Read to write of the 'Geometry of Fear', and several of them submitted work to the competition the following year for a monument to 'The Unknown Political Prisoner', won by a striking welded iron construction by Butler.

The attempt to marry the traditional subject-matter of art – landscape, figure and still life – with abstraction in a strongly emotional way was also characteristic of many painters and printmakers at this time. Peter Lanyon – a Cornishman, though only loosely associated with the painters who gathered at St Ives – painted powerful landscapes of his native land that reflected his Constructivist training with Ben Nicholson and Naum Gabo and a strong feeling for the natural world, transcending the picturesque of the Neo-Romantics. Hayter's cosmopolitan career had opened him to the art worlds of both Paris and New York, and the impact of Surrealism is evident in the evocation of the subconscious in his lines and forms.

1953

The boundaries between photography and fine art began to be blurred in the 1950s. Cecil Beaton used his prewar experience as a fashion and society photographer to compose an iconic state portrait of the new Queen in her coronation robes, while Bill Brandt, whose documentation of British life in the 1930s had made a most powerful impact, called on his early experience as an assistant to Man Ray in Paris for a series of monumental nudes, whose sculptural qualities were emphasized by the strong contrasts in his black-and-white prints.

Francis Bacon took photographs as a starting point for many of his paintings. He told David Sylvester: 'Through the photographic image I find myself beginning to wander into the image and unlock what I think of as its reality more than I can by looking at it.' In addition to the photographic sequences made by Eadweard Muybridge, which are implicit in many of his figure compositions, he made use of photos of friends, often found crumpled on the studio floor, for portraits. The series of popes, begun in 1951, had as its starting point photographs of Velázquez's portrait of Pope Innocent X, a work that obsessed Bacon, while the scream is derived from the scream of the nanny in Eisenstein's *Battleship Potemkin*. However, his pope was not intended as an image with a message and Bacon denied that it was his intention to create a tragic art: 'When you're outside tradition, as every artist is today, one can only want to record one's own feelings about certain situations as closely to one's own nervous system as one possibly can.'

CECIL BEATON
The Queen after her Coronation,
1953

Left: **BILL BRANDT**
Untitled Nude, 1953

Opposite: **FRANCIS BACON**
Study after Velázquez's Portrait of Pope Innocent X, 1953

The marriage of abstraction and figuration was rejected by a number of artists, who combined a more realist style with subject-matter related to the everyday life of ordinary people. L.S. Lowry had been painting his naive views of the industrial suburbs of Manchester since the 1920s, but he began to gain serious recognition as younger artists were choosing similar subject-matter for their own paintings. The 'New Realist' group formed by Derrick Greaves, Jack Smith (both born in Sheffield), Edward Middleditch and John Bratby was associated in the public mind with the new generation of realist novelists: John Wain's *Hurry On Down* established 'the Movement' in 1953, followed the next year by Kingsley Amis's *Lucky Jim*.

Hunstanton Secondary School in Norfolk, begun in 1949 and opened in 1954, was one of a small number of executed designs by the Smithsons. Although they are generally associated with the 'new brutalism' (named for the use of unadorned raw concrete, *beton brut*), this school is a rare British exercise in pure International Style, notable principally for the functional arrangement of rooms for group activity (on the ground floor) and classrooms filled with natural light (on the first floor), separated from the services, whose water tower is the building's striking vertical feature.

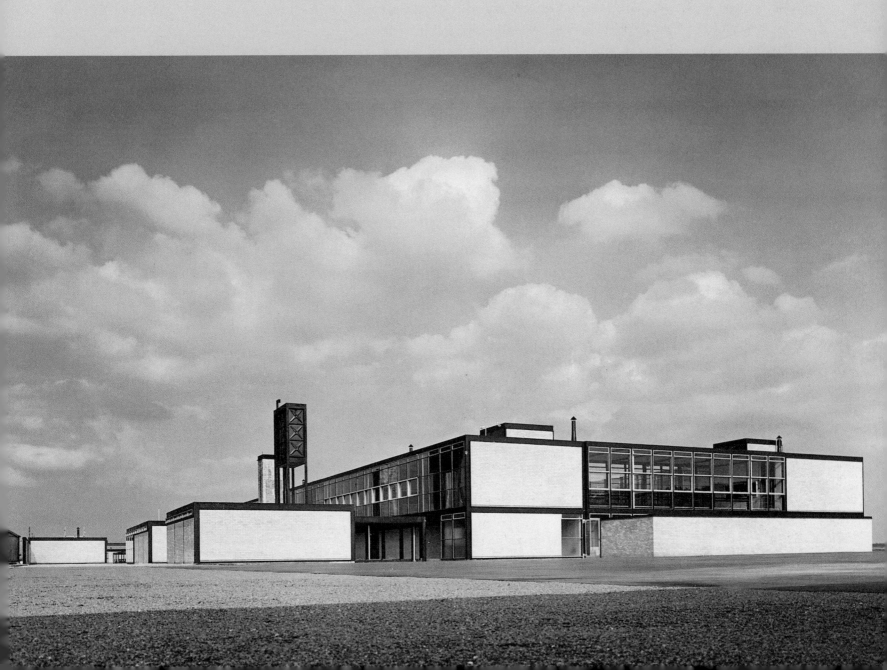

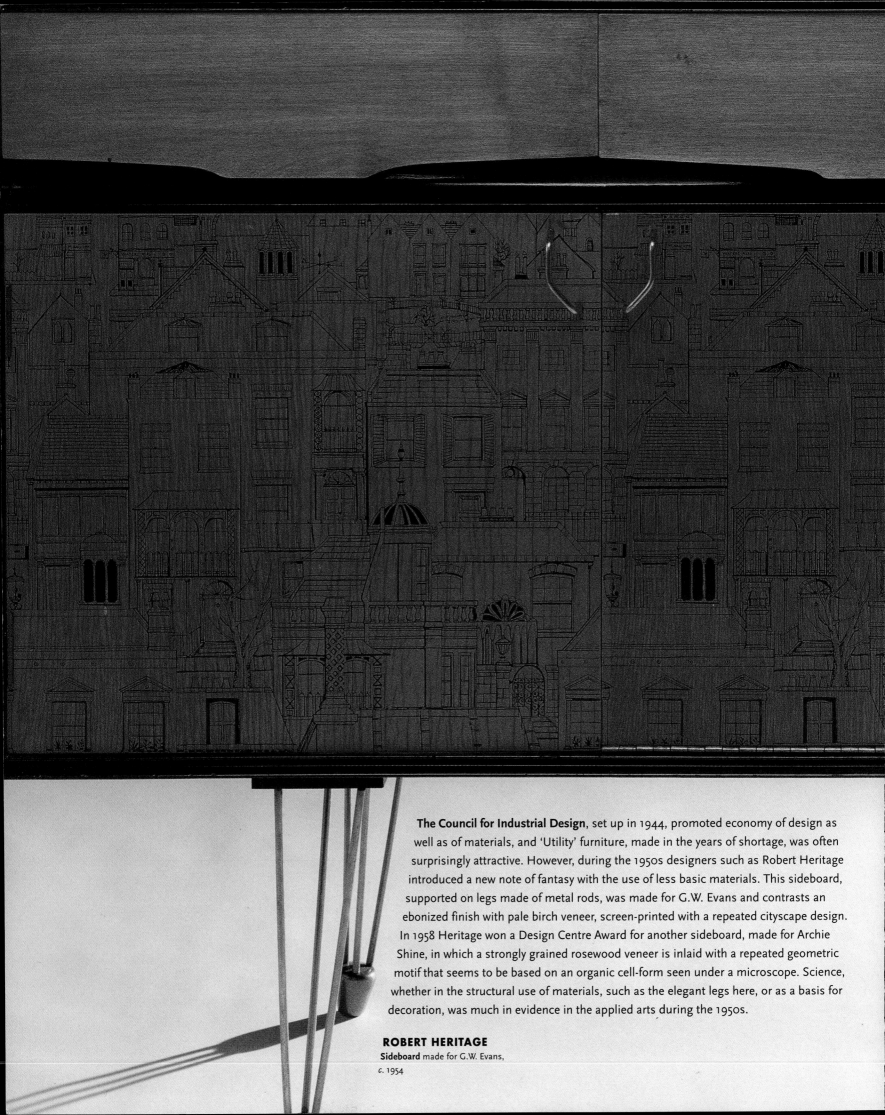

The Council for Industrial Design, set up in 1944, promoted economy of design as well as of materials, and 'Utility' furniture, made in the years of shortage, was often surprisingly attractive. However, during the 1950s designers such as Robert Heritage introduced a new note of fantasy with the use of less basic materials. This sideboard, supported on legs made of metal rods, was made for G.W. Evans and contrasts an ebonized finish with pale birch veneer, screen-printed with a repeated cityscape design. In 1958 Heritage won a Design Centre Award for another sideboard, made for Archie Shine, in which a strongly grained rosewood veneer is inlaid with a repeated geometric motif that seems to be based on an organic cell-form seen under a microscope. Science, whether in the structural use of materials, such as the elegant legs here, or as a basis for decoration, was much in evidence in the applied arts during the 1950s.

ROBERT HERITAGE
Sideboard made for G.W. Evans,
c. 1954

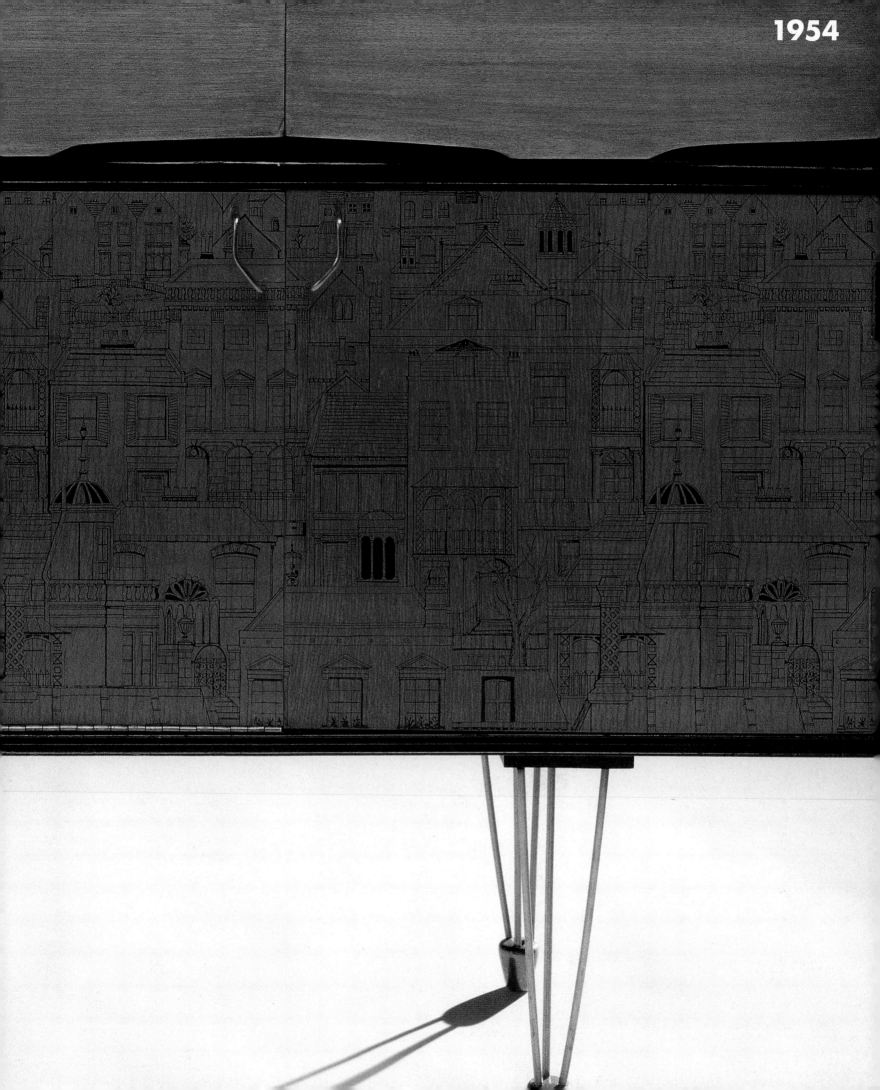

The outstanding development during the 1950s, on the itinerary of every foreign visitor interested in contemporary architecture, was the new Alton Estate at Roehampton, with its combination of high and low level buildings to accommodate some 9,500 people. It was an initiative of the London County Council, and the undulating site between Roehampton Lane and Richmond Park offered an opportunity, as Pevsner wrote, 'to apply Picturesque Principles to urban conditions'. Modernism had been adopted as the style of the welfare state, following the example of many socialist city and national governments in the 1930s, and it was the modernism of

Le Corbusier that was preferred to that of the German architects who had settled in the USA. Leslie Martin, chief architect to the LCC when the Roehampton scheme was initiated, wrote of Corb's 'Ville Contemporaine' that the plans were 'packed with ideas about housing, about environment, about traffic. They demonstrate that these things can be set down in measurable terms and can also be given a clear physical form.' Urban planning was one of the major concerns of local government, and it was undertaken with an optimism and certainty of purpose that often appears, with hindsight, to have been naive. Many urban tower blocks provided high-

density housing with no other amenities and were soon no better than the slum housing they had replaced, but projects like Roehampton, in its green setting, have proved at least a qualified success.

Another principle derived from Le Corbusier was the open-plan interior, which was introduced during the early 1950s. Examples by W.A. Allen and by the Architects Co-operative Partnership were illustrated in the *Daily Mail Ideal Home Book* for 1953–54, and a particularly successful one was the light-filled interior of the house at Farnley Hey designed by Peter Womersley.

Above: **LCC ARCHITECTS** Cadnam Point, Alton East Estate, Roehampton, 1951–55

PETER WOMERSLEY House at Farnley Hey, Yorkshire, 1953–55

In 1955 Nikolaus Pevsner gave his celebrated BBC Reith Lectures on 'The Englishness of English Art', and British artists at this time were earning increasing recognition on an international stage. Ben Nicholson (with Bacon, Freud and Butler) had been one of the British artists featured in the 1954 Venice Biennale, and in 1956 he was the first winner of the prestigious Guggenheim International Award. Since the 1930s, when he had been a member of the Abstraction-Création group in Paris and had become an admirer of Mondrian, Nicholson had been the leading abstract painter in Britain, and in the period since the war, working both at St Ives and in Italy, landscape – which Pevsner saw as a fundamental feature of English art – had played an increasingly important part in the structure of his compositions. Hepworth too, whose sculpture belonged to the European tradition of Brancusi, Arp, Picasso and Gabo, worked with natural materials that gave a local context to her serenely classical forms.

By contrast, the tortured metal surfaces of the figures by Lynn Chadwick (which were prizewinners at the 1956 Venice Biennale) exemplified the 'Geometry of Fear' and have a clear affinity with the 'new brutalism' of contemporary architecture. The same intensity of expression is found in the last paintings of David Bomberg, an artist who came to prominence with avant-garde work before World War I but had suffered decades of rejection and neglect as he developed his radical style, again chiefly through landscape painting. From 1945 to 1953 Bomberg taught at the Borough Polytechnic in London, where his courses were considered by the main art schools to constitute a danger to students. However, members of his 'Borough Bottega', notably Frank Auerbach and Leon Kossoff, built on his example to become some of the most distinguished and outward-looking British painters of the whole period.

Above: **LYNN CHADWICK**
Winged Figures, 1955

Left: **DAVID BOMBERG**
The Vigilante, 1955

Right:
BARBARA HEPWORTH
Curved Form (Delphi), 1955

Opposite:
BEN NICHOLSON
December 1955 (Night Façade), 1955

If France was still the dominant influence on women's fashion, Italian styles were taken as models not only for menswear but also for many home furnishings. The coffee bar, with its polished chrome espresso machine hissing steam, was a new feature of urban social life, and the blown-up engravings of Venice and Rome encouraged a taste for black-and-white decoration. Setting the style were the surreal classical decorations on the ceramics and furniture of Piero Fornasetti, stocked by all the smartest department stores, but Ridgway Potteries' 'Homemaker' service could be bought at Woolworth's, and it illustrates the fantasy with which furniture makers and designers were exaggerating many of the features of the 'organic' modernism of their models – with thin metal supports for furniture, bold geometric decoration and the ubiquitous houseplants, which were the dominant feature of Osbert Lancaster's 'Jungle-Jungle' style. Equally characteristic of ceramic design at this period were the patterns, many again with Italian echoes, produced for W.R. Midwinter by Jessie Tait ('Primavera' and 'Fantasy'), Hugh Casson ('Riviera' and 'Cannes'), Terence Conran, David Queensbury and other designers.

Above: **GEORGE HIM**
Schweppes advertisement, 1955–56

Left: **ENID SEENEY AND TOM ARNOLD**
'Homemaker' plate for Ridgway Potteries, 1955

Opposite: **JOHN CAVANAGH**
Slink Suit, 1955
Photo by **Norman Parkinson**

RICHARD HAMILTON
Just What is it that Makes Today's Homes
so Different, so Appealing?, 1956

Henry Moore was by now recognized throughout the world as the leading British artist of his time, and the public, monumental context of his new work was in some way an acknowledgment of this fact. He also began now to confront more heroic subjects – inspired perhaps by his visit to Greece in 1951: the great *King and Queen* (1952–53) and the antique warrior, which first appeared in his work in 1953. *The Fallen Warrior*, in which the hard limbs and shield seem to contrast a softness of flesh, reflects the sculptor's complete mastery of his chosen medium.

Vaughan was of the Neo-Romantic generation, but his monumental groups of male figures, which also owe much to classical tradition, are as anxiety-laden as the work of contemporary sculptors, evoking the spirit of Kafka, one of the presiding heroes of the literary world in postwar Britain.

Hamilton's little collage appeared in the catalogue of 'This is Tomorrow' and on one of the posters – though it was not part of the exhibit. Images were selected by Magda Cordell and Terry Hamilton from John McHale's collection of American magazines to reflect Hamilton's interests in 'man, woman, food, history and cinema', and Hamilton made the final choice and assemblage, very much in the spirit of McHale's own collages and those circulated by Paolozzi at the Independent Group's meetings. It has often been cited as a founding work of British Pop Art, but Hamilton wrote in the exhibition catalogue: 'We resist the kind of activity which is primarily concerned with the creation of style.... What is needed is not a definition of meaningful imagery but the development of our perceptive potentialities to accept and utilize the continual enrichment of visual material.'

KEITH VAUGHAN
Fourth Assembly of Figures, 1956

Below: **HENRY MOORE**
The Fallen Warrior, 1956–57

1957

BERNARD LEACH
Stoneware Pilgrim Bottle, *c.* 1957

Below: **WILLIAM SCOTT**
Orange Still Life with Figure, 1957

St Ives in the west of Cornwall became one of the most influential centres of art in 1950s Britain. Bernard and Janet Leach introduced a Japanese aesthetic to the practice of studio pottery, blending this with the functional English earthenware tradition, a tendency that would be most fully achieved in the work of Lucie Rie, the outstanding artist-craftsman of the whole period. A similar purity was an overriding characteristic of the – largely abstract – work of the group of artists who surrounded Ben Nicholson and Barbara Hepworth at their St Ives studio. Among the painters who regularly worked there were Bryan Wynter, Roger Hilton, Patrick Heron, Terry Frost, Alan Davie and William Scott. Scott, who regularly spent his summers at St Ives, had studied in Paris before the war and had also visited the USA in 1953, experiencing at first hand the works of the Abstract Expressionists – which were not exhibited as a group in London until 1956. The flattened forms of his still lifes and nudes animate the space of his richly painted canvases in a rare synthesis of European and American trends.

Two new prizes for artists were instituted in 1957: the John Moores prize for painting and the Design Council awards. Jack Smith's ironically titled *Creation and Crucifixion* was one of the most effective of his realist paintings, before he turned to a musically-derived abstraction. David Mellor's 'Pride' cutlery, designed for the Sheffield manufacturers Walker & Hall, was among the products recognized by the Design Council.

JACK SMITH
Creation and Crucifixion,
1957

DAVID MELLOR
'Pride' cutlery
for Walker & Hall, 1954
Winner of a Council of
Industrial Design award
in 1957

1958

Below: **JOHN BRATBY**
Four Lambrettas and Three Portraits of Janet Churchman, 1958

Right:
RICHARD STEVENS AND PETER RODD
'Chelsea' pendant lights, 1958
Glass fittings by Whitefriars Glass

Opposite:
EDUARDO PAOLOZZI
Japanese War God, 1958

Paolozzi translated the idea of collage into sculptural form, impressing a whole variety of objects into plaster, from which a sheet of wax casts could be made. These could be kept – like the cuttings he preserved from American pulp magazines – and incorporated into heads and figures, which combined the magic power of primitive figures with the rawness of Dubuffet's *art brut*.

John Bratby, who shared the British Guggenheim Award with Ben Nicholson this year, was the most prominent of the group of 'New Realists'. He disclaimed any social or political intent in his paintings, but their large scale, bold brushwork and vivid colours made them a powerful record of life in contemporary Britain: 'Art,' he wrote, 'expresses the feelings of its time'. This is one of a set of large canvases featuring art students; the Lambretta motor-scooters parked in the hallway were a Mod trademark.

The coloured glass lights owed more to the influence of Scandinavia, which was prominent in furniture, textiles, ceramics and glass in shops that specialized in modern interior design. Whitefriars Glass (see also p. 88), directed by William Wilson and with Geoffrey Baxter as its most innovative designer, produced many products with brightly coloured glass encased in a clear glass coating.

1959

The mannered sensuality of Armitage's figure sculptures maintained the dialogue between
figuration and abstraction within the framework of the twentieth-century European tradition
at a time when Paolozzi, Turnbull and Adams were making a more radical break with the past.
His gentler, more benign art never shared the anxiety of the figures by Chadwick and Turnbull.

Julian Trevelyan, one of the British artists to have taken part in Surrealist events and
exhibitions in London in the late 1930s, retained an element of fantasy in his postwar work,
but it contained no element of menace or subversion. His great sensitivity to line and texture
guided his activity increasingly towards printmaking.

The rule of taste was catered to by Heal's in London's Tottenham Court Road, where the
furniture Robert Heritage designed for Archie Shine, the pots of Hans Coper and Lucie Rie
and a collection of fabrics designed for the shop by leading artists, as well as many ordinary
household objects, encouraged a style of design that avoided the clichés so often associated
with the fifties: the fussiness of burgeoning neo-Victorian, the smart faux Regency of the
young David Hicks, or the palette-shaped tables with cocktail-stick legs associated with
the new TV culture.

JULIAN TREVELYAN
Portrait of the Bird that
Doesn't Exist, 1959

Right below:
HAROLD COHEN
Vineyard, 1959
Textile design for Heal's

Coventry was one of the cities hardest hit in the blitz, and the rebuilding of St Michael's church as a new cathedral after the war was intended as an act of reconciliation rather than triumph. The architect, Basil Spence, developed a contemporary style with many reminiscences of medieval church architecture (combining stone with pre-stressed concrete), and this Neo-Romantic approach was emphasized by the use of the tower and ruined walls of the old church as a forecourt to the new building, and by the design of its concrete rib vault being based on the gothic vault of the bombed building. The bronze group of the archangel Michael overcoming the devil was commissioned from Jacob Epstein, doyen of British sculptors, and it was to be his last work. The stained glass was commissioned from a number of artists: those in the Chapel of Unity, by Margaret Traherne, were donated by the German chancellor Konrad Adenauer, while the windows in the baptistery, made by Patrick Reyntiens, were designed by a leading Neo-Romantic painter, John Piper, who used an overall coordination of colour to unify the 198 panes of glass set into the stone wall; the font is made from a boulder found near Bethlehem. The outstanding feature of the interior is the tapestry portraying Christ in Glory that covers the sanctuary wall and was designed by Graham Sutherland. Coventry Cathedral became almost immediately one of the principal attractions for visitors to Britain, and it was here, on 30 May 1962, five days after the building was consecrated, that Benjamin Britten's *War Requiem*, a passionate plea for peace between all nations, was first performed.

Opposite: **BASIL SPENCE**
Exterior of Coventry Cathedral, 1954–62
with **JACOB EPSTEIN**'s sculpture
St Michael and Lucifer

Above: **GRAHAM SUTHERLAND**
Christ in Glory in the Tetramorph, 1955–61
Tapestry in Coventry Cathedral

Left: **JOHN PIPER AND
PATRICK REYNTIENS**
Stained-glass windows, 1958–62
in the baptistery of Coventry Cathedral
with the font in the foreground

1959

The great public projects – from the Festival of Britain to the reconstruction of bombed towns and cities – involved painters and sculptors as much as architects and engineers. New housing incorporated concrete reliefs; public sculpture was included in plans for new towns; enamel murals formed part of the designs for new factories and airports; and architects envisaged murals for many of their interiors. Among the younger artists to receive commissions were Gillian Ayres, who in 1957 executed large *tachiste* mural panels for the dining hall of South Hampstead School (for which Michael Greenwood was the architect), and Robyn Denny, whose *Great Big London* mural was designed for Austin Reed's store in Regent Street. Forty years later few of these works have survived: reliefs made by Pasmore and Coper have been sold; Ayres's murals have been destroyed; while Denny's is now in storage. Yet at the time it was prophetic of the sudden flowering of London as a centre of popular culture in the 1960s, the swinging city of music and fashion.

ROBYN DENNY
Great Big London, 1959
Mural for the Austin Reed store,
Regent Street, London

JUST AS DENNY AND SMITH EXPLAINED to John Minton that 'to your generation the thirties meant the Spanish Civil War; to us it means Astaire and Rogers,' so for the young generation of the nineties the sixties means the Beatles and Swinging London, although the atmosphere at the time was overshadowed by the unfreezing of the Cold War, the threat of nuclear bombs and the assassination of J.F. Kennedy. This violence was reflected in the radical new forms of artistic practice that were explored in an attempt to redefine the artist's role in society.

'The situation in London now' was the theme of an exhibition organized by Lawrence Alloway in September 1960 (followed by two sequels in 1961–63), which included paintings by a group of younger painters in thrall to American Abstract Expressionism. The works selected had to be abstract and over 30 square feet in size. Parallel to this new movement in painting was a revolution in sculpture brought about by Anthony Caro and his pupils at St Martin's School of Art, which first came to public notice in the 'New Generation' exhibition at the Whitechapel Gallery in 1965. The 'New Generation' sculptors abandoned the modelling and carving tradition of Henry Moore (to whom Caro, among others, had been an assistant) and ignored the 'Geometry of Fear', taking as their models the American artists David Smith and Kenneth Noland. By standing on the floor with no pedestals the works made the same direct impact on the spectator that the 'Situation' paintings had done, and their physical qualities were emphasized by the use of industrial materials – sheet steel, metal pipes or netting, fibreglass and acrylic plastic, often brightly coloured with commercial gloss paints.

Architecture, too, underwent a release from conventional notions of structure and planning, though few of the most visionary projects went beyond the planning stage, and many were clearly futuristic. The most significant was certainly the Fun Palace, projected around 1960 by Joan Littlewood, founder of Theatre Workshop, and planned by Cedric Price. This was designed as a multi-functional entertainment and community arts centre for East London, unenclosed and with no monumental architectural features, but made up of a flexible group of independent units, which could be rearranged by means of cranes running on overhead gantries. The intention – to plan for the unknowable – and the form were acknowledged by Richard Rogers as an inspiration for his later Centre Pompidou in Paris.

The new generation of artists were determined not only to make their works engage directly with their audience but also to enlarge this audience to include a far wider sector of the community, breaking down the barriers that middle-class taste had created. Their godfather was Marcel Duchamp, whose retrospective at the Tate in 1966 included the reconstruction of his *Large Glass* by Richard Hamilton. Duchamp lent historical weight to the current challenge to the capitalist art-market system and the assault on good taste mounted by the Pop Art movement. Subversion and liberation were the aim of many other initiatives. As early as 1961 Gustav Metzger demonstrated his Auto-Destructive Art as a protest against the arms race: he used acid to attack nylon sheeting, creating rapidly changing shapes until it was destroyed, so that the work was simultaneously auto-creative and auto-destructive. In the mid-decade John and Barbara Latham started the Artist Placement Group, through which artists would work in industrial concerns, not to create 'works of art' but to make work itself into art as a radical alternative to the production/profit structure of industry.

Towards the end of the decade the pop music industry, with its associated drug culture, began to offer an alternative system of patronage for underground and experimental art projects and to provide the public, in the words of *Oz* editor Richard Neville, 'with centres for fun, new culture and madness'. These included the Arts Laboratory set up by Jim Haynes in 1967 in an old warehouse in Drury Lane with a theatre, cinema, art gallery and workshop, the Middle Earth Club, and John Dunbar's Indica bookshop and gallery, which sold *International Times* and *Oz* and showed works by the Boyles and by kinetic artists. The police, in search of obscenity, were frequent intruders onto the art scene, and in 1966 – the year of Peter Brook's *Marat-Sade* production at the Royal Court theatre – closed a Jim Dine exhibition at Robert Fraser's gallery and arrested Gustav Metzger for his part in a 'Destruction in Art' happening which involved a dead sheep and a photograph of a man's penis projected on to the walls and the performers. In May 1968, following the student revolution in Paris, there were sit-ins at Hornsey and Guildford art schools; the students demanded that their teachers should acknowledge that art had changed and that the artist now had a new role to play in society.

THE ARTIST'S PROGRESS

David Hockney

IN 1957 I APPLIED TO THE ROYAL COLLEGE
of Art and the Slade with life drawings, life paintings and
figure compositions. I was accepted at the Royal College
painting department and went there in 1959. R.B. Kitaj,
a little older, an American in England on the GI Bill, was in
the same year and so were Allen Jones, Derek Boshier and
Peter Phillips.

Immediately after I started at the Royal College I realized
that there were two groups of students there: a traditional
group who carried on as they had done in art school, doing
still life, life painting, figure composition; and then what
I thought of as the more adventurous, lively students who
were more involved in the art of their time. They were doing
big Abstract Expressionist paintings on hardboard.

In fact what these more progressive students were doing
was a kind of pastiche derived from de Staël and other School
of Paris semi-abstractionists, Dubuffet, and de Kooning's
brand of lyrical abstraction. It was a kind of abstraction seen
in reproductions in art magazines and based on half-digested
and misunderstood influences of the New York School and
Abstract Expressionism. My training at the Bradford School
of Art had been traditional. So when I arrived at the Royal
College I didn't know what to do.

In 1956 there'd been a big exhibition at the Tate of
American Abstract Expressionists and Bryan Robertson had
done shows at the Whitechapel of Pollock and in 1961 Rothko.
Young students realized then that American painting was
more interesting than French painting of that time. I tried
my hand at it with pictures that were based on a mixture of
Alan Davie cum Jackson Pollock cum Roger Hilton. The first

student I got to know there was Kitaj. His painting
straightaway fascinated me. He was a great influence
on me and on a lot of people.

Kitaj was slowly doing these strange pictures and
we talked. He was doing pictures that were neither
figurative nor abstract in some ways, or both, refusing
to submit to a split between the two, as any good artist
would, pictures that reflected his own interests and were
idiosyncratic. He'd say to me, Why don't you paint subjects
you are interested in? But I still hadn't the nerve to paint
figure pictures; the idea of figure pictures was considered
really anti-modern, so my solution was to begin using
words, writing on the pictures. And then Ron said, Yes,
that's much more interesting. Then Richard Hamilton
visited the college. He saw that what some of us were doing
was really new and recognized it instantly as something
interesting. That's also when, among others who came to
look, I met Joe Tilson and Peter Blake, who were also doing
figure pictures in a new way.

At the 1961 'Young Contemporaries' exhibition at the
Whitechapel there was quite a stir created by Royal College
of Art students like Peter Phillips, Allen Jones, Derek Boshier,
Kitaj and Patrick Caulfield among others. Suddenly, at last,
there were paintings you could talk about again, instead of
just abstract formalist pictures. There was subject matter and
the idea of painting things from ordinary life, and that was
when everything was called 'pop art'.

Kitaj and I couldn't understand why the figure had to
disappear from modern art. What about Matisse and Picasso?
Of course the figure had not disappeared if you looked at it

another way, not at all. It was only a certain branch of the art world that said it had. One forgets how small an art world is or how many art worlds there are. I love the remark de Kooning made when Clement Greenberg said that it was not possible for a serious artist to paint a portrait now. De Kooning's reply was, Yes, and it's not possible not to.

What could Greenberg's statement mean? That the only portraits we could see were photographs, that is, seeing only in one particular way? This would mean that no future generation would be interested in making a depiction of a face in a way other than the photographic convention of the keyhole view-point way. But the fact is that we do have this very deep urge to depict – and depiction can't be left to the photographic way of seeing.

Kitaj and I would talk about this for a long time. And in 1976 the Arts Council had an exhibition which started at the Hayward Gallery and then toured the country, selected by Kitaj, called 'The Human Clay'. (I liked to quote the line from W.H. Auden's poem 'Letter to Lord Byron', 'To me Art's subject is the human clay'.) Among the thirty-five artists Kitaj showed were Michael Andrews, Frank Auerbach, Francis Bacon, Peter Blake, Patrick Caulfield, William Coldstream, Peter de Francia, Lucian Freud, Richard Hamilton, Allen Jones, Leon Kossoff, Leonard McComb, Philip Rawson and Euan Uglow. In his catalogue introduction Kitaj wrote: 'I thought I would try to look to what I believe to be the most basic art-idea, from which so much great art has come. I was looking mostly for pictures of the single human form....' And it was in the same text that he identified the possibility of a School of London. He wrote, 'There are artistic personalities in this small island more unique and strong and I think numerous than anywhere in the world, outside America's jolting artistic vigour.... If some of the strange and fascinating personalities you may encounter here were given a fraction of the internationalist attention and encouragement reserved in this barren time for provincial and orthodox vanguardism, a School of London might become even more real than the one I have constructed in my head. A School of real London in England, in Europe ... with potent art lessons for foreigners emerging from this odd, old, put upon, very singular place.'

The New Review printed a conversation between Kitaj and me in January–February 1977. In it I remarked that I was only really interested in the art of making still pictures because they're much more, infinitely more remarkable than moving images. It also seemed to me then, as it does now, that photography had been overrated. To make a picture with a camera, in the conventional way, is simply one way of making a picture, no more real than making it in your imagination and by your hand, indeed much less so. Greenberg's view of the emergence of abstract art is directly related to the mistaken belief that photography is true, realistic depiction. But the photograph can only be thought to be more 'real' than the drawing if it is seen not as an interpretation but as an objective record. The moment you think the photograph can be made differently, can be altered, all issues about the fixed view-point disappear and it becomes more interesting. If the view-point presented in a photograph is not fixed, everything becomes more interesting. The way we see the world is constantly changing. The idea that we have reached an 'objective' description of the world in a photograph is naive. I think this is rapidly changing, it has changed, and the false belief in the veracity of the photograph has been lost, revealed to be what it has always been, a convention. The photograph is an abstraction which we read as a record of reality; it is the same with television, with all photographic images. But there are richer, more complex and, yes, more true ways of depicting reality.

**DENYS LASDUN
AND PARTNERS**
Keeling House, Claredale Road,
London, 1955–60

Right: **DENYS LASDUN
AND PARTNERS**
Luxury flats, 26 St James's Place,
London, 1959–60

Opposite: **GORDON HOUSE**
Diagonal, 1960

The intention of the 'Situation' painters was to create a new relationship between painted space and the spectator, in which the painting became part of the environment and could not be viewed as a whole simply by a movement of the eyes. House, as a typographer and graphic designer (he produced an elegant 'group identity' for the 'Situation' exhibitions), saw his paintings in the context of the urban environment, likening his works to London Transport signs or the advertising messages on hoardings.

London was rapidly being rebuilt, and a variety of solutions was offered for the design of high-density high-rise buildings to replace old slums. Lasdun's fourteen-storey cluster tower in Bethnal Green had four angled wings with a central tower housing services; the fact that each wing had only two apartments per entry floor offered a greater sense of individuality than was the case in most tower-blocks. The elegant interrelationship of glazing with flat wall and balcony panels also characterized the luxury flats Lasdun built overlooking Green Park and facing the Palladian Spencer House – a startlingly modern structure for this prime site. Lasdun wrote that the harmonious relationship between the two buildings was achieved 'by each having a common concern with what is authentic in architecture of any time'.

ALAN DAVIE
Cornucopia, 1960

Below: **ELISABETH FRINK**
Harbinger Bird III, 1960

Although by now the mainstream of art had moved from Paris to New York, many British artists continued to produce striking work within a European context. The technique of assemblage, pioneered by Picasso before World War I, not only introduced materials that ran directly counter to the fine art practices still advocated in art schools but also allowed several layers of meaning to be incorporated in a work. George Fullard, who had been wounded severely during the war, produced a series of works, assembled from elements of scrap, on military themes treated with biting irony.

Elisabeth Frink, who had studied with Meadows, intensified the menace of her bird-figures with the crumpled skin of the bronze – reminiscent of the sculpture of Germaine Richier – and the sense of movement given by their top-heavy forms. The Scotsman Alan Davie filled his vivid canvases with a wealth of symbolic material, both ritualistic and – very much in the spirit of the times – Freudian. Davie was associated with the St Ives group, whose abstraction remained tied to figure, object or landscape, although his encounters with the American Abstract Expressionists and with primitive art left a clear impression on his work. His improvisatory method was analogous to his musical procedure as a jazz musician, and he saw his art as an attempt at 'the evocation of the inexpressible'.

Peter Blake had chosen the material of mass culture from his student days, and in Coronation year, just released from national service, he had done a little celebratory painting with several popular images, including a wall proclaiming 'Kilroy was here', while other, more nostalgic images featured children reading comics. His self-portrait holding an Elvis fan magazine shows a characteristic independence from the mainstream of Pop, with its typically English setting and its relish in the handling of materials. Although Blake is often included among the British Pop artists, there is a directness to his technique and expression and a lack of irony that has given his work as much independence of trends and movements as that of Hockney or Hodgkin.

The young generation of Pop artists made their mark at the 'Young Contemporaries' exhibition in 1961: the artists, mostly students or recent graduates from the RCA, included R.B. Kitaj, Peter Phillips, Allen Jones, Derek Boshier and Patrick Caulfield. Phillips was president of the group this year, and his *For Men Only* is an archetypal English Pop image, with the emblems, the pin-ups, the images of Marilyn Monroe and Brigitte Bardot, and the canvas divided like a games board. Boshier adopted more mundane objects for representation – toothpaste tubes, airmail letters, matchboxes – marking his canvases with tentative graphic figures and other forms.

The erotic lure of the automobile had been celebrated by Richard Hamilton in one of his earliest Pop pictures, *Hommage à Chrysler Corp.* (1957), in which a girl caresses a sleek American car. The E-type Jaguar was the first British car produced for the new 'affluent society' to earn the status of mechanical sex symbol.

Above:
**MALCOLM SAYER
AND WILLIAM HEYNES**
E-Type Jaguar, 1961

Right above:
PETER PHILLIPS
**For Men Only, Starring MM
and BB,** 1961

Right: **DEREK BOSHIER**
Airmail Letter, 1961

Opposite: **PETER BLAKE**
Self-Portrait with Badges,
1961 (detail)

HOWARD HODGKIN
Portrait of Mr and Mrs James Tower, 1962

Opposite: **DAVID HOCKNEY**
The Cruel Elephant, 1962

Howard Hodgkin's work, from the outset, had a quality of intimacy which set it apart from large-scale 'Situation' abstraction or the Pop artists' critical exploitation of mass culture. In the double portrait of the potter James Tower and his wife, Hodgkin places his sitters in a plain interior setting, simplifying the subject-matter but relishing the colour and quality of the paint.

David Hockney was a contemporary of the Pop artists at the RCA (he had shown some paintings based on a Typhoo tea carton in the 1961 'Young Contemporaries'), but his work generally drew on a very different range of references. He made a constant practice of drawing but felt inhibited at this point from including figures in his canvases – something that 'was considered really anti-modern'; instead he included words: 'And when you put a word on a painting, it has a similar effect in a way to a figure; it's a little bit of human thing that you immediately read; it's not just paint.' As a result, Hockney's early paintings have a pronounced graphic and narrative quality, like the prints on literary themes he was doing at the same period, and it was as a graphic artist that he first came to public notice.

THE CRUEL ELEPHANT

1962

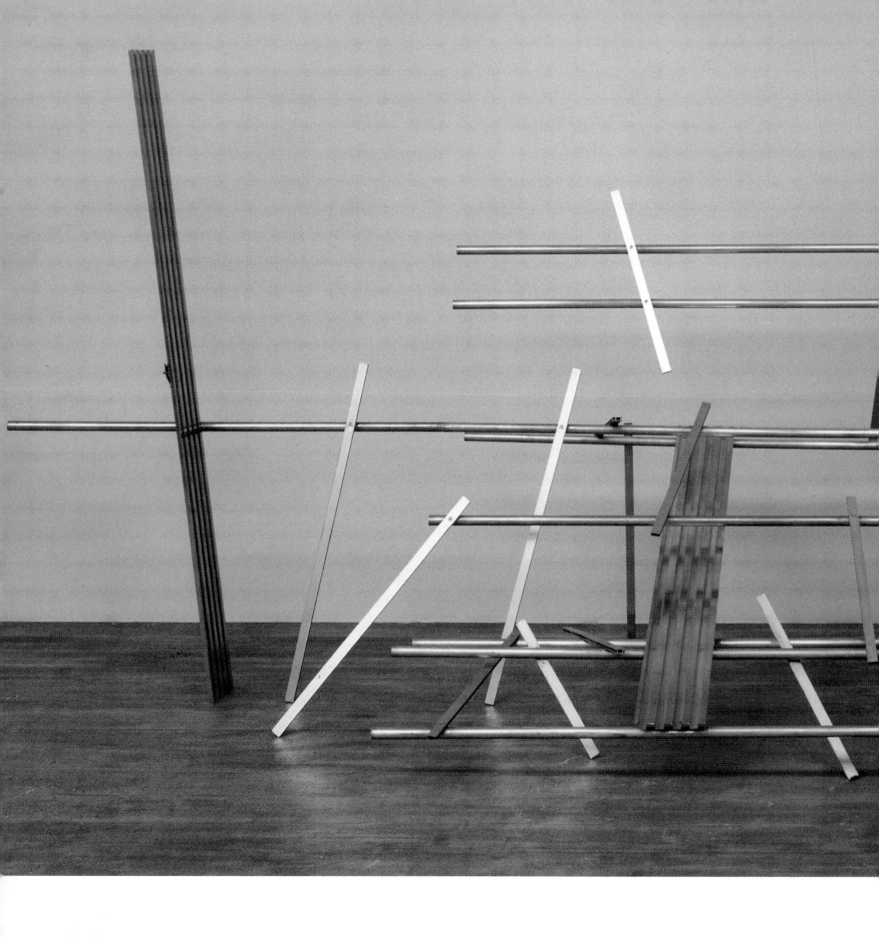

If Eduardo Paolozzi developed the most exciting figure sculpture derived from the sources that were inspiring the Pop painters, it was Anthony Caro who was the most innovative of the abstract sculptors. Like the 'Situation' painters, Caro had turned to America, and it was the work of Kenneth Noland and the great sculptor David Smith that gave him a new direction, leading him to abandon the figure sculpture modelled in clay or plaster and cast in bronze that he had done during the 1950s. His new work, made of welded industrially processed metal elements and often coloured, articulates space in a quite painterly way. The delicate intersections of *Hopscotch* imply movement – the ritualized dancing movements of the children's game carried out within a geometrical pattern chalked on the pavement. Like the abstract painters, Caro wanted his work to form part of the spectator's environment, and his sculptures stand directly on the floor, with no distancing plinth. 'I realized,' he said, 'that if you can make the floor act as part of the sculpture and not just [as a] base, the pieces will float.'

Robert Welch, whose fellow-students in the metalwork department of the RCA had included David Mellor and Gerald Benney, was notable especially for his use of stainless steel in services designed for industrial production that followed the contemporary taste for Scandinavian style, although his work in silver included a seven-rod candelabrum inspired by Jackson Pollock.

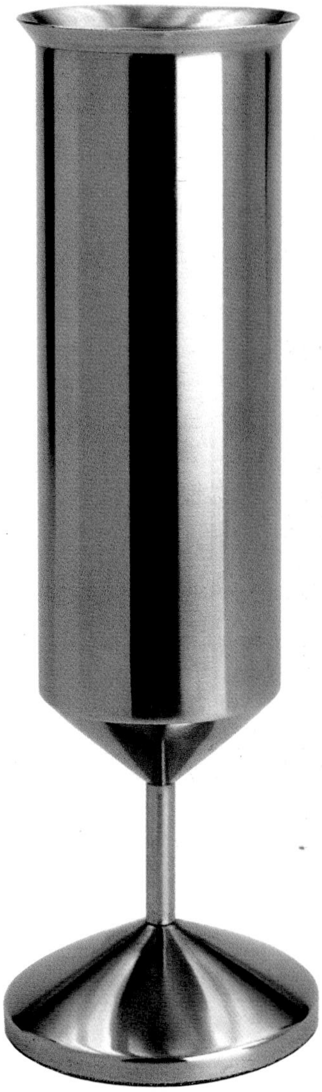

ANTHONY CARO
Hopscotch, 1962

Right: **ROBERT WELCH**
Vase from the 'Alveston' range
designed for Old Hall, 1962

Caro was the leader of a group of abstract sculptors associated with the St Martin's School of Art in London as teachers or students: Phillip King, David Annesley, Michael Bolus, Tim Scott and Isaac Witkin were all Caro students. King's work, using fibreglass and polyester as well as metal, is notable for its colour, which the sculptor saw as inherent in his material rather than a coating applied. His use of a range of pinks, in defiance of sculptural convention, imparts an air of playful sexuality to forms that are firmly grounded, like architecture.

Roger Hilton belonged to an older generation: he had studied in Paris before the war and, since the mid-1950s, had visited Cornwall, where he eventually settled, aligning himself with the St Ives group of painters, whose abstraction was based on the traditional subject-matter of art: still life, landscape and the human figure. At the same time, he had been profoundly influenced by Mondrian, and in the two versions of this composition (the earlier, *Oi yoi yoi*, is in the Tate) he experimented first by using the three primary colours with black, leaving the ground unpainted, and here with blue and yellow, omitting the red. In 1963 Hilton won the John Moores prize for the second time, and the following year he was awarded the UNESCO prize at the Venice Biennale.

Opposite: **PHILLIP KING**
Genghis Khan, 1963

Above: **ROGER HILTON**
Dancing Woman, 1963

Left: **LEWIS MORLEY**
Christine Keeler, 1963

Early in 1963 John Kasmin opened his gallery in London, and among the artists he showed that year were the Americans Kenneth Noland and Morris Louis, as well as Hockney, Richard Smith, Caro and John Latham. Latham had been interested in the paintings of Noland and Louis when he had visited New York in 1961, but his own work distanced itself from any kind of formalism, being loaded with several levels of meaning. He was deeply interested in the relation of art to theology and science, and in the nature of time. Latham invented the term 'event-structure' to describe his works, in which time-related components are independent of spatial presence, as in his use of a spray gun to apply paint, or the inclusion of books, 'time-activating instruments when read, while remaining the atemporal same otherwise'. The following year Latham made the first of his 'skoob towers' of burning books, in which the function of books, like the word, was reversed, making them unreadable – not to imply any contempt for literature, but to suggest that 'perhaps the cultural base had been burnt out.' Critics of Latham's 1963 show found the message of his art too strong – Bryan Robertson complained that it was 'like art criticism about paintings' – but his insistence, both in his work and his pioneering of the Artist Placement Group, that the role of the artist was not to produce 'works of art' to be channelled through the gallery system to the walls of a museum or a collector's house was to prove enormously influential on later generations.

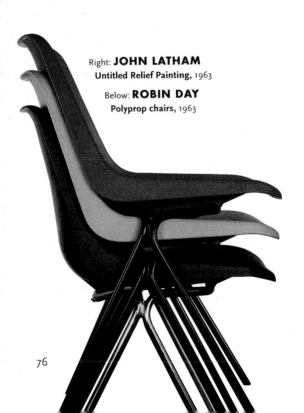

Right: **JOHN LATHAM**
Untitled Relief Painting, 1963

Below: **ROBIN DAY**
Polyprop chairs, 1963

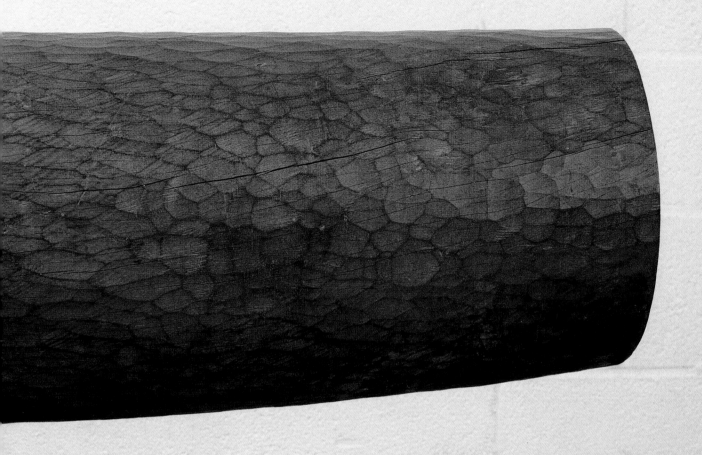

The early career of the sculptor William
Turnbull had many parallels with that of his
fellow-Scot Eduardo Paolozzi: both were
members of the Independent Group and took
part in 'This is Tomorrow' in 1956. However,
the time he spent in Paris in the late 1940s
had a strong influence on Turnbull's
sculptural practice, particularly his meetings
with Brancusi, Léger and Giacometti and his
discovery of primitive art in the Musée de
l'Homme. The series of idols and totemic
pieces he produced in the mid-1950s
established a form to which he returned
in the following decade. In the meantime,
Turnbull had been much impressed by
American Abstract Expressionist painting,
and he was also a leading contributor to the
'Situation' exhibitions.

WILLIAM TURNBULL
Spring Totem 2, 1963

BRIDGET RILEY
Crest, 1963

Bridget Riley had had her first solo exhibition at Gallery One in 1962, and the dazzling effects she created on the picture plane soon led to her work being saddled with the superficial label of 'Op Art'. Her mentor Anton Ehrenzweig, who taught at Goldsmiths College and was an inspiration to Paolozzi and many other artists of the period, wrote of Riley's 'conscious concern with the gradual variation of the single element which represents her theme'. He described how she had to avoid the danger of the picture plane being disrupted by parts of it becoming isolated: 'When the picture plane holds without breaking under the opposing strains, then the final unpredictable transformation takes place ... a mighty pulse skims through the entire picture plane, now lifting this or the other area to form a fleeting and swiftly crumbling pattern which need not have any correlative whatsoever in the objective composition.'

In Tess Jaray's early work (her first solo show was in 1963) the process of enlivening the painted surface is achieved by patterns with musical analogies derived from architectural perspective drawing.

Above: **TESS JARAY**
Minuet, 1963

Left: **MARTYN ROWLANDS**
Delta telephone, 1963

While **Max Clendinning furnished and decorated** his own Victorian house with bands of bright colour to redefine the interior space, Terence Conran introduced good basic design – derived largely from Scandinavian and Italian models – into his Habitat shops, revolutionizing the domestic surroundings of a whole generation of 'switched on' people.

The young sculptors of St Martin's followed Anthony Caro's lead in experimenting with the effect of materials and colour on the spatial qualities of abstract sculpture, while at the RCA the dominant influence on the young painters was their older, American fellow-student R.B. Kitaj. The collage of images in Kitaj's paintings represents an accretion of meanings intended by the artist. As with Latham, Kitaj's commentaries – whether articulated or implied – comprise an integral part of the formal existence of his works and give them a richness of association hardly paralleled in the fifty years under review: 'Some books have pictures and some pictures have books,' he wrote. This multi-layered quality, however, which opened so many avenues for young artists, was to prove a great stumbling-block for critics in the 1990s, who in wanting his art to 'speak for itself' tried to marginalize one of its essential elements. There is a great irony in the fact that one of the artists of great vision in Britain was driven into exile from his chosen country by the blindness of British critics. In 1996 Kitaj joined David Hockney, one of the artists to whom he had given decisive encouragement, in Los Angeles.

Left: **DAVID ANNESLEY**
Swing Low, 1964

Above:
TERENCE CONRAN
The first **Habitat** carrier bag, 1964

Right: **MAX CLENDINNING**
The designer's dining room, c. 1964

Opposite:
R.B. KITAJ
The Ohio Gang, 1964

Wittgenstein was always exhausted by his lectures. He was also revolted by them. He felt disgusted with what he had said and with himself. Often he would rush off to a cinema immediately after the class ended. As the members of the class began to move their chairs out of the room he might look imploringly at a friend and say in a low tone, 'Could you go to a flick?' On the way to the cinema Wittgenstein would buy a bun or cold pork pie and munch it while he watched the film. He insisted on sitting in the very first row of seats, so that the screen would occupy his entire field of vision, and his mind would be turned away from the thoughts of the lecture and his feelings of revulsion. Once he whispered to me 'This is like a shower bath!' His observation of the film was not relaxed or detached. He leaned tensely forward in his seat and rarely took his eyes off the screen. He hardly ever uttered comments on the episodes of the film and did not like his companion to do so. He wished to become totally absorbed in the film no matter how trivial or artificial it was, in order to free his mind temporarily from the philosophical thoughts that tortured and exhausted him. He liked American films and detested English ones. He was inclined to think that there could not be a decent English film. This was connected with a great distaste he had for English culture and mental habits in general. He was fond of the film stars Carmen Miranda and Betty Hutton. Before he came to visit me in America he demanded in jest that I should introduce him to Miss Hutton.

**ARCHIGRAM
(RON HERRON)**
Seaside Bubbles, 1965

Below: **RICHARD SMITH**
Tailspan, 1965

Opposite:
EDUARDO PAOLOZZI
**Wittgenstein at the Cinema Admires
Betty Grable,** 1965
From the **As is When** series

During the early 1960s Paolozzi had been using machine-parts in welded aluminium (sometimes painted) and chrome-plated steel to create sculptures of enormous presence. At one point he provided specifications for an industrial pattern-maker to produce parts to be assembled at a precision engineering firm. Paolozzi enjoyed the element of chance and risk-taking implicit in any collaboration, and this is found in his series of screenprinted collages, *As is When,* based on the life and writings of Ludwig Wittgenstein. He had earlier experimented with silk screens that could be randomly superimposed (one was used to decorate the Smithsons' office for Ove Arup), and he was, with Gordon House, one of the first to make extensive use of this medium for fine art.

The radical approach to architectural design embodied in Cedric Price's Fun Palace was reflected in a number of futuristic schemes. The Archigram Group produced a series of projects – Michael Webb's *Sin Centre* (1962), Peter Cook's *Plug-in City* (1964), Ron Herron's *Walking Cities* (1964) and others – that were clearly hypothetical in the solutions they offered to the problem of indeterminacy in future conditions but were nonetheless powerful manifestos calling for a fundamental change in the attitudes of architects and planners to the 'city' and the 'building'.

The Situationists' intention of making the scale and colour of a picture impose upon its environment was extended in the work of Richard Smith by the shaping of his canvas and its extension into real space, so that it becomes a kind of enveloping sculpture.

1965

Terry Frost, one of the St Ives abstractionists, who had lived in Cornwall from 1946 to 1962, was much in the public eye in the year he turned fifty, winning prizes in both the John Moores competition and in the Open Painting Exhibition in Belfast. Shapes and colours had become increasingly simplified in his work, but even at this period – unlike the Situationists – he preserved a sense of figuration within the traditional confines of the canvas.

Since Harold Macmillan had made his famous 'You've never had it so good' speech in 1957, affluence, which was increasingly enjoyed by the young, had effected a liberation in fashion and popular culture. The mid-1960s were the halcyon days of Swinging London, of sex, drugs and rock and roll. The prime image-maker of this culture was the photographer David Bailey, whose subjects included not only fashion models and the young and famous, but all those who fancied themselves young at heart. The spirit of the age was caught perfectly in the satirical film *Darling*, written by Frederick Raphael and directed by John Schlesinger, in which Julie Christie moves on from one representative of modish success to another – from journalist to business man to gay photographer to Italian prince.

Left:
JOHN SCHLESINGER
Darling, 1965

Above:
TERRY FROST
June, Red and Black,
1965

Opposite:
DAVID BAILEY
Jane Birkin, 1965

**MAURICE AGIS
AND PETER JONES**
Poster for **Space Place**, 1966

Above: **JOHN HOYLAND**
21.2.66, 1966

Left: **GEOFFREY BAXTER**
Drunken Bricklayers, 1966
Vases designed for Whitefriars Glass

Maurice Agis and Peter Jones extended the painters' exploration of space
and colour in a continuing project, which also had the aim of raising the
consciousness of a far wider audience to the products of artists' creativity.
Their work explored the perception of participants moving through an
active space as defined by panels and rods coloured red, blue and green:
'A spatial experience produces an awareness of self and as the experience
is capable of being shared by others it can provide a means of social
living.... An active spatial area can liberate our senses: resulting in a total
experience.' *Space Place* was first realized in a London basement in 1964,
but came to wider notice in 1966 when installed in the Museum of Modern
Art, Oxford, where dancers led by Yoko Ono performed within it.

John Hoyland was perhaps the finest of the 'Situation' painters,
producing a more painterly abstraction than his colleagues even during
the 1960s. Thereafter the texture of paint, dripped or freely brushed,
became increasingly important in his work, and his developing style
carried the ideals of abstraction into a period when young painters were
preoccupied with very different concerns. 'Paintings are not to be
understood,' Hoyland has said, 'they are to be recognized.'

MARY QUANT
Miniskirt, *c.* 1966

Below:
WILLIAM TUCKER
Memphis, 1966

Opposite: **GILLIAN AYRES**
Umbria, 1966

Mary Quant was the designer who established a consciously British style of fashion during the 1960s, owing little or nothing to Paris or Milan or New York. She had opened her boutique Bazaar in the King's Road, Chelsea, as early as 1955 and soon began designing clothes herself. The most obvious feature of her Mod look was the miniskirt – by mid-decade several inches above the knee – but the overall image that she promoted was what *Life* magazine in 1960 described as 'a kooky schoolgirl'. By devoting her energy to the ready-to-wear clothes wholesaled by her Ginger Group for the young woman on the street, she made the latest fashions immediately accessible and established 'Swinging London' as a world centre of fashion.

Gillian Ayres had been the most gestural of the 'Situation' painters, the closest to *tachisme*, but during the early 1960s the forms in her work became more hard-edged, while by the middle of the decade her colours changed, partly in response to the experiments she undertook with her students in 1965–66, projecting filtered lights onto still lifes.

William Tucker, one of Caro's pupils at St Martin's, was particularly concerned to demystify the art of the sculptor, taking it off its pedestal metaphorically as well as literally. He produced a striking white plastic sculpture in 1961–62 based on the interior volumes of milk bottles, and at the end of the decade was able to write: 'The sculptural object was finally freed from the residual structure of the human figure, the inhibitions of expensive materials and complex craft processes.'

Posters, like rock music, were appropriated by the young generation as their own form of art, and their eclectic origins produced a new artistic genealogy, ranging from art nouveau and Aubrey Beardsley – exhibited at the Victoria and Albert Museum in 1966 and notorious because posters of his work had been seized by the police – to icons of rock music and the cinema, images taken from American Pop and abstract art, and the fluid shapes and vibrant colours of psychedelia. Michael English (sometimes working in partnership with Nigel Waymouth as Osiris Posters) was a most prolific poster designer, and his work and its derivatives defined the imagery of the fashion culture of London's King's Road and Carnaby Street, producing a form of commodified, consumable art that perfectly suited the bold layouts of the new magazines, led by *Nova*.

Equally removed from mainstream 'art' were the experiments of Mark Boyle and Joan Hills: both their randomly framed 'Presentations' of squares of junk in London streets and the lightshows, such as *Son et Lumière for Bodily Fluid*, created in their Sensual Laboratory. These were first shown at various venues in London and then taken on a US tour with Soft Machine and Jimi Hendrix. In a way that was as radical as Latham or Metzger, the Boyle family challenged the meaning, function and traditional media of art objects, introducing random methods of selection, a reliance on natural processes and an essential quality of impermanence.

Above: **NIGEL WAYMOUTH AND MICHAEL MAYHEW**
Granny Takes a Trip façade in King's Road, Chelsea, featured in **Nova** magazine, April 1967
Photography and design by **Harri Peccinotti**

Right: **MARK BOYLE AND JOAN HILLS**
Sensual Laboratory Lightshow,
c. 1967–68

Opposite: Collection of posters, many by **MICHAEL ENGLISH**, including his **UFO Love Festival** poster, 1967

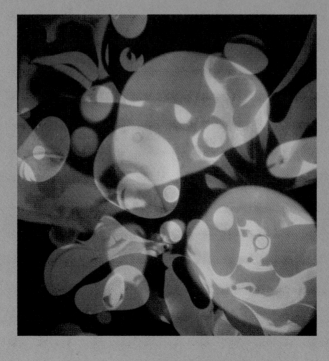

TONY RAY-JONES
Chatham May Queen, 1968

Opposite: **STUART BRISLEY**
Ritual Murder Nodnol, 1968

The continuing erosion of the boundaries of art meant that photography was perceived in a new way – not only artfully composed and manipulated images such as Man Ray and the Surrealists had produced, but photographs whose subject-matter, like that of contemporary painting, was everyday life. Tony Ray-Jones's mixture of irony and humour had its origins in his love of the cinema, while he acquired much of his technical skill in the years he spent in the USA, where he was strongly affected by the 'Street Photography' movement; however, his best works are his views of English life. In 1968 he wrote: 'My aim is to communicate something of the spirit and mentality of the English, their habits and their way of life, the ironies that exist in the way they do things, partly through tradition and partly through the nature of their environment and mentality. I have tried to present some of these daily anachronisms in an honest and descriptive manner, the visual aspect being directed by the content.... I wish to record the "English way of life" from my particular point of view before it becomes more Americanized.'

The enactment of eccentric rituals in public places as a form of living three-dimensional art characterized the early examples of performance art in Britain, which followed Happenings and Performances in continental Europe, Japan and the USA. Stuart Brisley studied in Munich and Florida after the RCA and from 1963 had been making perspex constructions and kinetic works. It was after the student sit-in at Hornsey Art School, where Brisley was teaching, in May 1968 that he staged his first performance, *Ritual Murder Nodnol* (a reversal like 'skoob'), enacted in Hyde Park. Later performances increasingly focused on the artist's own body, generally in rituals of endurance, self-cruelty and conflict that acted as artistic metaphors for human behaviour.

Patrick Heron remained an archetypal St Ives painter; early in
his career he had been close to the Leachs and to Nicholson and
Hepworth; his artistic formation derived from the examples of
Matisse and Braque; and from the 1960s his work became
increasingly concerned with the spatial effects created on the
canvas by colour within enclosed abstract forms, generated by
the rocks and features of the Cornish landscape. In his view, 'there
is no such thing as non-figuration. The best abstraction breathes
reality: it is redolent of forms in space, of sunlight and air.'

Liliane Lijn and the Greek sculptor Takis, whose kinetic works
had been exhibited in Paris earlier in the 1960s, contributed to the
extension of art into light and movement, which British artists such
as the Boyles and Peter Sedgley were already investigating. Lijn's
explorations of light and movement were shown at the Indica
Gallery and (like Sedgley's coloured 'video discs') were also made
into multiples. Five years earlier she had written: 'I want to walk
thru the transparent world of photon light, work with the source of
light ... capture electron images.' Two exhibitions around this time
gave wider currency to these new ideas: 'Cybernetic Serendipity',
organized by Jasia Reichardt at the ICA in 1968 and Theo Crosby's
show of kinetic art at the Hayward Gallery in 1970. Both looked
forward some twenty-five years to a time when the capabilities of
computers and a wider acceptance of the possibilities of interactive
art would offer a new generation of artists one of their most fruitful
fields for development.

Opposite **PATRICK HERON**
Orange in Deep Cadmium
with Venetian, 1969

Right **LILIANE LIJN**
See Thru Koan, 1969

Above **TERRY GILLIAM**
animation still from the
Monty Python's Flying Circus
television series, 1969

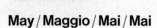

May / Maggio / Mai / Mai

Monday Lunedì Montag Lundi	Tuesday Martedì Dienstag Mardi	Wednesday Mercoledì Mittwoch Mercredi	Thursday Giovedì Donnerstag Jeudi	Friday Venerdì Freitag Vendredi	Saturday Sabato Samstag Samedi	Sunday Domenica Sonntag Dimanche	Monday Lunedì Montag Lundi	Tuesday Martedì Dienstag Mardi	Wednesday Mercoledì Mittwoch Mercredi	Thursday Giovedì Donnerstag Jeudi	Friday Venerdì Freitag Vendredi	Saturday Sabato Samstag Samedi	Sunday Domenica Sonntag Dimanche
28	29	30	1	2	3	4	5	6	7	8	9	10	11
12	13	14	15	16	17	18	19	20	21	22	23	24	25
26	27	28	29	30	31	1	2	3	4	5	6	7	8

DEREK BIRDSALL
Pirelli Calendar, 1969
Photos by **Harri Peccinotti**

Opposite: **ALAN ALDRIDGE**
Cover design for **The Beatles
Illustrated Lyrics,** 1969

Opposite below:
ALLEN JONES
Table, 1969

The erotic element of Pop Art, which had been such a powerful weapon against the stifling rule of good taste, was taken over with little sense of irony into commercial design. Derek Birdsall had designed the first Pirelli Calendar in 1964, and his use of Harri Peccinotti's photographs is provocatively oral within a cool, elegant design. Alan Aldridge, whose Dalíesque poster for Andy Warhol's *Chelsea Girls* won a Design & Art Directors' Award this year, used a sensual cartoonist's technique for his *Beatles Illustrated Lyrics*.

Allen Jones's fetishistic furniture took the pin-up imagery of early Pop into three-dimensional sculpture. It was David Hockney who brought this subject-matter to the attention of Jones, who made extensive use of it in paintings and prints: after seeing Jones's *Hermaphrodite* (1964), one of several variations on amalgamated male-female images, Hockney pointed out that this idea was paralleled in popular fetishistic illustration. The directness of Jones's sculpture – since it is certainly neither frivolous nor misogynistic – has a disturbing power, which seems to have been an inspiration to sculptors in the 1990s.

By the end of the decade the achievements of British Pop had, in the eyes of many of the public, been swamped by American Pop Art – especially the photographic screen prints of Andy Warhol. The gallery director Robert Fraser had introduced many of the American artists to the British public, and he appears in Richard Hamilton's *Swingeing London '67*, derived from a press photograph (by John Twine, published in the *Daily Sketch*) showing Fraser and Mick Jagger arriving at court for the trial of the Rolling Stones on drugs charges at Chichester in June 1967. The title of the work – one of a series of silk-screen paintings – makes an ironic comment on the clash of values between *Time* magazine's nomination of London as the 'Swinging City' (April 1966) and the swingeing prison sentences imposed by the judge, which confirmed the inability of the English legal system to come to terms with the new conventions of personal freedom in society.

The work of both Hamilton (whose *Toaster* was joint winner of the John Moores prize in 1969) and Joe Tilson was at its closest to American art at this moment. Tilson's three-dimensional enlargement of a 35mm colour slide was one of a host of 'multiples' (extensions of the idea of the limited edition original print) which were appearing in art galleries at this time. These included sculptures by William Pye as well as works by Pop artists Allen Jones, Dick Smith and Derek Boshier.

JOE TILSON
Transparency,
The Five Senses,
1969

Right:
RICHARD HAMILTON
Swingeing London '67,
1968–69

THE EFFECTS OF THE POLITICAL RADICALISM of 1968 registered immediately on the British art world. The rejection of traditional methods, subjects and concepts, which had previously been tentative and unfocused, became far more widespread and could no longer be ignored. A new view of the artist and his work was strongly influenced by American thinking: Donald Judd defined a work of art in his celebrated dictum, 'If someone calls it art it's art', while John Cage opined that 'Art, instead of being an object made by one person, is a process set in motion by a group of people. Art's socialized. It isn't someone saying something, it's people doing things, giving everyone (including those involved) the opportunity to have experiences they would not otherwise have had.' The seventies saw British artists seriously engaged in developments such as minimalism, conceptual art, kinetic and cybernetic art, behavioural art, video art, happenings, body art, air art and environmental art, while the relationship of art to technology and art to information, the processes of art, ritual, game theory and structuralism overshadowed aesthetics. In this sense, as artists cut loose from formal individual artistic practice, the decade marked an end to the long 'avant-garde' chapter in the history of western art: as Robert Hughes wrote, 'By 1975 all isms were wasms'.

The world of professional artists was extraordinarily fragmented. Quite apart from traditionalist Royal Academicians, many of the pioneers of an older generation were still active during the 1970s – Moore, Hepworth, Nicholson, Sutherland, Burra; and among the Neo-Romantics John Piper, Michael Ayrton, Edward Bawden, John Nash and John Craxton; among postwar developments in painting, 'New Realism', the 'School of London', St Ives abstractionism, Situation abstractionism, Pop Art, Op Art and Constructionism all continued to be developed actively, while in sculpture Armitage, Paolozzi and Caro represented movements that seemed to international observers to be Britain's most significant contribution to new art. However, the rising young generation found little to interest them in all of this.

Young, socially committed artists felt that the audience for art was too narrow, laying the blame on the 'artworld', a perceived conspiracy between the Arts Council, the Tate, the London art galleries, leading critics, and art schools, whose constituent members ensured their own self-perpetuation. Artists looked actively for alternative forms of art that defied commercial exploitation, that would be 'unsellable', for studio and exhibition spaces untouched by artworld influence, and for a press that would judge their activity by their own criteria. Ironically, many of their activities received active support from 'artworld' institutions, especially the Arts Council, liberally feeding the hands that bit them while drawing the fire of the philistines. In 1978, a landmark year for feminist art in Britain and one in which the artist Rasheed Araeen published his *Preliminary Notes for a Black Manifesto*, a group of artists put on an exhibition in the Arts Council's Serpentine Gallery, organized by Richard Cork, editor of *Studio International*, called 'Art for Whom?' Their collective statement expressed the conviction that 'the artist should engage with as many as possible of the working people who think art has nothing to do with them.... We would like society to regard artists as having an active part to play in dealing with the human, social and political issues which affect everyone's existence.'

Real popularity, however, was to be found elsewhere. Eighteen-year-olds had gained the vote in 1970, and the mood of the decade – foreshadowed in Stanley Kubrick's film of Anthony Burgess's *A Clockwork Orange* (1971) – was captured for young people by Punk, a highly original and wholly anti-authoritarian youth movement, which had a profound effect on popular culture, especially music, design and fashion. The year that Malcolm McLaren launched the Sex Pistols, 1975, was coincidentally when unemployment reached its highest figure since the war and Margaret Thatcher's supporters engineered the 'Milk Street coup' that won her leadership of the Tory party. Alienation from consumer society and its rules led to alternative artistic strategies, which were to become increasingly significant.

Nevertheless, the preceding boom years had seen important developments in British design and architecture. New architectural projects were embarked upon during the decade by Foster, Rogers, Stirling, Wilson and Hopkins, among others, while 1972 saw the foundation of the design partnership Pentagram by the architect Theo Crosby, graphic designers Alan Fletcher, Colin Forbes and Mervyn Kurlansky, and industrial designer Kenneth Grange. Their integrated approach to design was based on the belief that 'both designer and client would achieve superior creative results through cross-disciplinary collaboration'. The influence of Pentagram's principles in a world where branding, identity, image and styling had become a measure of success was overwhelming.

TELEVISION AND THE ARTS

Melvyn Bragg

THE MOST ENCOURAGING ASPECT of this superficially inauspicious alliance between the Arts (often bagged by the Few through centuries) and Television (sprouted fully grown into the middle of the first century of The People) is how quickly it has been consummated.

While sceptics and doubters and feudal Lords of the old Arts shook their heads, before our very eyes the livelier, more robust, more inventive artists and commentators seized on this new invention with delight.

Picasso was filmed working on a painting, Kenneth Clark brought a magnificent pageant of Western Civilization into millions of homes throughout the world, Bacon, Hockney, Hodgkin; Mailer, Pinter and Toni Morrison; Bergman and Truffaut, Walton and the Beatles, Nureyev and Martha Graham, Callas and Pavarotti and the list goes on and on, all embraced the small screen.

Artists saw in television a way to reach new and larger audiences. Television saw in artists a richness of subject which is only now, in the second phase following that early excitement, beginning to be explored in the detail which it deserves and which can make such an impact.

Television producers have used the interview in many forms to allow artists an unprecedented freedom of intimate contact with massive audiences. They have developed techniques of close up and skilful cutting, borrowing from feature films. They have also developed commentary and contextualization borrowing from biography and radio. In my opinion this has enabled some television arts documentaries to claim a little of art for themselves.

There are impediments – the size of the screen being the most obvious in dance and opera for instance. But just as in watching sport on television, we elasticate and re-invent with ease the size and even the smells of what we see on a screen – so in the arts we imagine what it 'really' is from the clues given. What we bring helps compensate for what we lose. Not entirely, that can never be. But it is a happier marriage than anyone could have dreamed of. Literally tens of millions of people have already enjoyed the company of the work of artists hitherto totally off the radar of their expectations. And the archive which is being built up will ensure that the pleasure in the television programme may have a posterity, just as the art itself may have a posterity. Now they go hand in hand, the recorder and the recorded, the artist shaping the world and television attempting to give shape to the world of the artist.

ADVANCING PHOTOGRAPHY

Martin Harrison

PHOTOGRAPHY, DESPITE BEING a democratic, protean medium with wide cultural resonance, has not had a smooth ride in Britain in the second half of the twentieth century. First, class barriers had to be breached. On the popular level a photographer was fixed somewhere between a camp character with artistic pretensions, huddled mysteriously under a blackcloth and 'painting with light', and a 'Flash!Bang!Wallop!' wedding merchant. Higher up the scale, Tony Armstrong-Jones's marriage to Princess Margaret helped enormously, and soon David Bailey, precocious usurper at *Vogue,* was hailed by Cecil Beaton for sparking a revolution that allowed the photographer, formerly 'a sort of inferior tradesman', to 'go anywhere'.

In 1949, British photography had lagged behind the USA and much of Europe: only Bill Brandt and Cecil Beaton could claim international stature. According to the American critic John Szarkowski, Britain had 'forgotten its rich photographic past, and showed no signs of seeking a photographic present.' The early modernist thrust of advertising photography had dissipated after World War II, pictorialism and society portraiture survived but were in terminal decline, and even photojournalism was slipping past its *Picture Post* peak. But the situation was turned around in the sixties with the rejuvenation of magazine photography, and by the end of the decade even bastions of the art establishment had begun to be pierced, with photography exhibitions at the National Portrait Gallery. Smaller private galleries sprung up in the 1970s, both in and out of London, and there was an important revival in the publishing of photography books.

Simultaneously, though, a schism developed between 'art' photography and applied photography that dated back to the unresolved high art versus mass media debate of the 1950s. Following the crossover of thirties Neo-Romantics like Nash and Piper, some of Britain's leading artists – Francis Bacon, Peter Blake and Richard Hamilton for example – had made imaginative use of photography, but their photographer contemporaries, such as Roger Mayne, John Deakin and Nigel Henderson, had to await postmodern historians for re-evaluation. Today, the divisions between past and present, high and low are less evident: a new generation of magazine photographers, led by figures like Rankin and Corinne Day, is sought after worldwide, while Martin Parr, Donovan Wylie and Richard Billingham intriguingly bridge the printed page and the gallery wall. The new millennium – the dazzling digital future – will begin with photography. Yet it remains unrepresented by a national gallery in England's capital; for anyone passionate about the medium, this would set the seal on a half-century of remarkable progress.

Hockney's double portrait
of the fashion designers Celia
Birtwell and Ossie Clark,
begun in spring 1970 and
completed early in 1971, marks
a moment of achievement but
also a crisis in his work. The
artist wrote: 'What I wanted to
achieve by such a big painting
was the presence of two
people in this room. All the
technical problems were
caused because my main aim
was to paint the relationship
of these two people.' However,
the almost Victorian
naturalism of the work, which
no doubt accounts for its huge
popularity at the Tate Gallery,
proves to be something of
an obstacle to an appreciation
of its formal and aesthetic
qualities – to such an extent
that Hockney's subsequent
works make more of the actual
process of marking lines and
applying colour, whether in
drawings, prints or paintings.
From the mid-1970s he also
began to work with collages
of polaroid photographs,
using them to produce a
faceted picture space like that
in cubist portraits by Picasso,
the artist whose work has been
an inspiration for Hockney
throughout his career.

DAVID HOCKNEY
Mr and Mrs Clark and Percy,
1970–71

The work of Metzger, Latham, Brisley and the Boyles, as well as the early environmental sculptures of Richard Long and Barry Flanagan, had suggested a new context for the work of art, relating it both to the functions of the artist's living body and to his environment and ecology. Bob Law, who had worked as a painter, potter and carpenter in St Ives and had exhibited in 'Situation', derived the scale of his paintings from human proportions. He is best known for his paintings executed entirely in black, but from 1970 he began to make white paintings marked with the outline of a rhombus (based on a drawing he had made ten years earlier).

Michael Craig-Martin's minimalist sculptures had been included in the first exhibition of conceptual art in London – 'When Attitudes Become Form' at the ICA in September 1969. The work shown there introduced the latest tendency in American sculpture, focusing on the mental impact of accepting apparently unfashioned objects as 'works of art'.

Gilbert and George defined their art not as performance but as living sculpture. They themselves, painted in gold and metallic colours, were their own subject. *The Singing Sculpture*, enacted robotically and ritualistically over eight hours to a repeated record of Flanagan and Allen's 'Underneath the Arches', was first presented, as *Our New Sculpture*, at St Martin's School in 1969. In 1970 there were presentations in Germany, Italy and Scandinavia and at the Nigel Greenwood Gallery, then in 1971 at the Sonnabend Gallery, New York. This marked an impact of British art on the American scene, where previously only groups like the Beatles and the Rolling Stones or the British Pop painters had made any real impression.

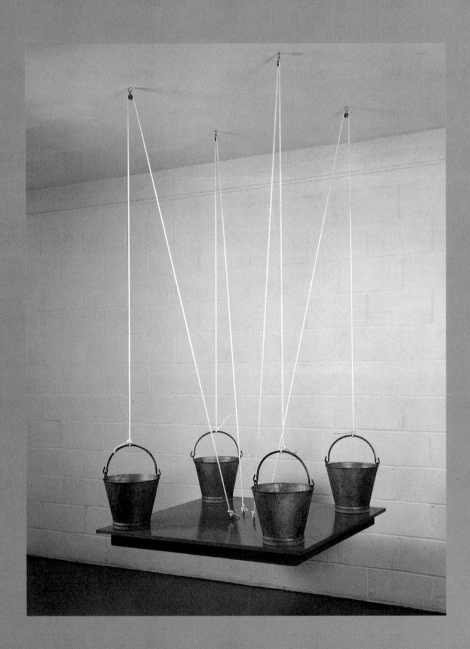

MICHAEL CRAIG-MARTIN
On the Table, 1970

Right above: **BOB LAW**
In front of his painting
Number 95 Mister Paranoia IV,
1970

Opposite:
GILBERT AND GEORGE
The Singing Sculpture, 1971
Photo by **Lord Snowdon**

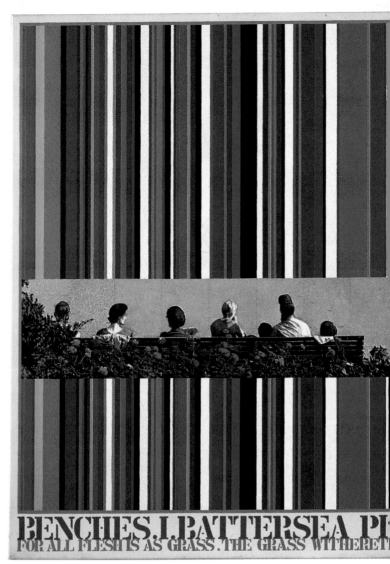

Left above: **SUSANNA HERON**
Bracelet, 1971

Above: **TOM PHILLIPS**
Benches, 1971

Left: **PATRICK CAULFIELD**
Interior with Room Divider, 1971

The subject-matter and techniques of Pop Art continued to be extended in a number of distinct ways. Patrick Caulfield belonged to the original Pop generation, arriving at the RCA only a year after Kitaj, Hockney, Boshier and Jones, but the imagery he refers to is not the stuff of pulp magazines but rather the children's early reader or the furniture catalogue. His style in both painting and printmaking has remained remarkably constant, although intrusions of illusionistic realism have sometimes been used to heighten the ironical references to consumer society. In its conversion of images into signs, Caulfield's style influenced younger artists such as Michael Craig-Martin.

Tom Phillips has a more complex and more literary approach, which in its manipulation of existing images from postcards and other popular sources – generally with an implicit political message,

as in *Oh Miss South Africa* (1975) – is clearly indebted to Richard Hamilton. Words, almost always applied in stencil lettering, play an important role in his paintings, as does the serialization of the colours used in a work, here applied in bands of random width. These techniques offer a parallel to contemporary semiological criticism of art, which applied the structuralist theories of Claude Lévi-Strauss to decode meanings implicit in the work which were entirely distinct from the artist's specific intentions. One of Phillips's important projects from the late 1960s and throughout the following decade was his work on *A Humument* (first published in book form in 1980), a 'treated' Victorian novel (by the obscure William Hurrell Mallock) whose pages are painted and typed over to obliterate or partially obliterate most of the text, leaving words and phrases that become significant in their new context.

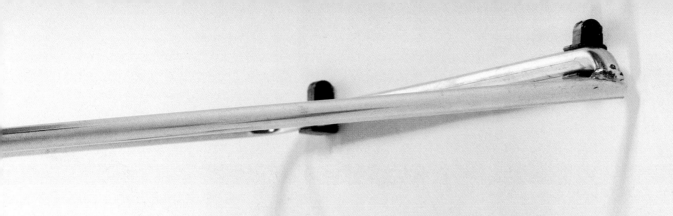

The Omkstak chair, with seat and back support made from stamped steel, became an icon of the school of High-Tech design, whose architectural symbol was to be the Centre Pompidou in Paris (1976) designed by Richard Rogers and Renzo Piano. Kinsman was inspired by one of the earliest designs for a stacking chair, Hans Coray's Swiss 'Landi Stuhl' of 1938, which had used a single moulded sheet of stamped aluminium alloy on a tubular frame, but the Omkstak chair is distinctive for the elegant lightness of its design and its glossy, painted industrial finish.

A fellow-student (and early collaborator) with Gilbert and George at St Martin's sculpture school, McLean's work was always more openly subversive. *Posework for Plinths* satirized both the obsessive reclining figures of Henry Moore's oeuvre and the Caro school's determination to place sculpture directly on the ground. 'All the discussion,' McLean wrote, 'centred on the proclamation that sculpture should be placed on the floor and not on a base. It seemed to me quite daft that adults should spend their time like that. It dawned on me that what it was really about was making a name for oneself.' This statement was made at the time of McLean's neo-Dada one-day 'retrospective' at the Tate Gallery in 1972, where the main exhibit consisted of a thousand catalogues placed on the floor which the spectators were invited to pick up and take away.

RODNEY KINSMAN
Omkstak chair, 1971

Right: **BRUCE McLEAN**
Posework for Plinths 1, 1971

1972

The **South Bank site** of the Festival of
Britain had remained bleak for many years
after the Tory government which came to
power in autumn 1951 had swiftly
demolished all the exhibition buildings
and sculptures, with the exception of the
Royal Festival Hall. An overall plan for
the area was prepared in 1953 by the
LCC architects' department led by
Leslie Martin, but (apart from the
undistinguished Shell Centre, 1956–63,
by Robertson and Smith) the principal
buildings were not started until the 1960s:
the Hayward Gallery and two concert halls
(1965–68) by the (now) GLC architects'
department and the National Theatre
(1961–76) by Sir Denys Lasdun. Each of
these buildings has proved extremely
successful from a functional point of view,
but the public has never warmed to the
brutalist aesthetic of their architecture,
and the informally planned concrete
terraces, on which Pye's sculpture stands,
have always been much criticized. The
whole complex is due to be rebuilt.

The LCC had pioneered the
commissioning of public sculptures, and
Zemran is the most successful of several
works on the South Bank site. Pye, whose
work has affinities with Paolozzi's
aluminium pieces of the 1960s, is at his
best on a monumental scale, and he
completed a number of important
commissions during the 1970s. Several
works of the mid-seventies incorporated
water, and the rhythmic patterns made
by a film of water over metal have inspired
much of his later work. Also in 1972 the
Peter Stuyvesant Foundation, which
had been building a collection of recent
British painting and offering bursaries
to artists, embarked on its City Sculpture
Project, planning for works to be erected
in Newcastle, Liverpool, Sheffield,
Birmingham, Cardiff (a sculpture by Pye),
Cambridge, Southampton and Plymouth.

WILLIAM PYE
Zemran, 1972

BILL GIBB
Fake ponyskin jacket and
tight-hipped flared skirt, 1972
Photo by **Clive Arrowsmith**

Opposite:
WENDY RAMSHAW
Ring set, 1971
Winner of a Council of
Industrial Design award in 1972

Below:
JOHN McCONNELL
Biba logo

Bill Gibb, who had studied at St Martin's and the RCA was named *Vogue* magazine's Designer of the Year in 1970. Throughout the decade, until the recession reduced the scale of his business in the late seventies, he was one of the most innovative names in the British fashion world. Among his most fruitful collaborations was that with Kaffe Fassett on knitwear, which gave new life to a type of garment ignored by most designers. Gibb was a brilliant draughtsman, and the swirls of his party dresses, with their surprising combinations of pattern and fabric, transform the lines of his drawings into three dimensions.

Biba, Barbara Hulanicki's fashion label, began selling by mail order in 1964, and she opened her trendsetting store on Kensington High Street in 1969. The unmistakable house style of the packaging was designed by John McConnell, who received a D&AD award that year for the Biba corporate identity. Biba underwent a huge expansion in the early 1970s, buying the Derry & Toms store in 1972, but the plans were overambitious and the store closed in July 1975.

Wendy Ramshaw's jewelry has always been inspired by an eclectic interest in arts in other media and from other civilizations: one of the most influential London exhibitions in recent years had been of the work of Magritte at the Tate in 1969, and the lathe-turned projections on the ring sets Ramshaw designed at this period recall the wooden 'bilboquets' that appear so often in the work of the Belgian Surrealist; at the same time, the mixture of gold and coloured stones recalls the treasures of Tutankhamun (exhibited in Paris and then at the British Museum in 1972). The sets of dress rings (which could be worn singly or as a cluster on one finger) were displayed on perspex stands and in this form could be viewed as autonomous works of art. They won a London Design Award in 1972.

British studio pottery entered a brilliant phase in the second half of the century, as the long tradition of earthenware that reached back to the medieval period was transformed by the influences of Japan (in the work of the Leach family), of Africa (in Michael Cardew and his pupils) and of the purest traits of the Wiener Werkstätte style (in Lucie Rie's pots). Hans Coper, born in Germany, worked with Rie for several years and out of their collaboration he developed a repertory of forms and techniques which lend his pots a presence that is similar to that of sculpture. The shapes are generally composite, and while ostensibly retaining the form of a vase, they relate strongly to Cycladic and other primitive figures. The surfaces were often ground down to reveal an astonishing richness of colour – of clays and glazes – emerging from the surface range of creams and browns.

Stephen Buckley's work is characterized by an emphasis on the materials of painting (supplemented by other unorthodox media) subjected to a whole range of destructive and constructive processes – from shredding and burning to weaving, wrapping, screwing and nailing. He developed the shaped canvas used by abstract painters and by the Pop artists, turning the support for his paintings into elaborate assemblages of panels, strips of canvas and other accretions. The images were assembled in the same fragmented forms. Buckley's compositions remain abstract, but the titles are evocative of the personal associations of his works.

Above: **STEPHEN BUCKLEY**
Chestnuts, 1972

Opposite: **HANS COPER**
Stoneware thistle form pot, *c.* 1972

Two of the outstanding painters to emerge during the 1950s were Leon Kossoff and Frank Auerbach (five years Kossoff's junior). Both were included in the group of figurative painters (with Bacon, Freud and Andrews) that Kitaj in 1976 designated the 'School of London', painters who bravely swam against the tide of abstraction, conceptualism and late Pop. There are strong similarities between them both in their free handling of paint and in their subject-matter: scenes of London near their studios and portraits of close friends. However, Kossoff's landscapes are full of human activity, although his figures always seem trapped, unable to escape the restrictions of the material world; his paint is applied by dragging, dripping and flicking, making it hard for the eye to focus on the image conveyed by the broken surface of the canvas. Auerbach's paint is put on in fierce slashing strokes made with a brush, a knife or even the artist's hands. In his earlier works the repeated applications built up a solid, almost sculptural, accretion of colour, particularly in his figure compositions, but later he would scrape away the earlier layers leaving a fragmentary history covered by the new application of paint.

Above:
LINDSAY ANDERSON
Still from the film **O Lucky Man,** 1973
Production design by **Jocelyn Herbert**

Left: **LEON KOSSOFF**
**Dalston Junction Ridley Road Street
Market, Stormy Morning,** 1973

Opposite:
FRANK AUERBACH
**Looking Towards Mornington
Crescent Station – Night,** 1973

The Byker redevelopment in Newcastle is a pioneering scheme in the humanization of the mass housing unit. Erskine had adopted a participatory practice in his earlier work in Sweden, consulting future inhabitants of his buildings in an office on the building site at a very early stage. He was aware that the neo-brutalist use of materials advocated by the Smithsons aroused hostility, and he introduced colour, naturalistic materials and elements of quirky surprise in the design. The building is a continuous curving structure built around the edge

of an area that at the time was in the process of transition, but the surface is broken up both at ground level and vertically by variations in the materials. This gives the impression of almost organic growth, like the natural development of a village, rather than the imposition of a total design scheme. The reaction against modernist architecture, particularly by the introduction of traditional elements with historical connotations, gave rise to the eclectic practice which became known as postmodernism.

RALPH ERSKINE
Byker Wall, Newcastle-upon-Tyne, 1969–80

1975

Norman Foster responded to the public rejection of modernism by taking modernism itself into a new phase. He completely enclosed his buildings in a glass skin (here the panes of the glass curtain wall are divided by translucent silicone rather than by steel or masonry), with services contained in the roof space, thus creating an extremely flexible interior environment, while externally the transparency reduces the apparent solidity of the building – reflecting the surrounding townscape by day, and at night dissolving as the interior is lit from within. Although Foster's work soon earned the label 'High-Tech', he himself sees his buildings rather as incorporating 'appropriate technology'.

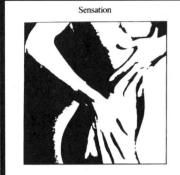

Sensation	ContraDiction	Logic

Create a little sensation
Feel the difference that everyone can see
Something you can touch
Property
There's nothing to touch it

You've got it
You want to keep it
Naturally. That's conservation
It conserves those who can't have it
They don't want to be conserved
Logically, that's contradiction

Everything you buy says something about you
Some things you buy say more than you realise
One thing you buy says everything
Property
Either you have it or you don't

Above: **VICTOR BURGIN**
Sensation, 1975

Opposite: **FRANCIS BACON**
Three Figures and Portrait, 1975

Below right: **JOHN DAVIES**
Head with Shell Device, 1973–75

Below: **F.H.K. HENRION**
Logo for the National Theatre, 1975

NT

Conceptual art – in which the art object is replaced by images, words, signs and sensual signals that allow the spectator to participate actively by making a mental construct of the work – took many forms: performance, living sculpture, cake art, environmental or land art were three-dimensional, sculptural forms, while two-dimensional images, texts, diagrams and photographs might serve either to record or document an ephemeral work or stand in for the work itself. The leading British conceptual artist was Victor Burgin, who parodied the images and slogans of advertising to suggest that the familiar signs of consumerist society could be reinterpreted in an anti-materialistic way.

In Bacon's multiple portrait of his lover George Dyer (who had died in 1971) the domestic interior, with painted walls, skirting board and picture hanging on the wall, is made theatrical by the definition of other spatial boundaries marked as though by spotlights or stage props, while the view from above and exposed spine of the figure on the left suggest it could be an anatomy theatre (where Rembrandt's Dr Tulp might perform) rather than a place of entertainment.

Davies had first included a mask-like shell in his portrait of Robert Sainsbury (1973), and he used the device to create a disturbing 'interrupted realism' that parallels his more elaborate compositions in which figures dressed in actual clothing are confined – or, as with his acrobats, liberated – by structures of wood and string.

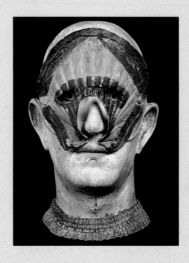

Several important contributions to the debate on the role of women as artists were made in the late 1980s, a time when the role of women in architecture and other male-dominated fields became increasingly accepted. The assertion of sexuality became an important theme, though it was one that found many different forms of expression. Bridget Bailey used materials traditionally crafted by women to create analogies of the female sex. The painted three-dimensional fabrics she made by a process of steam-moulding and pleating produce a sculptured surface that acts both as disguise and metaphor for the body it is designed to enclose.

Paula Rego's enigmatic narrative paintings and prints, with their recurrent themes of rebellion and escape from dominant authority, recall her experiences as a child brought up under Salazar's dictatorship in Portugal. Sometimes using figures from children's literature (*Nursery Rhymes*, 1989, and *Peter Pan*, 1992, are two suites of prints) or drawing on art of the past or outsider art, her compositions can be strangely disturbing: 'I paint to give fear a face', she has written.

Eva Jirična has appropriated the language of High-Tech architecture and animated it with rich curves to provide a dramatic setting for a discotheque.

Above: **PAULA REGO**
The Policeman's Daughter, 1987

Left: **EVA JIRIČNA**
Interior of **Legends** nightclub, London, 1987

Opposite: **BRIDGET BAILEY**
Hand-painted, steam-pleated silk organza, 1987

Above:
ANDY GOLDSWORTHY
Blades of grass
creased and arched
secured with thorns
Penpont, Dumfriesshire
14 August 1988

Left:
MICHAEL ROWE
Conditions for Ornament No. 6,
1988

Environmental sculpture, pioneered in Britain in the sixties and seventies by Flanagan and Long, was given a new direction by the work of Andy Goldsworthy. Rather than working primarily with earth or stones to alter features of the environment, he creates objects, but in order to portray nature in a state of change he uses flowers, leaves, twigs and branches of trees, snow, ice – so that these objects are necessarily impermanent. Their continued visibility depends on the richly coloured photographs he makes of them. At the same time, he insists, 'All my work still exists in some form.... Each work grows, stays, decays – integral parts of a cycle which the photograph shows at its height, marking the moment when the work is most alive.'

The dissolution of categories within the broad realm of 'sculpture' has spilled over into the work of craftsmen, whose field of activity, traditionally the making of useful pieces, is often concerned with the creation of objects more closely akin to works of art. While forms or materials indicate the expected function, placing the pieces in a very specific context and defining their relationship with the ambient space, objects such as the vessels in Michael Rowe's *Conditions for Ornament* series may have no effective utilitarian purpose. Indeed, Rowe, a teacher at the RCA and leading theoretician of the decorative arts, has evolved a new metaphorical, conceptual, role for objects created by an innovative practice of the traditional processes of craftsmanship.

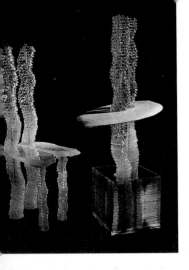

Below:
STEVEN CAMPBELL
Painting Influenced by the Foot
of a Chair and the Top of a Building,
1988

Opposite: **RON ARAD**
The Big Easy Volume 2, 1988

Top: **DANNY LANE**
Solomon chair and table, 1988

Above: **NIGEL COATES**
Genie stool, 1988

Right below: **TOM DIXON**
'S' chairs, 1988

Chairs have become a favoured form for many artists to create objects that are imbued with all the associations of a functional article designed to support the human body while at the same time aspiring to the condition of art – what Richard Rogers has described as 'usable artwork'. Ron Arad, Danny Lane and Tom Dixon all showed their furniture in Arad's One Off showroom, opened in Covent Garden in 1981, where initially Arad and Dixon created 'recycled furniture'. The examples shown here indicate how the generalized form of the chair can be adapted to a highly appropriate sculptural use of the materials chosen: glass for Lane, bent steel for Dixon, and polished welded stainless steel for Arad. The architect Nigel Coates, by contrast, makes elegant use of technology – the wooden seat of his stool is joined like a human pelvis – for a stool designed to provide comfort by promoting ideal posture.

Glasgow – rather than Edinburgh – has been an important artistic centre throughout the century, but the number of leading Glasgow artists in the 1980s – Steven Campbell, Ken Currie, Adrian Wiszniewski, Peter Howson, Stephen Conroy and Douglas Gordon, among others – has led to the label 'New Glasgow School' being applied to the figurative painting several of them have practised. Campbell started as a performance artist before spending five years in the USA. His paintings are tableaux of disquieting rituals, the elusive meaning of which is conveyed by the gestures of the characters. He himself has acknowledged the influence of Bruce McLean and Gilbert and George, not only on his own performances but on his paintings, while the long shadow of Magritte is also plain to see.

Bill Woodrow's sculpture demonstrates the artist's commitment both to his art and to the issues of his time. His work of the early eighties was characterized by his cutting of familiar objects – a guitar, a chainsaw or a bicycle – from washing machines and other household appliances, both old and new objects forming part of the work of art, generally connected by an umbilical strip of metal. More recent works are more complex, some being cast in bronze, but the separation and joining of familiar but unrelated readymade and fashioned parts produces works which impose their presence very strongly on the spectator: their configurations imply a story being told, but the thread of the narrative remains elusive. In *Let's Eat Fish* the groups of letters on the floor spell FISH OUT OF WATER, while the individual upright letters make the word S-O-F-T.

Peter Greenaway, who is a painter and exhibition curator as well as a film director, constructs his films – variations on the themes of sex and murder – as works of art with the power to disturb and disorientate the spectator, rather than simply provide entertainment: 'I wanted to make a cinema of ideas, not plots, and to use the same aesthetics as painting, which has always paid great attention to formal devices of structure, composition and framing.'

Right: **BILL WOODROW**
Let's Eat Fish, 1988

Left: **PETER GREENAWAY**
Still from the film **Drowning by Numbers**, 1988

Craigie Aitchison belongs to the generation of artists who came
to prominence in the 1950s, and his own first one-man show was
in 1960 at the Beaux Arts Gallery, which had supported the 'Kitchen
Sink' artists as well as the 'School of London'. His figurative
paintings nevertheless have strong affinities with the 'New
Figuration' of younger painters in the 1980s. The simplicity,
purity and directness of his work has sometimes been described
as childlike, but it is the result of a ruthless process of reduction,
both of composition and subject-matter: 'I do mostly black people,
dogs, religious pictures and still lifes', he has said.

Stephen Conroy, nearly thirty years Aitchison's junior, creates
a deliberately anachronistic atmosphere both by his technique and
the appearance of his characters. The formal action of his interior
scenes appears to take place in some late Victorian dreamworld,
not unlike the fairy world painted by Peter Blake. He has explained
that he wants to recreate the 'sense of dissonance' he finds in the
work of Degas and Sickert, whose paintings of ordinary life appear
to uncover such disturbing undertones.

Both Georgina Godley, with her Surrealist-inspired padded and
sculpturally shaped garments, and Georgina von Etzdorf with her
richly patterned fabrics also provoke an uneasy sense of déjà vu.

Above: **GEORGINA GODLEY**
Corrugated Strides, 1989
Silk taffeta trousers

Right: **STEPHEN CONROY**
Che Gelida Manina, 1988–89

Opposite:
CRAIGIE AITCHISON
Portrait of Patrice Felix Tchicaya,
1989

Below: **GEORGINA VON ETZDORF**
Invitation to the **Rhythm & Blues** collection,
Autumn/Winter 1989

IN THE DESULTORY POLITICAL DECADENCE of the mid-nineties a new generation of British artists and designers came of age; they had been taught to pursue economic as well as aesthetic goals, but, alienated from the mainstream of society, they turned this lesson against the world of their predecessors. Their response was to produce work that excluded all but their own age-cohort: the enemy of the old avant garde, the middle class, was replaced by the enemy of youth, the middle-aged. Taste became meaningless and was eclipsed by Style. Postmodern irony pervades nineties art, and artists' ambivalent take on the artworld was summed up in Chris Ofili's response to the announcement by the fashion star Agnès B that he had won the 1998 Turner Prize: 'Where's the cheque?'

Many of the practices of the 1960s have been taken up again: Rachel Whiteread's casts have a precedent in William Tucker's casts of the interiors of milk bottles (*Ceremonial*, 1961–62); the intense focus on the body and its fluids – remember *Dr Strangelove* – goes back to the hero of sixties artists, Marcel Duchamp, as well as the Boyles; Antony Gormley's self-casting recalls Roy Adzak's half-positive, half-negative *Human Columns* of 1966; Cornelia Parker's deconstructions echo the auto-destructive art of Gustav Metzger; while computer, kinetic and interactive art has its roots in Jasia Reichardt's 'Cybernetic Serendipity' exhibition at the ICA in 1968. However, with the passing of thirty years, the goals appear to be very different: personal rebellion rather than social revolution, and an attempt to take over rather than to subvert the art market.

The economic conditions for art have changed considerably, both with major new commissions for architects and designers funded from the National Lottery and with the colossal influence of Charles Saatchi, the maecenas of 'New British Art'. Not only has he supported and collected young artists, he has defined the school and established a wider market for its work by his highly successful sale of 130 works in December 1998 – undertaking to reinvest the proceeds in a new young generation, both through purchase grants and by funding bursaries at the RCA, Goldsmiths and Chelsea School of Art.

The advance of postmodernism has blurred the dividing lines between old categories. For many potters, glassmakers, jewellers, metalworkers and furniture designers function has become a secondary consideration – or is of no consequence at all – while the work of documentary or fashion photographers, film and video makers, and graphic designers working on paper or in electronic media is art as much as that of a painter or a sculptor or a printmaker. The notion of an 'artwork' has also been extended in other directions during the decade, merging with the concept of 'lifestyle': installations and artist-run galleries have included the work of young artists such as Richard Foster, who has treated the office environment as art (echoes of Latham's Artist Placement Group), or Peter Harris and Charles Avery, for whom curatorial activity as well as performance becomes art.

It should be emphasized once again that 'New British Art' – given a comprehensive showing in the 1997 'Sensation' exhibition at the Royal Academy – has not had a monopoly of the decade. The majority of the artists, designers and architects whose work is included in the book are still alive and active, and the many overlapping layers of the artworld resemble a brilliant collage – that process which more than any other can stand as a metaphor for the creativity of the past fifty years, whether for the combination of different levels of meaning and expression in a single work, for the use of appropriation to stir hidden analogies or for the capacity to communicate aesthetic, moral and social values.

The nineties were ushered in by the exhibition 'Freeze', curated in 1988 in a disused warehouse in the London docks with consummate professionalism by Damien Hirst. The works included were by his fellow-students at Goldsmiths College. Hirst is in many ways the representative artist of these years – not because of the media celebrity he has achieved, but because, for all the irony with which his work is presented, he is a dedicated artist with a command of an extraordinarily wide range of modes. His work with living and dead creatures – from butterflies to sharks to sheep – is balanced by a subtle and perceptive sense of colour and process in works that define a new kind of postmodern minimalism. He understands clearly his purpose as an artist: 'Art is about life, and it can't really be anything else. There isn't anything else.'

THE TURNER PRIZE   Nicholas Serota

FOR MUCH OF THE NINETIES the level of public interest in the visual arts has been so striking that it is difficult to remember that until quite recently the audience in Britain for contemporary art has been relatively small. In 1964 more than 50,000 people visited the Rauschenberg exhibition at the Whitechapel and in the same year 90,000 saw the Gulbenkian Foundation survey exhibition, 'Painting and Sculpture of a Decade '54–'64', at the Tate; but these were exceptional numbers. Generally an attendance figure of more than 25,000 has been regarded as remarkable. While British artists in the postwar period have won prizes at the Venice Biennale, or have been honoured with major exhibitions abroad, their achievements have rarely raised public acclaim at home, at least not until each generation approaches the age of sixty.

In the 1960s Bryan Robertson's Whitechapel Gallery was an honourable exception to this rule, regularly presenting important shows of younger and middle-generation British artists. Paradoxically his departure from the Whitechapel in 1968 coincided with several developments in which we may trace the roots of the remarkable growth in audiences for contemporary art which has occurred during the 1990s.

Between 1965 and 1970 the opportunities to see contemporary art outside the commercial galleries were dramatically transformed. Within this short period occurred the opening of the Hayward Gallery and an enlarged ICA on the Mall in 1968; Norman Reid's reorganization of the displays at the Tate placing greater emphasis on the modern and international dimensions of the collection, followed by a much more adventurous and high-profile series of exhibitions of artists then in their forties, such as Warhol, Hamilton, Lichtenstein and Oldenburg; the opening of new venues such as the Arts Lab or the new Space studios at St Katherine's Dock in which initiatives by artists created space for performance, installation and events; and the opening or reorientation of a group of independent regional galleries,

often funded in part by the Arts Council and dedicated to showing new developments in contemporary art, with the Arnolfini in Bristol, Midland Group in Nottingham, Ikon Gallery in Birmingham, Richard Demarco in Edinburgh, and the Museum of Modern Art in Oxford. Finally, in 1970 the Arts Council opened the new Serpentine Gallery in Kensington Gardens, specially dedicated to showing the work of younger artists.

However, these promising developments did not immediately create a new audience. Press and television hostility to contemporary art remained fierce, and was fuelled in 1976 as the Tate came under attack following the discovery that it had earlier acquired Carl Andre's sculpture *Equivalent VIII* ('The Bricks'). For several years thereafter the Tate remained on the defensive in respect of its activities in the contemporary field and this loss of confidence spread as successive institutions, such as the Hayward and the ICA, were pilloried for their support of supposedly extreme positions in contemporary art.

It was therefore a bold move by the new director of the Tate, Alan Bowness, when in 1983 he responded with enthusiasm to an idea, promoted by the newly formed support group called the Patrons of New Art and based on a suggestion from the architect Max Gordon, that a prize be instituted for the visual arts. His hope was that the prize would do for the visual arts what the Booker Prize, established in 1968, had recently begun to do so successfully for contemporary literature: stimulate public debate and interest and thereby broaden the audience for the new novel.

Initially, like the Booker, things did not go well. There were arguments about the name, the 'Turner' Prize supposedly taking in vain the name of Britain's most distinguished painter. The first winner was an expatriate, the almost unknown Malcolm Morley. There was disquiet about the inclusion of curators or critics in the field and about pitting established means to be an artist in the contemporary world. All its programmes were therefore constructed on the principle of student-centred learning. From the beginning of their course, every student is expected to make independent work – where both the form and the content are of their own choice – which then becomes the subject of tutorial and group discussion. This retrospective approach to teaching is intended to guide but not dictate the direction and concerns of the student's work, to encourage independent thinking and expressive diversity. The aim is to help students develop those characteristics that are essential to sustaining creative activity over a lifetime in a rapidly changing world: productive self-criticism, self-discipline and self-confidence.

I believe that one of the principal reasons the generation of young artists who graduated from Goldsmiths in the late eighties had such an immediate and profound impact on the international perception of British art was that they continued the critical dialogue that had characterized their education into the art world beyond the school. Every exhibition, every interview, every social event became an opportunity to extend awareness and to discuss ideas, feelings, concerns and values. More and more artists were drawn into this dialogue of work and words, and for the first time in memory London could be seen to be generating rather than just responding to the central discourse that characterizes and propels contemporary art of international interest.

Many factors, from the grand to the grassroots, are necessary for a city to become a representative centre of contemporary art both nationally and internationally: substantial and active museums, public exhibition spaces, commercial galleries, alternative spaces, affordable studios, fabrication facilities, publications, critics, collectors and, of course, art schools. But more than anything else a centre needs artists – a concentration and a diversity of good artists from the country as a whole who in turn attract other artists from around the world. Ironically, the success of the art schools in educating the extraordinary number of good artists drawn to London has created an art world in which the schools themselves are no longer the critical centre. And yet the art schools have probably never been more important, not if London is to remain the nationally representative focus for art – as Paris was in France and New York the United States – and is to sustain the quality of creative self-renewal that has characterized the past decade.

**DAVID BOWIE
AND DAVID MALLET**
Stills from the video **Ashes to Ashes**,
1980

The **speed at which the boundaries** between commercial and 'fine' art were
dissolving increased with the new decade. Video art, which was in its infancy as
an 'art form', and cinema were boosted by the experimental techniques facilitated
by the large budgets available for promotional pop music videos and for television
commercials. David Bowie had already appeared in feature films, including Nicolas
Roeg's *The Man Who Fell to Earth*, and between 1979 and 1987 he made more than
a dozen promotional videos in association with director David Mallet which greatly
expanded the boundaries of the form. Advertising agencies also employed new
design techniques, aimed at promoting the 'image' of a brand rather the qualities
of a product. The restrictive rules governing tobacco advertising encouraged a style
of visual punning that was deeply indebted to Magritte, and the Benson & Hedges
Gold campaign, started in the 1960s, continued to be showered with awards.

In contrast to these competitive male worlds, feminist art also began to
blossom. Susan Hiller's training as an anthropologist has led her to describe
her work as 'retrieving and reassembling a collection of fragments', but her
Sentimental Representations, composed principally of rose petals embedded
in acrylic, is also a quiet assertion of feminism in its evocation of a quilt – the
archetypal womanmade artefact in our civilization – not only for the process
by which it is made but for the associations and memories that are implicit in it.
For Hiller distinctions of rationality and irrationality, present and past, fact and
memory are manmade.

**COLLETT DICKENSON
PEARCE & PARTNERS**
Benson & Hedges advertisement, 1980
Art direction by **Neil Godfrey**

Opposite: **SUSAN HILLER**
**Sentimental Representations in Memory of
my Grandmothers (Part 1 for Rose Ehrich),**
1980–81

MIDDLE TAR As defined by H.M. Government
H.M. Government Health Departments' WARNING:

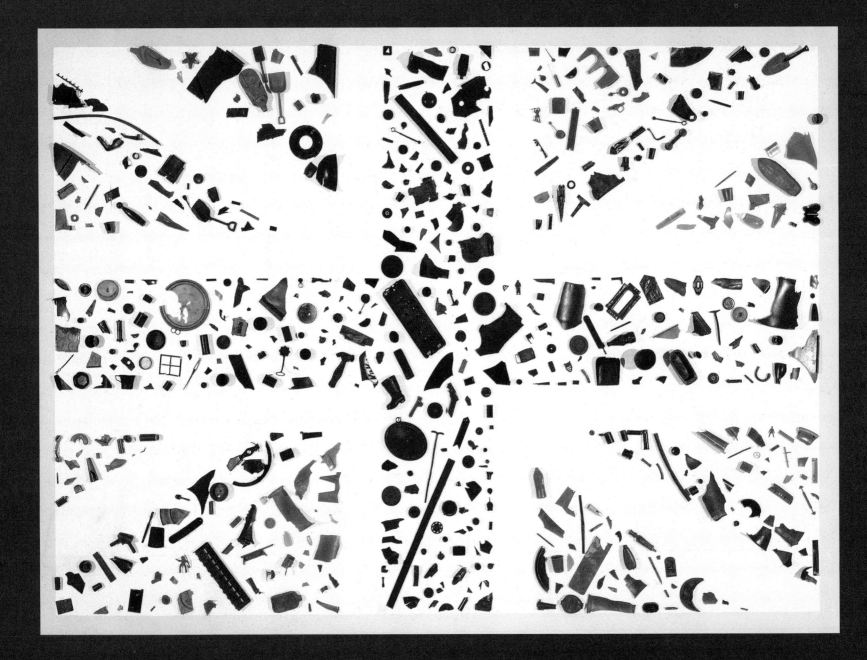

The sculptural work of the late 1960s and the 1970s, which encompassed performance, auto-destruction, land art and the negation of the museum object, gave way to a less radical practice in the work of the 'New British Sculptors', who included Tony Cragg, Bill Woodrow, Richard Deacon and Richard Wentworth and were effectively promoted by Nicholas Logsdail of the Lisson Gallery. Cragg employed urban detritus rather than the traditional materials of sculpture, but his large assemblages use the familiar materials and

images of everyday life, which gives them an immediacy that allows them to be appreciated by a broader artworld. *Britain Seen From the North*, in which the artist contemplates a map of Britain from a position far removed from the seat of power, was installed in his first major British exhibition – at the Whitechapel Gallery – where all the pieces (*Postcard Union Jack*, *Crown Jewels*, *Soldier*, *Polaris*, *Everybody's Friday Night*) had ironic political overtones in the euphoric atmosphere leading to the royal wedding of Charles and Diana that year.

Above: **TONY CRAGG**
Britain Seen From the North, 1981

Opposite: **TONY CRAGG**
Postcard Union Jack, 1981

149

Bridget Riley's black and white paintings produced extraordinarily strong physical and metaphysical effects, but she was already experimenting with greys and then colour in the mid-1960s. However, the colours of many works she painted in the eighties were influenced by a trip she made to Egypt in 1979–80. Riley has emphasized the natural basis of her work: 'I draw from nature, I work with nature, although in completely new terms. For me nature is not landscape, but the dynamism of visual forces – an event rather than an appearance – these forces can only be tackled by treating colour and form as ultimate identities, freeing them from all descriptive or functional roles.... I choose a small group of colours and juxtapose them in different sequences, to provide various relationships and to precipitate colour reactions. These colour *events* are delicate and elusive.'

Elizabeth Fritsch, one of the most successful British potters, uses coloured patterns both decoratively and, in combination with a slanting rim, to produce perspective effects that seem to contradict the flattened shape of the pot itself. This counterpoint is reflected in the musical titles she frequently bestows.

Above:
ELIZABETH FRITSCH
Optical Pot, 1981

Right: **DANIEL WEIL**
Radio in a welded PVC envelope, 1981

Opposite: **BRIDGET RILEY**
Sea Cloud, 1981

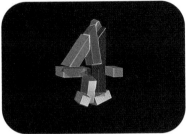

Gilbert and George gave up their roles as 'living sculptures' in 1977 and from 1980 turned mainly to huge photo pieces, which have something of the appearance of stained glass. In *Naked Faith* they appear themselves, standing against flowers, symbols of sex, with boys from London's East End who represent ideal manhood.

i-D magazine was the journal of record for eighties street style. The back cover of issue no. 2, which featured a punk with a Mohican haircut, stated: 'i.D. is a Fashion/Style Magazine. Style isn't what but how you wear clothes. Fashion is the way you walk, talk, dance and prance. Through i.D. ideas travel fast and free of the mainstream....'

The expansion of television included a new independent channel, Channel Four, with its inventive logo, and TV AM, Britain's first breakfast television station, whose headquarters were converted by Terry Farrell from a garage to create the first truly postmodern building in Britain. Its identity is represented with symbolic contextual references: the curving front façade is designed as a billboard screen with colouring based on a sunrise; the central atrium has a gigantic floating classical pediment and a ziggurat stair; while the back wall over a canal is decorated with nine boiled-egg finials.

JAKE TILSON
Bar, The Highstreet SW1, 1983

Opposite:
STEPHEN FARTHING
The Nightwatch, 1983

Below: **ALISON WILDING**
Pond, 1983

The image of modern life in the city became a favoured subject in the 1980s for many artists, who were returning to a more traditional figuration with its roots in Pop Art, even if their techniques remained unconventional. Jake Tilson's dioramas are assembled, like the collages of Kurt Schwitters, from unconsidered items of urban debris, and they complement his work as a designer and producer of artists' books and journals. Stephen Farthing's paintings approach the progress and relentless encroachments of modern technology in home and office environments with a mixture of exhilaration and alarm.

Alison Wilding's sculptures, which always show a rich delight in the varied materials used (here copper, slate and stone), are related to those of the 'New British Sculptors'. A feature of her work is the relationship of two contrasted and separated elements – representing a dichotomy of which the male-female interpretation is only a part – which gives the spectator an insistent reminder of the ties that connect art and life.

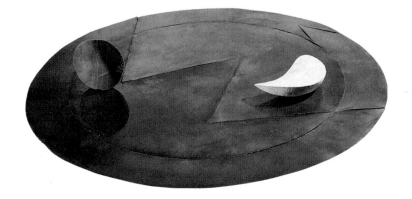

1983

Flanagan's sculpture, which underwent several sudden changes in the course of his career, was especially striking in the late 1960s when, like Richard Long and Bruce McLean, he challenged the Caro-dominated formalist orthodoxy at St Martin's. His early 'soft sculptures' were made of sand, part-filled sacks, rope and a variety of materials, in which the natural force of gravity and a clear indication of the process by which the work was made were conditioning features. Although his leaping bronze hares, begun in the late 1970s, became his best-known works, Flanagan began to work soon afterwards on a series of 'carvings', executed by Italian craftsmen as large-scale realizations of forms he had himself fashioned by folding and squeezing lumps of clay.

At Ian Hamilton Finlay's Scottish 'Little Sparta', as in an eighteenth-century garden, the individual works are part of an overall programme, the aim of which is to evoke a spirit of revolutionary classicism. The fragmentary inscription shown here, carved by Nicholas Sloan, was installed at the time of Finlay's celebrated dispute with the local council – the 'Little Spartan War' – which the artist saw as representing the conflict between law and culture, in which his own role was akin to that of a French Revolutionary hero.

Manchester became an important centre for music and popular culture during the 1980s with the success of Factory Records and the Hacienda club, set up by Tony Wilson and Peter Saville. Saville's record cover for New Order typifies postmodern design in its appropriation of a nineteenth-century floral still life (complete with colour-scale).

Opposite: **BARRY FLANAGAN**
Carving No. 1, 1983

Above: **IAN HAMILTON FINLAY WITH NICHOLAS SLOAN**
The Present Order is the Disorder of the Future, 1983

Right: **PETER SAVILLE**
Power, Corruption and Lies, 1983
New Order album cover

1983

Richard Deacon's sculptures reflect the artist's strong feeling for lyric poetry, so that their abstract form is laden with a wealth of ideas: 'Making has some profound relationship with language. One of the prime functions of language is to describe or reform the world. It is something that is neither yours nor mine, but is ours and lies between us and the stuff out there. Making is not dissimilar.' He describes himself as a 'fabricator' and considers that part of his duty as an artist is to bring the spectator back in touch with the materials of art and the way in which they are joined and manipulated to create the final work. The poetry depends on the way in which they are put together. Surfaces and joins are therefore of great importance, and they are able to enhance the sense that the form of the work divides internal from external space, as if it were covered by an invisible membrane. In this way his sculpture gives shape to experience: 'it mediates and models a notion of what the world is like'.

RICHARD DEACON
Two Can Play, 1983

1984

Below: **NEVILLE BRODY**
Cover of **The Face** magazine,
featuring T-shirts by **Katharine
Hamnett**, June 1984

Below right:
MALCOLM GARRETT
The Reflex, 1984
Duran Duran single cover

Opposite: **JOHN HILLIARD**
Dark Shadow, 1984

Both Brody and Garrett were designers whose work developed from the liberated typography of the album cover and its associated publicity materials. In his pioneering art-direction of *The Face* Brody showed his ability to absorb the ferocity of Punk style, with its use of collage techniques and rough typefaces, but also its models – from Dada procedures to Russian revolutionary Constructivism – and produce something that communicated with a more directed impact, encouraging readers/spectators to challenge their own assumptions about design. The application of these principles to widely distributed magazines paralleled developments in pop music and fashion, creating a genuinely popular form of art – anti-'art' in its opposition to what was perceived as the emptiness and inhumanity of minimalism or the easy commercialism of American late Pop styles. If Brody's work itself became widely imitated in commercial styling, even its derivatives remained close to an original visual experience.

Dark Shadow was part of Hilliard's exhibition *Vanitas*, intended as a *memento mori* for a friend and drawing heavily on art-historical precedents. The double-image produced in a mirror – the traditional iconographic emblem of Vanity – was extended to include a whole range of other threatening images of *Doppelgänger*.

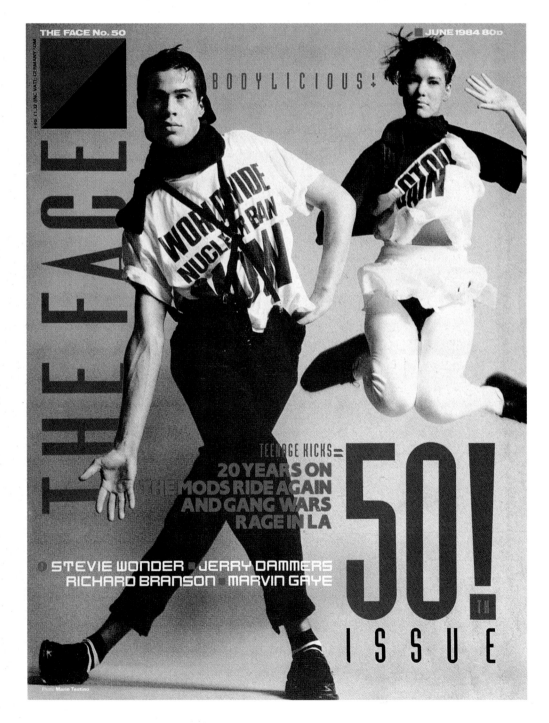

1984

Hodgkin, who has never formed part of any school or movement, has nevertheless prolonged one of the recurrent aims of British artists in the second half of the century: the attempt to combine abstraction and representation. For Hodgkin representation is both physical and metaphorical, and while the vivid colours and broad brushstrokes might suggest works quickly achieved, his paintings are in fact the result of a long and painstaking process. The subject – as often as not clearly referred to by the title (here a lone figure in bed) – is the starting point, but it has to be 'somehow transmuted, transformed or made into a physical object, and when that happens, when that's finally been done, when the last physical marks have been put on and the subject comes back ... then the picture's finished and there's no question of doing anything more to it.'

Allington was one of a number of sculptors who entered art school at the end of the 1960s and sought a renewal of sculpture by focusing more clearly on the 'poetic object'. He is typically postmodern in his interest in both classicism and kitsch – and the way in which they can merge into one another – so that his pastiche baroque cornucopia of plastic tomatoes hints at a romantic longing for an unattainable past. Allington also makes exceptional drawings for hypothetical sculptures, which display a fantasy and quality of line that is reminiscent of Saul Steinberg.

Below: **EDWARD ALLINGTON**
The Groan as a Wound Weeps, 1984

Right: **HOWARD HODGKIN**
Clean Sheets, 1982–84

1984

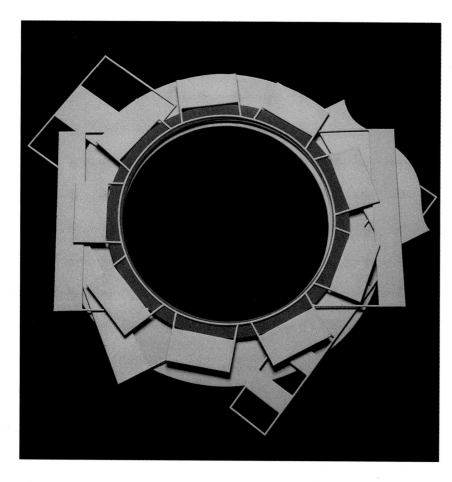

DAVID WATKINS
Voyager, 1984
Neckpiece

Opposite: **RICHARD LONG**
Piemonte Stone Circle, 1984

Below:
RICHARD WENTWORTH
Fin, 1983–84

By the 1980s Long was almost one of the elder statesmen of European art, but the elegance of his stone circles exhibited in baroque palaces still suggested the sublime purity of the natural environment which has always been his medium. His earliest works, such as *A Line Made By Walking England*, created in 1967 in just the way its title suggests, had made a dramatic impact because they were so different from the prevailing formalism of the 'New British Sculpture' of St Martin's. While McLean had parodied Moore and Caro in his performances, Long introduced a new conceptual element to sculpture: the marks and arrangements he made in the landscape were not only immovable but often impermanent, so that the work existed through its documentation – photographs, maps, itineraries. There was a clear distinction between Long's work and American 'Land Art', which claimed possession of the land it used: 'My interest was in a more thoughtful view of land and nature, making art both visible and invisible, using ideas, walking, stones, tracks, water, time, etc. in a flexible way…. I prefer to be a custodian of nature, not an exploiter of it.'

The found elements that are combined in Wentworth's sculptures are manufactured, and his practice suggests delight and irony in equal measure; the pieces are, like so many postmodern works, serious without solemnity. Wentworth has maintained a photographic record – entitled *Making Do and Getting By* – of 'situations that attracted' him, showing improvised solutions that have been devised to cope with problems posed by modern city living.

Voyager, made of neoprene-coated steel and wood, is a neckpiece that has been described admiringly by Barbara Maas as 'of archaic simplicity and computer aided design'. Watkins's neckpieces are conceived not as jewelry for the purpose of adornment, but as body sculptures which restrict the movement of the wearer, acting as a metaphor for and drawing attention to the body.

The Schlumberger Research Centre in Cambridge was designed to accommodate both a large space for the testing of heavy oil-drilling equipment and laboratories and offices where computer modelling and other research can be carried out. Completed in 1985, it was extended in a second phase of building between 1990 and 1992. The most striking feature of the original structure is the triple tent (the upper part of the central tent is seen in the photograph), whose roof is suspended on either side from four sets of twinned masts. The tent covers the test station and a winter garden, while the offices and laboratories run in parallel ranges along its lower parts on either side. Michael Hopkins has allowed the structure of masts, trusses, cables and fabric (engineered by Anthony Hunt in collaboration with Ove Arup) to dictate the

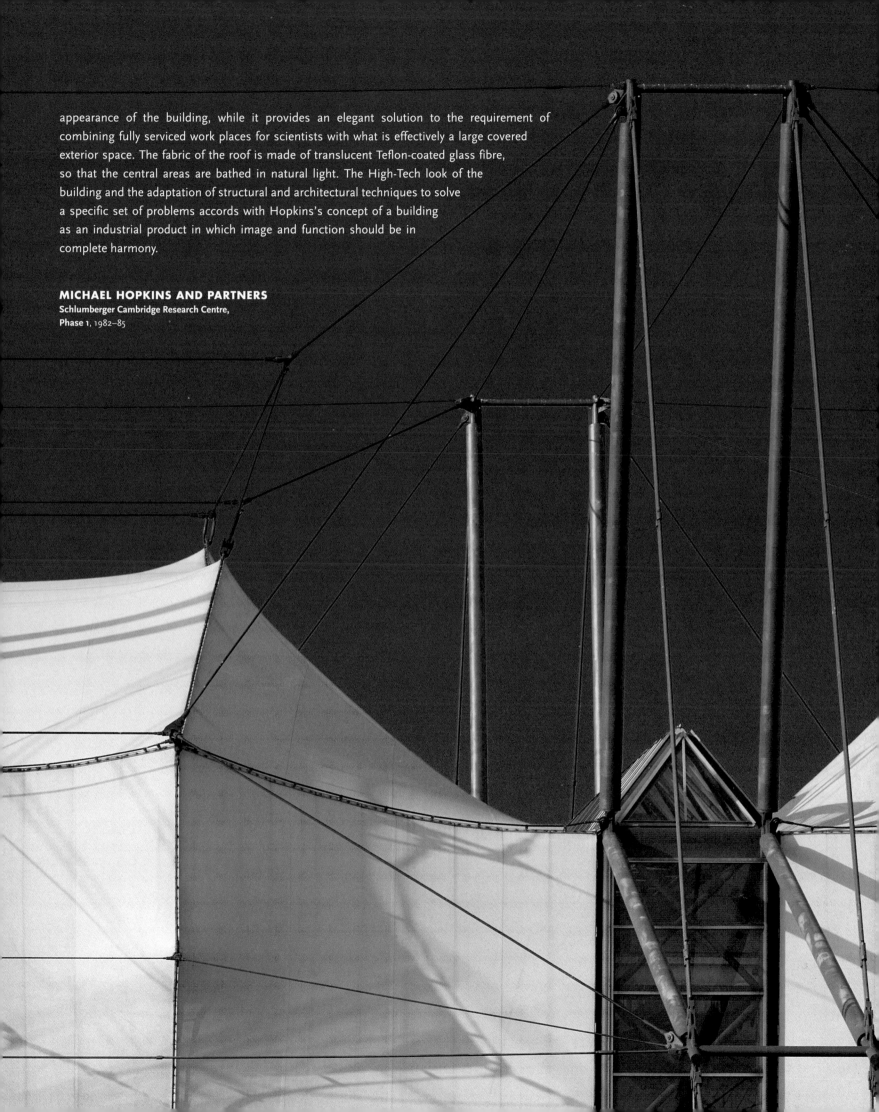

appearance of the building, while it provides an elegant solution to the requirement of combining fully serviced work places for scientists with what is effectively a large covered exterior space. The fabric of the roof is made of translucent Teflon-coated glass fibre, so that the central areas are bathed in natural light. The High-Tech look of the building and the adaptation of structural and architectural techniques to solve a specific set of problems accords with Hopkins's concept of a building as an industrial product in which image and function should be in complete harmony.

MICHAEL HOPKINS AND PARTNERS
Schlumberger Cambridge Research Centre,
Phase 1, 1982–85

Art & Language – whose collaborative work has always been carried out in the name of the group – was founded in 1968, and has been one of the most powerful forces for conceptual art in Britain. The theoretical basis of their work, which was extensively analysed in their journal *Art-Language*, was founded in Marxism and structuralist semiotics, so that the aims of their art are social and political rather than aesthetic. The have consistently questioned the cultural status of the artist by concentrating on the relationship between the art object and its context. Their techniques have included printed texts based on dialogue between the members of the group, but since the end of the 1970s, when the two practising artists have been Michael Baldwin and Mel Ramsden, they have returned to studio practice, although the intent of works like those 'in the style of Jackson Pollock' – which include a series of *Portraits of V.I. Lenin in Cap* – have been clearly ironical. This irony is equally evident in their *Incidents in a Museum* series, which depicts imaginary installations of Art & Language works in New York's Whitney Museum of American Art, one of the key institutions that supported American modernism.

Timney-Fowler's fabrics represent the most appropriate application of postmodern characteristics to interior design. Classical and baroque imagery, a retrospective homage to Italian style of the 1950s and a surrealist wit in the combinations of printed sources are used with a strong feeling for the materials and for the processes they undergo.

Left: **ART & LANGUAGE**
Index: Incident in a Museum V, 1985

Below: **TIMNEY-FOWLER**
Textile from the **Neoclassical** collection, 1985

David Mach's best-known works have been his sculptures created by the accumulation of familiar objects – heads made from wire coat-hangers or matches, buildings from tyres, or his celebrated *Train* at Doncaster (1997) from engineering bricks. The ambiguity of the result is matched by the combination of wit and aggression in their making, while the shock of recognition offered by both subjects and materials has won him genuine popularity. In the 1980s Mach produced several large-scale installations in which groups of objects appeared in an environment consisting of piles of newspapers or magazines carefully arranged to suggest a powerful natural phenomenon like a tidal wave or a river in spate. The principle of sculptural collage and transformation practised by Paolozzi (and previously by Picasso) has been rehabilitated by Mach after a period when the unqualified identity of the sculptural object had been beyond question.

DAVID MACH
Fuel for the Fire, 1986

Left: **MARTIN PARR**
New Brighton
From **The Last Resort** project,
published 1985–86

Above: **CALUM COLVIN**
Death of Venus, 1986

Opposite:
HELEN CHADWICK
Vanity II, 1986

During the 1980s photography and other reprographic processes were incorporated into art works in many new ways. The ecclesiastical appearance of Gilbert and George's photo pieces or the neo-cubism of Hockney's polaroid collages indicated that the photograph could be manipulated successfully as an artistic medium as well as used to document performances or processes that were impermanent. Helen Chadwick exploited the ambiguous nature of photography in a corpus of work that also made use of food, household fluids and human and animal body products in disarmingly colourful and attractive patterns and arrangements. The contrast between blossoming (preserved by photographs) and decay (in the actual materials exhibited) was a recurrent theme, and she applied this to herself, for her work is essentially autobiographical. *Vanity II* shows the decorated body of the artist holding a mirror which reflects her own installation *Of Mutability* (1984–86), a platform decorated with sculptural and photographic images of transience.

Calum Colvin also made use of photography in his series of works portraying goddesses and heroes: he subverts and deconstructs the icons of classical western art by placing them in surroundings of 1970s junk. Botticelli's Venus emerges not from the waves but from a clutter of dolls, a plastic table and a goldfish bowl.

Martin Parr follows photographers such as Brandt, Ray-Jones and McCullin in documenting the underside of life in Britain. His pictures of New Brighton, a dilapidated seaside resort for Liverpudlians on the Wirral, taken in 1983–85, were published in book form as *The Last Resort* with a commentary by Ian Walker.

JAMES STIRLING AND MICHAEL WILFORD
Clore Gallery, Tate Gallery, London, 1980–86

The return to representation in painting was concerned principally with the human figure, and Lisa Milroy's still life paintings stand out from contemporary work. They are painted from memory, and there is a strong sense of detachment in her repeated images of everyday objects – shirts, shoes, ironmongery, tyres – executed on a huge scale, but within an entirely neutral space. The almost photographic realism gives them the nature of documentation: of mentally constructed assemblages or installations.

Matt's Gallery, opened in 1979 in an East End warehouse by Robin Klassnik, was one of the first spaces specifically designed for artists to exhibit installation works, offering something midway between the pushy commercial galleries and museum or art gallery exhibition spaces. Richard Wilson's *20/50* was first exhibited there before its long-term installation in the Saatchi Gallery. It consists of a room filled with used sump oil, over which the spectator walks on a narrowing, rising steel plank, so that the reflection on the surface of the visually impenetrable liquid produces a strong sense of disorientation, but also an impression of great beauty. Wilson works on an architectural scale with familiar elements and materials with which alarming displacements are made, creating a highly effective interior form of environmental art.

LISA MILROY
Tyres, 1987

Opposite:
RICHARD WILSON
20/50, 1987

Several important contributions to the debate on the role of women as artists were made in the late 1980s, a time when the role of women in architecture and other male-dominated fields became increasingly accepted. The assertion of sexuality became an important theme, though it was one that found many different forms of expression. Bridget Bailey used materials traditionally crafted by women to create analogies of the female sex. The painted three-dimensional fabrics she made by a process of steam-moulding and pleating produce a sculptured surface that acts both as disguise and metaphor for the body it is designed to enclose.

Paula Rego's enigmatic narrative paintings and prints, with their recurrent themes of rebellion and escape from dominant authority, recall her experiences as a child brought up under Salazar's dictatorship in Portugal. Sometimes using figures from children's literature (*Nursery Rhymes*, 1989, and *Peter Pan*, 1992, are two suites of prints) or drawing on art of the past or outsider art, her compositions can be strangely disturbing: 'I paint to give fear a face', she has written.

Eva Jirična has appropriated the language of High-Tech architecture and animated it with rich curves to provide a dramatic setting for a discotheque.

Above: **PAULA REGO**
The Policeman's Daughter, 1987

Left: **EVA JIRIČNA**
Interior of **Legends** nightclub,
London, 1987

Opposite: **BRIDGET BAILEY**
**Hand-painted, steam-pleated silk
organza,** 1987

Above:
ANDY GOLDSWORTHY
Blades of grass
creased and arched
secured with thorns
Penpont, Dumfriesshire
14 August 1988

Left:
MICHAEL ROWE
Conditions for Ornament No. 6,
1988

Environmental sculpture, pioneered in Britain in the sixties and seventies by Flanagan and Long, was given a new direction by the work of Andy Goldsworthy. Rather than working primarily with earth or stones to alter features of the environment, he creates objects, but in order to portray nature in a state of change he uses flowers, leaves, twigs and branches of trees, snow, ice – so that these objects are necessarily impermanent. Their continued visibility depends on the richly coloured photographs he makes of them. At the same time, he insists, 'All my work still exists in some form.... Each work grows, stays, decays – integral parts of a cycle which the photograph shows at its height, marking the moment when the work is most alive.'

The dissolution of categories within the broad realm of 'sculpture' has spilled over into the work of craftsmen, whose field of activity, traditionally the making of useful pieces, is often concerned with the creation of objects more closely akin to works of art. While forms or materials indicate the expected function, placing the pieces in a very specific context and defining their relationship with the ambient space, objects such as the vessels in Michael Rowe's *Conditions for Ornament* series may have no effective utilitarian purpose. Indeed, Rowe, a teacher at the RCA and leading theoretician of the decorative arts, has evolved a new metaphorical, conceptual, role for objects created by an innovative practice of the traditional processes of craftsmanship.

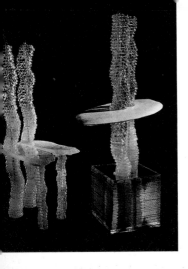

Below:
STEVEN CAMPBELL
Painting Influenced by the Foot
of a Chair and the Top of a Building,
1988

Opposite: **RON ARAD**
The Big Easy Volume 2, 1988

Top: **DANNY LANE**
Solomon chair and table, 1988

Above: **NIGEL COATES**
Genie stool, 1988

Right below: **TOM DIXON**
'S' chairs, 1988

Chairs have become a favoured form for many artists to create objects that are imbued with all the associations of a functional article designed to support the human body while at the same time aspiring to the condition of art – what Richard Rogers has described as 'usable artwork'. Ron Arad, Danny Lane and Tom Dixon all showed their furniture in Arad's One Off showroom, opened in Covent Garden in 1981, where initially Arad and Dixon created 'recycled furniture'. The examples shown here indicate how the generalized form of the chair can be adapted to a highly appropriate sculptural use of the materials chosen: glass for Lane, bent steel for Dixon, and polished welded stainless steel for Arad. The architect Nigel Coates, by contrast, makes elegant use of technology – the wooden seat of his stool is joined like a human pelvis – for a stool designed to provide comfort by promoting ideal posture.

Glasgow – rather than Edinburgh – has been an important artistic centre throughout the century, but the number of leading Glasgow artists in the 1980s – Steven Campbell, Ken Currie, Adrian Wiszniewski, Peter Howson, Stephen Conroy and Douglas Gordon, among others – has led to the label 'New Glasgow School' being applied to the figurative painting several of them have practised. Campbell started as a performance artist before spending five years in the USA. His paintings are tableaux of disquieting rituals, the elusive meaning of which is conveyed by the gestures of the characters. He himself has acknowledged the influence of Bruce McLean and Gilbert and George, not only on his own performances but on his paintings, while the long shadow of Magritte is also plain to see.

Bill Woodrow's sculpture demonstrates the artist's commitment both to his art and to the issues of his time. His work of the early eighties was characterized by his cutting of familiar objects – a guitar, a chainsaw or a bicycle – from washing machines and other household appliances, both old and new objects forming part of the work of art, generally connected by an umbilical strip of metal. More recent works are more complex, some being cast in bronze, but the separation and joining of familiar but unrelated readymade and fashioned parts produces works which impose their presence very strongly on the spectator: their configurations imply a story being told, but the thread of the narrative remains elusive. In *Let's Eat Fish* the groups of letters on the floor spell FISH OUT OF WATER, while the individual upright letters make the word S-O-F-T.

Peter Greenaway, who is a painter and exhibition curator as well as a film director, constructs his films – variations on the themes of sex and murder – as works of art with the power to disturb and disorientate the spectator, rather than simply provide entertainment: 'I wanted to make a cinema of ideas, not plots, and to use the same aesthetics as painting, which has always paid great attention to formal devices of structure, composition and framing.'

Right: **BILL WOODROW**
Let's Eat Fish, 1988

Left: **PETER GREENAWAY**
Still from the film **Drowning by Numbers,** 1988

Craigie Aitchison belongs to the generation of artists who came to prominence in the 1950s, and his own first one-man show was in 1960 at the Beaux Arts Gallery, which had supported the 'Kitchen Sink' artists as well as the 'School of London'. His figurative paintings nevertheless have strong affinities with the 'New Figuration' of younger painters in the 1980s. The simplicity, purity and directness of his work has sometimes been described as childlike, but it is the result of a ruthless process of reduction, both of composition and subject-matter: 'I do mostly black people, dogs, religious pictures and still lifes', he has said.

Stephen Conroy, nearly thirty years Aitchison's junior, creates a deliberately anachronistic atmosphere both by his technique and the appearance of his characters. The formal action of his interior scenes appears to take place in some late Victorian dreamworld, not unlike the fairy world painted by Peter Blake. He has explained that he wants to recreate the 'sense of dissonance' he finds in the work of Degas and Sickert, whose paintings of ordinary life appear to uncover such disturbing undertones.

Both Georgina Godley, with her Surrealist-inspired padded and sculpturally shaped garments, and Georgina von Etzdorf with her richly patterned fabrics also provoke an uneasy sense of déjà vu.

Above: **GEORGINA GODLEY**
Corrugated Strides, 1989
Silk taffeta trousers

Right: **STEPHEN CONROY**
Che Gelida Manina, 1988–89

Opposite:
CRAIGIE AITCHISON
Portrait of Patrice Felix Tchicaya,
1989

Below: **GEORGINA VON ETZDORF**
Invitation to the **Rhythm & Blues** collection,
Autumn/Winter 1989

IN THE DESULTORY POLITICAL DECADENCE of the mid-nineties a new generation of British artists and designers came of age; they had been taught to pursue economic as well as aesthetic goals, but, alienated from the mainstream of society, they turned this lesson against the world of their predecessors. Their response was to produce work that excluded all but their own age-cohort: the enemy of the old avant garde, the middle class, was replaced by the enemy of youth, the middle-aged. Taste became meaningless and was eclipsed by Style. Postmodern irony pervades nineties art, and artists' ambivalent take on the artworld was summed up in Chris Ofili's response to the announcement by the fashion star Agnès B that he had won the 1998 Turner Prize: 'Where's the cheque?'

Many of the practices of the 1960s have been taken up again: Rachel Whiteread's casts have a precedent in William Tucker's casts of the interiors of milk bottles (*Ceremonial*, 1961–62); the intense focus on the body and its fluids – remember *Dr Strangelove* – goes back to the hero of sixties artists, Marcel Duchamp, as well as the Boyles; Antony Gormley's self-casting recalls Roy Adzak's half-positive, half-negative *Human Columns* of 1966; Cornelia Parker's deconstructions echo the auto-destructive art of Gustav Metzger; while computer, kinetic and interactive art has its roots in Jasia Reichardt's 'Cybernetic Serendipity' exhibition at the ICA in 1968. However, with the passing of thirty years, the goals appear to be very different: personal rebellion rather than social revolution, and an attempt to take over rather than to subvert the art market.

The economic conditions for art have changed considerably, both with major new commissions for architects and designers funded from the National Lottery and with the colossal influence of Charles Saatchi, the maecenas of 'New British Art'. Not only has he supported and collected young artists, he has defined the school and established a wider market for its work by his highly successful sale of 130 works in December 1998 – undertaking to reinvest the proceeds in a new young generation, both through purchase grants and by funding bursaries at the RCA, Goldsmiths and Chelsea School of Art.

The advance of postmodernism has blurred the dividing lines between old categories. For many potters, glassmakers, jewellers, metalworkers and furniture designers function has become a secondary consideration – or is of no consequence at all – while the work of documentary or fashion photographers, film and video makers, and graphic designers working on paper or in electronic media is art as much as that of a painter or a sculptor or a printmaker. The notion of an 'artwork' has also been extended in other directions during the decade, merging with the concept of 'lifestyle': installations and artist-run galleries have included the work of young artists such as Richard Foster, who has treated the office environment as art (echoes of Latham's Artist Placement Group), or Peter Harris and Charles Avery, for whom curatorial activity as well as performance becomes art.

It should be emphasized once again that 'New British Art' – given a comprehensive showing in the 1997 'Sensation' exhibition at the Royal Academy – has not had a monopoly of the decade. The majority of the artists, designers and architects whose work is included in the book are still alive and active, and the many overlapping layers of the artworld resemble a brilliant collage – that process which more than any other can stand as a metaphor for the creativity of the past fifty years, whether for the combination of different levels of meaning and expression in a single work, for the use of appropriation to stir hidden analogies or for the capacity to communicate aesthetic, moral and social values.

The nineties were ushered in by the exhibition 'Freeze', curated in 1988 in a disused warehouse in the London docks with consummate professionalism by Damien Hirst. The works included were by his fellow-students at Goldsmiths College. Hirst is in many ways the representative artist of these years – not because of the media celebrity he has achieved, but because, for all the irony with which his work is presented, he is a dedicated artist with a command of an extraordinarily wide range of modes. His work with living and dead creatures – from butterflies to sharks to sheep – is balanced by a subtle and perceptive sense of colour and process in works that define a new kind of postmodern minimalism. He understands clearly his purpose as an artist: 'Art is about life, and it can't really be anything else. There isn't anything else.'

THE TURNER PRIZE Nicholas Serota

FOR MUCH OF THE NINETIES the level of public interest in the visual arts has been so striking that it is difficult to remember that until quite recently the audience in Britain for contemporary art has been relatively small. In 1964 more than 50,000 people visited the Rauschenberg exhibition at the Whitechapel and in the same year 90,000 saw the Gulbenkian Foundation survey exhibition, 'Painting and Sculpture of a Decade '54–'64', at the Tate; but these were exceptional numbers. Generally an attendance figure of more than 25,000 has been regarded as remarkable. While British artists in the postwar period have won prizes at the Venice Biennale, or have been honoured with major exhibitions abroad, their achievements have rarely raised public acclaim at home, at least not until each generation approaches the age of sixty.

In the 1960s Bryan Robertson's Whitechapel Gallery was an honourable exception to this rule, regularly presenting important shows of younger and middle-generation British artists. Paradoxically his departure from the Whitechapel in 1968 coincided with several developments in which we may trace the roots of the remarkable growth in audiences for contemporary art which has occurred during the 1990s.

Between 1965 and 1970 the opportunities to see contemporary art outside the commercial galleries were dramatically transformed. Within this short period occurred the opening of the Hayward Gallery and an enlarged ICA on the Mall in 1968; Norman Reid's reorganization of the displays at the Tate placing greater emphasis on the modern and international dimensions of the collection, followed by a much more adventurous and high-profile series of exhibitions of artists then in their forties, such as Warhol, Hamilton, Lichtenstein and Oldenburg; the opening of new venues such as the Arts Lab or the new Space studios at St Katherine's Dock in which initiatives by artists created space for performance, installation and events; and the opening or reorientation of a group of independent regional galleries,

often funded in part by the Arts Council and dedicated to showing new developments in contemporary art, with the Arnolfini in Bristol, Midland Group in Nottingham, Ikon Gallery in Birmingham, Richard Demarco in Edinburgh, and the Museum of Modern Art in Oxford. Finally, in 1970 the Arts Council opened the new Serpentine Gallery in Kensington Gardens, specially dedicated to showing the work of younger artists.

However, these promising developments did not immediately create a new audience. Press and television hostility to contemporary art remained fierce, and was fuelled in 1976 as the Tate came under attack following the discovery that it had earlier acquired Carl Andre's sculpture *Equivalent VIII* ('The Bricks'). For several years thereafter the Tate remained on the defensive in respect of its activities in the contemporary field and this loss of confidence spread as successive institutions, such as the Hayward and the ICA, were pilloried for their support of supposedly extreme positions in contemporary art.

It was therefore a bold move by the new director of the Tate, Alan Bowness, when in 1983 he responded with enthusiasm to an idea, promoted by the newly formed support group called the Patrons of New Art and based on a suggestion from the architect Max Gordon, that a prize be instituted for the visual arts. His hope was that the prize would do for the visual arts what the Booker Prize, established in 1968, had recently begun to do so successfully for contemporary literature: stimulate public debate and interest and thereby broaden the audience for the new novel.

Initially, like the Booker, things did not go well. There were arguments about the name, the 'Turner' Prize supposedly taking in vain the name of Britain's most distinguished painter. The first winner was an expatriate, the almost unknown Malcolm Morley. There was disquiet about the inclusion of curators or critics in the field and about pitting established names against Young Turks. There was also, increasingly, a sense of predictability, given that five of the first six winners were precisely the artists who had constituted the first shortlist in 1984. Above all there was dismay that the small size and hasty fashioning of the annual Turner Prize exhibition seemed to deny the public any real opportunity to become familiar with the work of the shortlisted artists. The prize lacked confidence and any real sense of public engagement.

In 1991, following the withdrawal of another commercial sponsor, the prize was relaunched under the sponsorship of Channel 4 Television. The new sponsor provided more substantial television coverage and a new format was created to ensure a more evenly balanced field by the introduction of an age limit of fifty. The Tate at last made a serious commitment to a more effective display of each artist's work. Furthermore, there was a real attempt to communicate with a broader public through a catalogue and extensive programme of discussions which by the mid-nineties had extended beyond London to a series of debates held in galleries across the country. However, the success of the prize as a focus for an annual debate about the state of contemporary art, accompanied by cartoons and feature articles in the national press, owes less to these changes in rubric and means of promotion than to the changing character of contemporary art in the nineties.

The 1991 shortlist was notable because the oldest artist, Anish Kapoor aged thirty-seven, appeared an elder statesman beside the others, who were all well under thirty. Most of the broadsheet critics were outflanked by this sudden emergence of a new generation and reacted adversely. Even more striking was the fact that two of four nominees were women. In the first four years of the prize, before the formal shortlist was abandoned for the years 1988 and 1989, only two women had been nominated compared with twenty-one men. By contrast in the years 1991–98 fourteen of the thirty-two nominees were women. Furthermore, while the new art of the eighties had been seen to reaffirm the commitment to the more traditional craft practices of painting and sculpture, the new art of the nineties was often more directly expressive of the issues and predicaments of everyday life and employed the more contemporary means of the photograph, film and video.

Quite suddenly, it seemed that art could be young, female and directly connected to the viewer's daily experience. Given that the majority of the Tate's public is below the age of thirty-five, this change brought an immediate sense of identification for a large part of the audience and their enthusiasm, communicated by word of mouth rather than through a press which was either uncomprehending or hostile, began to have an impact on the numbers visiting the exhibition. A climate was created in which an audience, stimulated by the work of their peers and pursuing their own curiosity, responded directly to the work without waiting for the endorsement of the older critics. Experiencing contemporary art had become, like cinema, a much more general part of young people's lives.

Of course, the attention given to the Turner Prize is only one manifestation of a much wider change in attitudes which has also seen an extraordinary growth in the number of artist-run gallery spaces and an increase in the audiences for contemporary art at other London venues, such as the Serpentine, Hayward, ICA and Whitechapel, not to mention Charles Saatchi's personal gallery in north London. The Saatchi Gallery, which opened in 1985, has set the pace through its dramatic exhibitions, initially of the work of major American and European artists but increasingly of younger artists, presented on a scale which no public institution can quite emulate.

Nevertheless, the Turner Prize is now the focus of this much wider public interest and has become an event in the national calendar much more eagerly anticipated than anyone might have predicted even ten years ago.

The metaphysical quality of Anish Kapoor's sculpture comes from the sense of envelopment the spectator experiences on looking into the apparently infinite depth of its colour-saturated cavities, a sense of the sublime. Colour, pure pigment, has always been a key element in Kapoor's sculptures, and he sees it in terms of a Jungian archetype: 'Colour has an almost direct link with the symbol-forming part of ourselves.... It is just there.' His concern as a sculptor is 'to make sculpture about belief, or about passion, about experience, that is, outside of material concerns.'

ANISH KAPOOR Untitled, 1990

Having originally used photography as a means of documenting his work, Boyd Webb came to see the photograph itself as the work of art and the elements represented, whether made or manipulated, as only stages in its creation. He works on a large scale – *Mezzanine* is a colour photograph covering nearly two square metres – and his concern for the political and ecological mismanagement of our world is expressed by his representations of apparently parallel worlds in which familiar objects have unfamiliar properties.

Vivienne Westwood was one of the key players in the Punk movement of the 1970s, her partnership with Malcolm McLaren bringing about a conjunction of music, style and design that touched every aspect of the artistic world. After their collaboration ended in the early 1980s, the force of Westwood's subversive creativity remained highly influential in the world of fashion, although directed towards a much more mainstream audience: 'I realized that by attacking the establishment I'd become a victim; the only true way to make a difference is through ideas, not rebellion.'

The television series *Spitting Image* was another major force of social and political critique in the 1980s, satirizing Margaret Thatcher throughout her years of power in Britain.

PETER FLUCK AND ROGER LAW
Spitting Image puppet of Margaret Thatcher, 1990

Opposite:
VIVIENNE WESTWOOD
From the **Portrait** collection,
Autumn/Winter 1990

Right: **BOYD WEBB**
Mezzanine, 1990

Left: **RAY FLAVELL**
Greenpiece, 1991

Opposite: **CORNELIA PARKER**
Cold Dark Matter: An Exploded View,
1991

Below: **NEVILLE BRODY**
Poster for the typeface **F State,**
from **Fuse 1,** 1991

Cornelia Parker uses processes of destruction and deformation, finding and assembling, on both a physical and a mental level, to produce works of art that force the spectator to re-evaluate the properties of the physical world. Cold dark matter is the name scientists give to the indefinable substance that holds the universe in equilibrium, and it is applied here to a work made from fragments of a greenhouse blown up by the army under the artist's instructions and reassembled around a lightbulb in a gallery installation. Much of Parker's work is devoted to showing how destructive processes can transform objects creatively, allowing their new structure to form part of a system that exists side by side with the everyday world.

The typography and language research project *Fuse* was set up in 1990 by Brody with FontShop International to explore the assumptions of typography in the light of digital technology and renew the design of type from first principles. In *Fuse* magazine, edited by Jon Wozencroft, current uses of type are explored and their authoritative nature subverted: 'Access to digital typography empowers more people with the tools to question and develop alternative forms of visual language.'

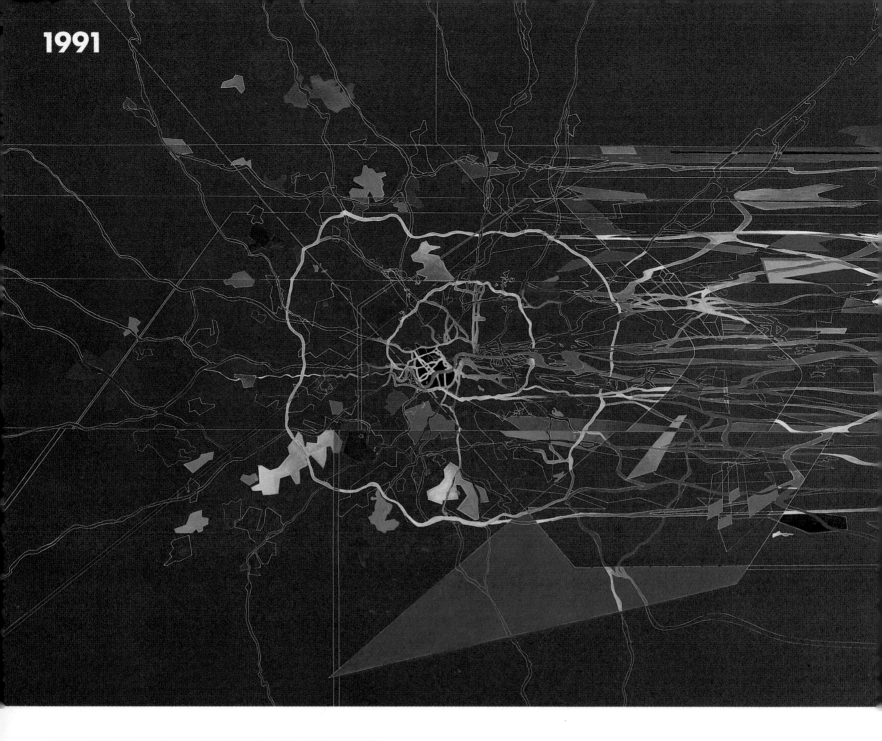

ZAHA HADID
London 2066, 1991

Left: **PETER DOIG**
The Architect's Home
in the Ravine, 1991

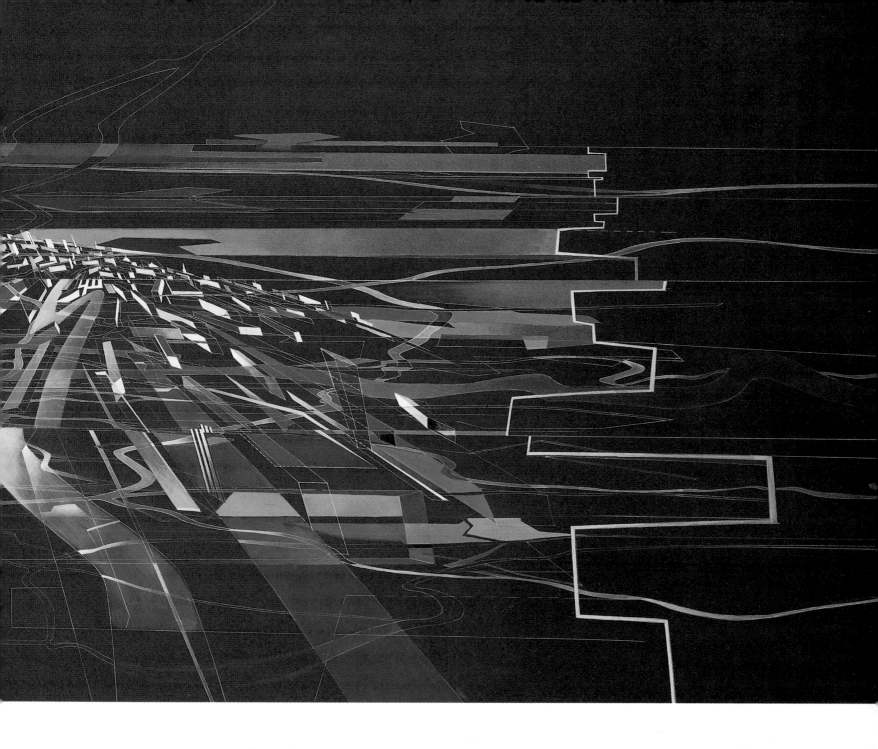

Zaha Hadid has been recognized as one of the most innovative architects working in Britain, and her winning entry in the competition for a new home for the Welsh National Opera in Cardiff in the mid-1990s would have been one of the finest new buildings in Britain, but the project was abandoned. Hadid's paintings based on computer models are particularly striking, and in her plan for London in the second half of the twenty-first century the brushstrokes, moving to the east, 'cut new section-lines of air and area for what we believe could be new areas for buildings, for it is the very intersection of vertical structures to the ground where public activities would be intensified in this new plan.' Kenneth Frampton has written of Hadid: 'The space she creates stretches constantly towards the infinite, racing for the sun.... For her, the modern project is not only incomplete, it has hardly even begun.'

Peter Doig's paintings, predominantly snow scenes recalling his native Canada, are disarming in that the wistful mood invoked by the image depicted is disturbed by the physical presence of the veil of paint representing snow. The artist seems to be playing two roles, portraying both human creativity and the force of nature.

Freud's paintings of the human figure are without precedent in British art, and the sense of monumentality in his works of the 1990s is particularly evident in his paintings of the colossal – and outrageous – performance artist Leigh Bowery. Freud always paints with his model present, and the intimacy of the relationship between painter and subject is so strongly conveyed that, since the 1950s, his work has provoked hostility as well as admiration. Working through a period when Mondrian, Duchamp and Magritte have presided over so many artists, Freud has looked rather to the old masters, Watteau or Velázquez, though he is no less of his time than the contemporary 'Young British Artists'.

Gary Hume achieved a huge early success in the late 1980s with a series of large neo-minimalist paintings of hospital doors executed in house paint, and the three door-sized panels that make up *Naturalist* are an extension of this theme in which figurative elements and new textures are introduced. Hume says of his work: 'I just do simple things. Describing anxiety and love and beauty, sadness and pathetic hopes.'

Peter Chang, whose technical expertise comes in part from his youthful employment making reproduction antiques, uses recycled plastic for his massive bracelets because of its 'present day integrity' and for the pleasure of turning rejected waste material into lasting, precious objects: 'Plastics, unlike some natural materials are basically characterless, anything you make out of them only adds'.

PETER CHANG
Bracelet, 1992

Opposite: **LUCIAN FREUD**
Back View (Leigh Bowery), 1992

Below: **GARY HUME**
Naturalist, 1992

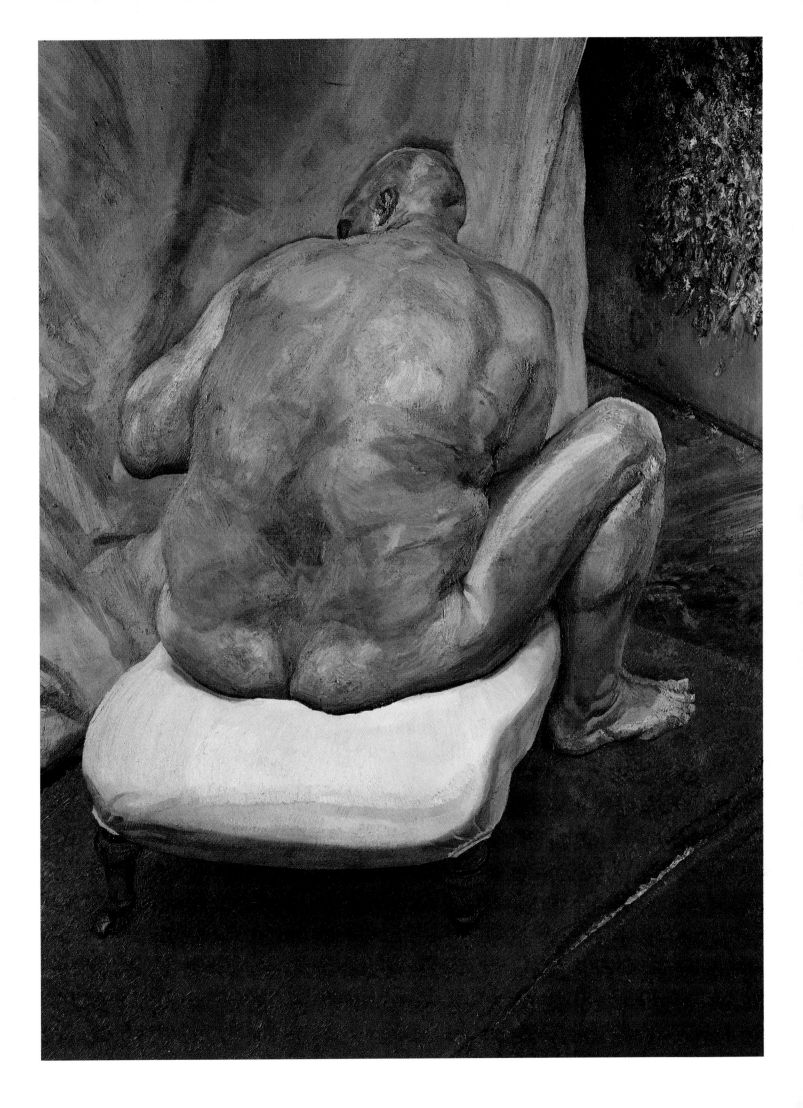

Shirazeh Houshiary's sculptures have a mystic connection with the earth. Many of her earlier works, such as the monumental *Temple of Dawn* (1987) in Münster, used soil or clay as part of their material, while in more recent works light and dark metals, gold, silver, copper, lead, are used with symbolic significance. Like *Licit Shadow* (1993), in which six divided trays were arranged in a cosmic circle, *Bright Night in Dark Day* symbolizes the sun within the planetary system with its six rows of six squares, while the honeycomb arrangement 'evokes the ripples of water which break the light from above'. Each row in either direction has light and dark equally distributed in all possible permutations: their equality symbolizes 'the original androgynic state', while 'the dance of light and dark ... points to the multiplicity of our being'.

Caroline Broadhead makes art in the form of clothes, giving a sense of movement, as though of participation in a performance, by the curved seams with which the panels of fabric are stitched together. Her figures have a presence as sculptures that evoke nineteenth-century artists' fantasies of living clothes, like Max Klinger's *A Glove*.

Industrial design had dominated the furniture market in the postwar period, but a 'craft revival' began in the 1970s in which the skill of workmanship applied to individual pieces again became the defining quality. Fred Baier was a leading figure in this movement, and his work is notable for the way in which the expressive assembly of metal forms takes precedence over functional considerations.

CAROLINE BROADHEAD
Wobbly Dress II, 1992

Right above: **FRED BAIER**
Steel chairs, 1992

Opposite:
SHIRAZEH HOUSHIARY
Bright Night in Dark Day, 1992

Rachel Whiteread's sculptures are casts – in plaster, rubber or resin – of the inside of things, and there is an unexpected sense of déjà vu in the perception of a surface that lies so close to a familiar surface; we seem to see things we know very well but have never before been able to grasp. *House* – a cast of the last house to be demolished in an East London street – drew public attention to Whiteread, not only for its scale, but because the solid interior seemed to have trapped a host of collective and private memories. There were many protests when the local council would not allow it to stand permanently, but as it was a work about impermanence and about memories it is perhaps fitting that, like many conceptual works, its own existence depends on records and memory.

Sean Scully's artistic education was in Britain, but he has lived in the USA since 1975 and the characteristic style of his work since 1980 – bold horizontal and vertical stripes on large, often composite, canvases – belongs to the tradition of American abstraction. He sees abstraction as a form of 'non-denominational religious art ... the spiritual art of our time.'

Opposite:
RACHEL WHITEREAD
House, 1993

Below: **SEAN SCULLY**
Vita Duplex, 1993

DOUGLAS GORDON
Psycho, 1993

Opposite: **JULIAN OPIE**
Imagine You are Driving, 1993

Below: **TERENCE CONRAN**
Quaglino's ashtray and salt and
pepper pot, 1993

Douglas Gordon's *Psycho* hitchhiker (heading for the motel?) was made in connection with the artist's *24 Hour Psycho*, a showing of Hitchcock's film slowed down to two frames per second so as to last a complete day. It was silently back-projected onto a screen set up in the middle of a room, allowing the spectator to move around the image, and the appropriation and manipulation of the original gave rise to complex tensions: expectations were constantly frustrated because the action did not move fast enough, while surprising details became visible that would normally pass unperceived. Gordon's concern is the psychological effect of the moving image on the spectator as voyeur: 'it is about a human drive of real desire to see what shouldn't be seen.'

Julian Opie's painted steel sculptures done just when he left college were an immediate success and his work was widely exhibited before he had turned thirty. More recently he has explored simplification and simulation in a world of infinitely changing systems. Moving through his installations is like finding oneself inside a computer game, as the artist poses the question: at how many removes are we from reality?

1993

Most of Antony Gormley's sculptures consist of lead body cases made from plaster casts of his own body. These generalized body forms, bent crouched or stretched out, are frequently grouped in large installations. *Field for the British Isles* is a work of a different kind (a reworking of a project first produced in Mexico in 1989), in that most of the figures are small (just over 8 cm high), but there are some 40,000 of them. They were made by 100 people from a community in St Helen's, Lancashire, who worked together under the artist's direction, while deciding the scale and shape of each figure for themselves. Each work is therefore individual, but they form an integral mass. The artist has described the collective experience of making *Field* as a kind of harvesting, 'tilling the earth with your own hands, but instead of making something grow, it's the earth you are forming directly. The harvest comes from within the people, or the thing that is growing comes out of the people. Everyone has their own row and throughout the project they continue to do row after row on the same strip like the old medieval strip field and they build up a very strong relationship with that patch of earth. Those gazes they are seeding in the clay look back at them as they are working, suggesting that consciousness is not only inside. I see it as a kind of soul garden.'

ANTONY GORMLEY
Field for the British Isles, 1993

Below: **NICK PARK**
Still from the animated film
The Wrong Trousers, 1993

Damien Hirst has become by far the best known British artist of the 1990s, principally because of his use of animals confined within glass tanks – an analogy of the museum vitrine – whether a lamb, the cross-section of a cow and her calf, or a rotting head with maggots and flies enacting a perpetual cycle of life and death. Like Francis Bacon, an artist whom he much admires, Hirst's intention is to portray the condition of living creatures without a trace of sentimentality, and this message is in part conveyed by the evident labour and attention with which the works are made.

Mona Hatoum took her art to an extreme of self-reference in *Corps Etranger*, in which an endoscopic film of the exterior and all the interior orifices of the artist's body were projected within a large viewing cylinder onto the floor, accompanied by the sound of her breathing, pulse and heartbeat. For Hatoum the human body represents both vulnerability and resistance in a context that can be interpreted both personally and politically.

Mark Wallinger uses the metaphor of horseracing for his commentaries about artistic identity. *Half-Brother* is composed of half-portraits of two horses born from the same mare.

Above:
MARK WALLINGER
Half-Brother (Exit to
Nowhere/Machiavellian),
1994

Opposite:
DAMIEN HIRST
Away From the Flock,
1994

Opposite above:
MONA HATOUM
Corps Etranger, 1994

DONOVAN WYLIE
Children from the A46 site playing
in a nearby field, 1994
From the **Losing Ground** project, 1993–95

MAT COLLISHAW
Leopardskin Lily, 1995

The artworld of the 1990s was less conducive to direct social protest than had been the case in the 1960s and 1970s, so that much of the most powerful work in this field came in photography. For two years Donovan Wylie followed a group of 'New Age travellers' from a country site between Stroud and Bath, where they lived in what one of the women described as 'paradise', to the appalling misery of their broken lives in the East End of London after the Criminal Justice Act had forced them to move on.

Howard Sooley documented the shingle garden created by the artist and film director Derek Jarman in the years when he was dying of AIDS. In the shadow of the bulk of Dungeness nuclear power station, Jarman developed an extraordinarily beautiful garden, with flowers and plants adapted to the coastal ecology interspersed with found objects that make it into a living sculptural installation.

Mat Collishaw uses photography to make art: in 1995–96 he created a series of flowers overlaid with animal imagery or with photographs of diseases. Jon Thompson has written that the contrast of the natural and the artificial produces 'an almost populist version of the beautiful; the attraction and repulsion involved in the deceptive or aberrative image, where it also assumes something of the authority of a closely observed truth.'

DEREK JARMAN
The artist's garden, Dungeness, Kent
Photo by **Howard Sooley**, 1995

Minimum, the 'excitement of empty space', is John Pawson's ideal. He advocates the pursuit of simplicity in architecture, art and design, where in his search for harmony, reason and truth the designer reduces or condenses 'every component, every detail and every junction ... to its essentials'.

JOHN PAWSON
Interior of the architect's house
in Notting Hill, 1992–95

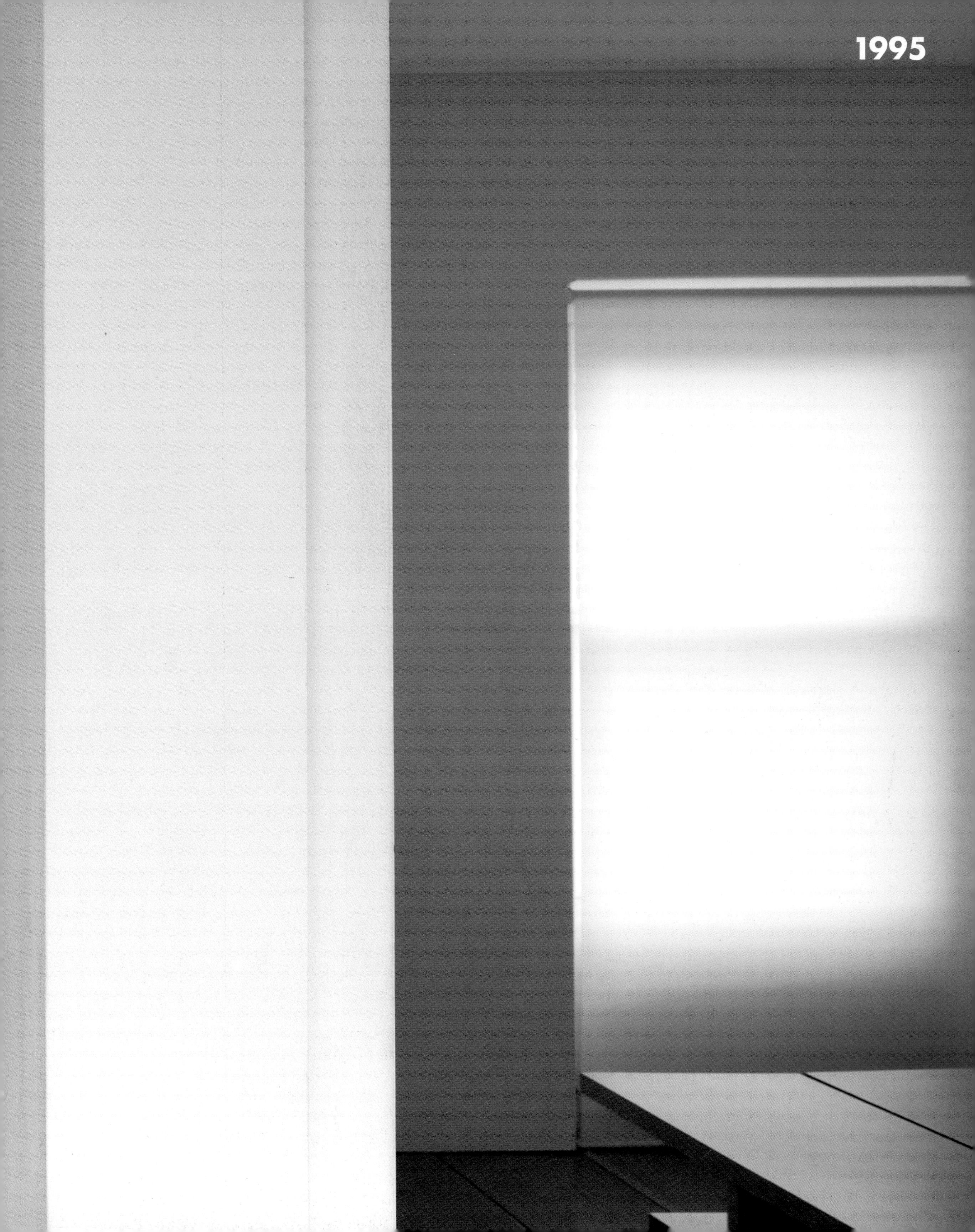
1995

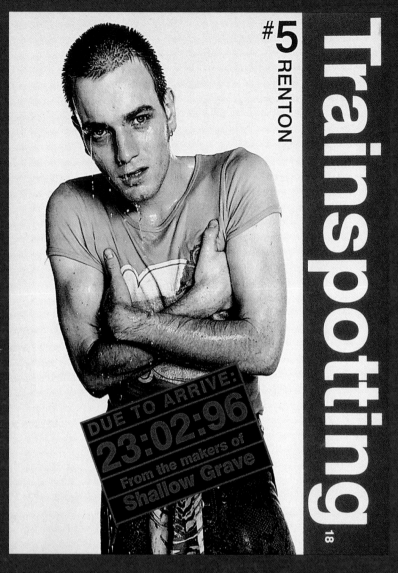

#5
RENTON

Trainspotting 18

DUE TO ARRIVE:
23:02:96
From the makers of
Shallow Grave

orange™

SAM TAYLOR-WOOD
Pent-Up, 1996

Right: **GILLIAN WEARING**
60 Minutes Silence, 1996

Gillian Wearing works as a 'documentarist', using video and photography to penetrate the inner lives of her subjects at a level quite distinct from the role-playing forced on them by late twentieth-century society. *60 Minutes Silence*, one of the works for which Wearing was awarded the 1997 Turner Prize, is a revealing video for which the group of police men and women undertook the testing task of keeping still and silent for an hour.

Sam Taylor-Wood's videos suggest more extreme situations: the panoramic multi-screen video projection of *Pent-Up*, first shown at the Chisenhale Gallery, shows separate monologues, the isolated intensity of which is only broken when, briefly, there seems to be some communication across the screens.

Designers Republic and Tomato are two of the most innovative young design groups (while Wolff Olins is one of the most old-established and distinguished). Tomato came to prominence with their poster and credits for Danny Boyle's film *Trainspotting*. These reflected the values of the film itself, which with its wit and pathos, tenderness and violence, demanded acceptance, rather than reactionary condemnation or liberal sympathy, for the life of the heroin-addicts it depicted. 'The point is,' as one of the characters says, 'you've got to find something new.'

Opposite left:
DESIGNERS REPUBLIC
Present, 1996
CD artwork for Sun Electric

Opposite right: **TOMATO**
Poster for the film **Trainspotting**,
1996

Opposite below:
WOLFF OLINS
Corporate identity for
Orange™, 1996

1996

The work of Jake and Dinos Chapman relies on the changed sensibilities that are reflected in the stylish black humour of contemporary cinema. Recreating Goya's *Great Deeds Against the Dead* from the *Disasters of War* in the form of fibreglass shop-window dummies negates the traditional concept of taste, as do their equally disturbing groups of joined pubescent children (sometimes with their facial features replaced with adult sexual organs). The Chapmans make the mutant mannequin figures more real by dressing them in wigs and Fila trainers: 'The shoes stop them from becoming classical sculptures. They return to the shop window.... It ruins the notion that they are aberrations. It denies the dysfunctional aspect by implying that they are dynamic and flexible; it proposes that they are better than – beyond – humans.' The Chapmans' insistence on a new set of values is characteristic of their generation's desire to revive the impact and appeal of art.

In these conditions, photography and fashion have become closer than ever to fine art. The artist whose work best sums up the spirit of this period is Rankin, who with Jefferson Hack founded the magazine *Dazed and Confused* in 1991. His photographs – whether portraits of celebrities or fashion shots – are blatantly commercial but have created a new, very British, chic in their flouting of all the advertisers' conventions. With characteristic irony Rankin writes: 'One thing you have to remember about my work is, it has no style.'

Above: **INFLATE**
UFO Light, 1996
Designed by **Nick Crosbie**

Right: **JAKE AND DINOS CHAPMAN**
Zygotic, 1996

Opposite: **RANKIN**
Hungry, 1996

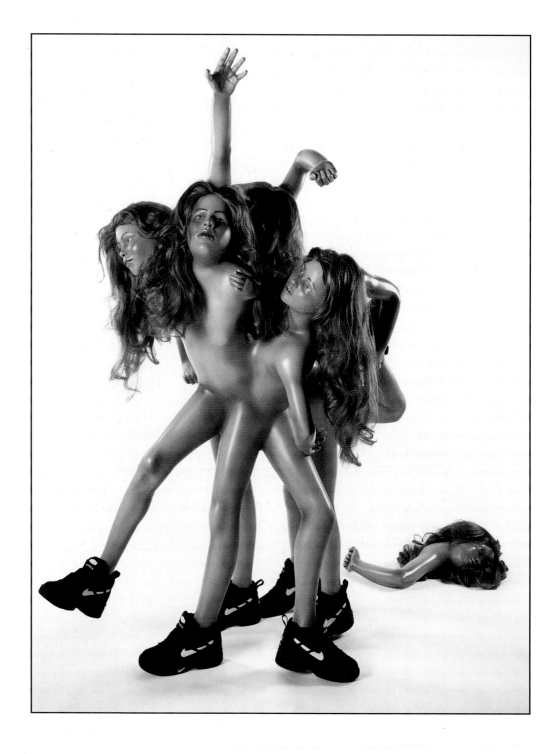

JENNY SAVILLE
Shift, 1996–97

Below: **PHILIP EGLIN**
Seated Nude, 1996

Opposite: **CHRIS OFILI**
The Holy Virgin Mary, 1996

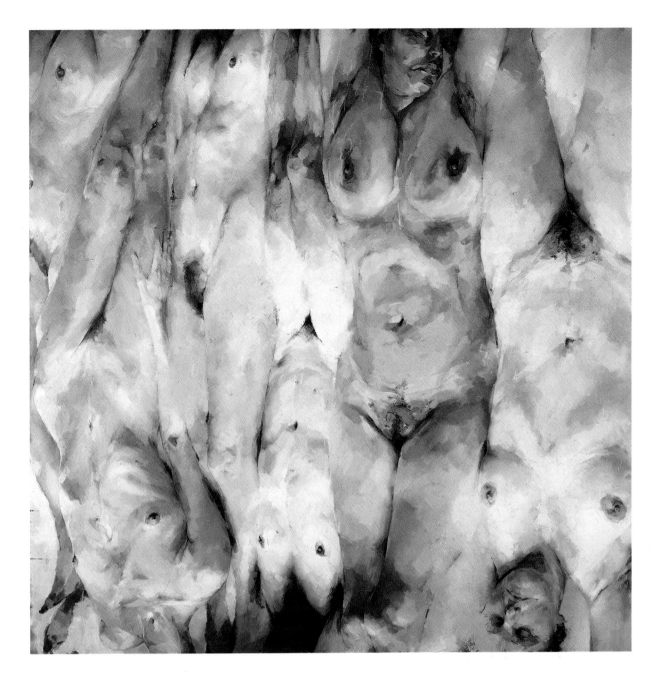

Chris Ofili achieved media notoriety by including elephant dung among the materials in his paintings – including a 1993 self-portrait entitled *Shithead* – but this notoriety has obscured the intention: to integrate something tangibly African into the work of a British black artist working in the 1990s. The juxtaposition of emblems representative of a confused cultural identity – the dung, clippings of female genitals from porn magazines, the obsessional pattern-making based on rock paintings in Zimbabwe, the Christian reference of the title – results in a joyous resolution that defies social and cultural prejudice, whether it is the open hostility of racism or the fearful indulgence of white liberalism.

Jenny Saville's huge paintings of female nudes (*Shift* measures 3.65 metres square), done from photographs and from the model, can be seen as a step beyond feminist argument. By adopting a style that seems to derive from that of Lucian Freud, who has often faced accusations that he has exploited women's bodies, she forces each spectator to confront his or her own prejudices about the tradition of the art-school life class and the representation of the nude in western art.

Like many recent ceramists, Philip Eglin has moved from pottery to sculpture. Drawing on the tradition of Staffordshire flatback figures, he constructs figures (generally female nudes) by folding and modelling sheets of clay that he has already decorated, using transfer printing techniques, with images often inspired by graffiti – a reminder of the statues covered with graffiti in his home town, Harlow New Town.

Alexander McQueen's impact on the fashion world has been like that of the 'Sensation' artists on the artworld – a dramatic entrance greeted with shock, envy and then a realization of the close affinities these artists have to the roots of their own art. McQueen came to fashion through working as a tailor's cutter, but the outré sexiness and sophistication of the *Bellmer La Poupée* collection (one of his earliest shows) fully justified the title's reference to the fetishist Surrealist artist. McQueen's talent as a creator of wearable clothes led to his appointment as chief designer of Givenchy in 1997 in succession to John Galliano.

Galliano, now chief designer for Dior, made his first impact in his degree show at St Martin's in June 1984 with a collection based on French eighteenth-century models. His designs are derived from an outrageously eclectic series of sources handled with an extravagant operatic romanticism.

Nick Knight's acute sense of colour and form and his technical skill not only with the camera but also with techniques of computer enhancement have made him the ideal artist to record British fashion at a time when it has the reputation of leading the world.

Left:
ALEXANDER McQUEEN
From the **Bellmer la Poupée**
collection, Spring/Summer 1997
Photo by **Nick Knight**

Opposite: **JOHN GALLIANO**
Necklace for Christian Dior,
Autumn/Winter 1997–98
Photo by **Nick Knight**

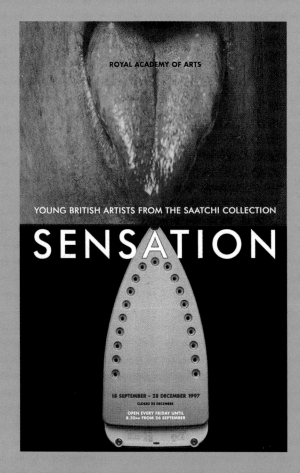

Fiona Rae was one of the painters who came to prominence in the late 1980s in 'Freeze'. Her works of this period were often painted collages of images appropriated from both 'high' and 'low' art, deconstructed and reassembled. More recently she has made variations on a format in which a black and white ground, painted with strong indications of gesture and movement, both underlies and invasively spills over precisely painted discs, whose circular bands are painted in vibrant colours. Her biography in the *Sensation* catalogue suggests that 'the paintings seek to resolve the conflict between pure abstraction and figurative representation in the age of postmodern appropriation'.

The design group Why Not Associates wrote of their 'Sensation' poster: 'it's the right image for the show because it's about context, seemingly innocuous images and objects transformed by the context in which they are presented. We thought about the aggressive nature of the work, a lot of which is to do with bodies and everyday objects ... the idea was skin, that's where sensations come from, someone said heat, and immediately we could see those shapes in our heads.'

Above: **WHY NOT ASSOCIATES**
Poster for the '**Sensation**' exhibition at the
Royal Academy of Arts, 1997

Right: **JAMES DYSON**
Dyson Dual Cyclone™ DC02, 1995
Winner of the Design Council Award
for European Design in 1997

Opposite: **FIONA RAE**
Untitled (Sky Shout), 1997

Below: **MAAZ**
Doorknobs, 1997

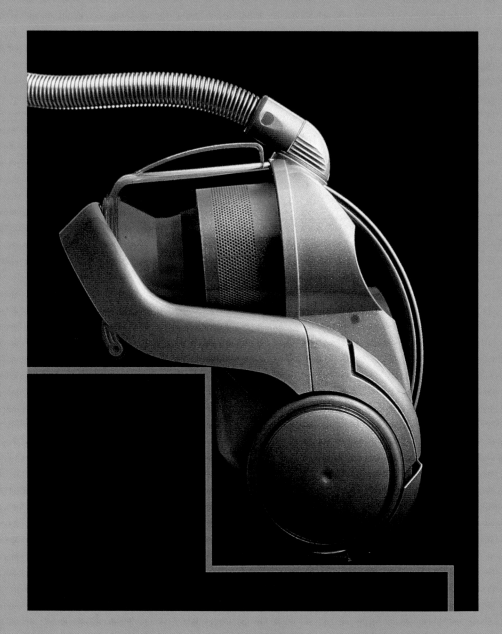

The site for the new British Library in Somers Town near St Pancras Station was acquired in 1976 – although the architect had worked on a project to replace the library centred around the old domed Reading Room in the British Museum since 1962. Wilson's building, considerably reduced from the originally approved plans, was finally opened to readers in 1998 and the transfer of all books is due to be finished during 1999. Rather than try to put the clock back with an indulgence in postmodern decorative features, the design of the library follows the lead of the true non-conformists of the international Modern Movement – identified by the architect as Wright, Aalto, Asplund, Scharoun, Melnikov and Kahn – who approached the 'travesty of thirties architecture promoted as the international style' in a spirit of creative doubt. While the principal material of the library echoes Gilbert Scott's St Pancras Station (seen in the background of the photograph) Wilson's aim has been to avoid false monumentality and to respond to the needs of the reader, whose prime requirements are a quiet well-lit space with easy accessibility to books.

Tom Hunter's photograph, part of a series documenting a community of squatters in Hackney, is derived from *Girl Reading at an Open Window* by Jan Vermeer, an artist whom Hunter sees as having taken 'average, working class people for his subjects, portraying them in real, commonplace situations, giving them dignity'. The work won the John Kobal Photographic Portrait Award for 1998, and the whole series of photographs was acquired by the Saatchi Collection. Hunter is a representative of the new 'Neurotic Realism' movement, identified and collected by Charles Saatchi in the late 1990s and the subject of a series of exhibitions, the first of which was mounted at the Saatchi Gallery in January 1999.

Above: **COLIN ST JOHN WILSON**
British Library, London, 1982–98

Opposite: **TOM HUNTER**
Woman Reading Possession Order, 1998

Michael Craig-Martin's work has always been concerned with the relationships of ordinary objects with art, with the spectator and with the mediating space. These relationships raise the issues of representation and of the artist as *auteur*. Much of Craig-Martin's most recent work has taken the form of gallery or museum installations, in which the architectural features of the room are the given elements, the context in which the objects painted on the brightly coloured walls – with illusionistic simplicity but bewildering dimensions – establish their particular presence. The artist has written: 'The world in front of our eyes is extraordinary. The difficulty is in seeing what is in front of our eyes. The difficulty for the artist is in acknowledging what he sees.' 'The experience you have as a viewer, at the moment of viewing – that is the experience of a work of art.'

MICHAEL CRAIG-MARTIN
Room 3 from **Always Now**, a site-specific
project at the Kunstverein, Hanover, 1998

Ian Davenport first exhibited in 'Freeze', but his work is in many ways more traditional than that of his fellow exhibitors, being concerned both with abstraction and with process – the interaction between control and chance. His paintings are made by pouring paint, so that the hand of the artist is obscured, and the textures of the different media used – household gloss paint, industrial matt paint and varnish – determine the forms that the channels of paint take, though the artist remains in charge. As he has written, 'The structure of the painting is formed by the paint running into itself. Each of my paintings has evolved from a very deliberate process, not from intuitive marking.'

Don Brown's smooth-cast, life-size self-portraits are smartly dressed in casual clothes, sometimes wearing sunglasses to emphasize the attitude of cool detachment. The idea, as Adam McEwen has written, 'is about making nothing so that it can be everything; showing the world without speaking'.

The development of the Worldwide Web as a medium for advertising and recreation has opened opportunities for artists as well as designers. Following Web artist William Latham's experimental *Organic Art*, the 'Serious Games' show (1997) at the Barbican included the work of artists such as Ann Whitehurst; Henry Newton Dunn has produced a brilliant series of images for Levis; while AudioRom both on the Web and at the ICA have shown the imaginative possibilities of interactive multi-media projects. In *Shift Control*, a work produced in CDRom format which won a 1998 BAFTA award, the active observer accesses different graphic devices to modify and generate sounds.

DON BROWN
Don, 1998 (detail)

Right: **JONATHAN IVE**
iMac, 1998

Opposite: **IAN DAVENPORT**
Poured Painting: Lime Green, Pale Yellow, Lime Green, 1998

Below: **AUDIOROM LTD**
www.audiorom.com, 1998
News page from the AudioRom website

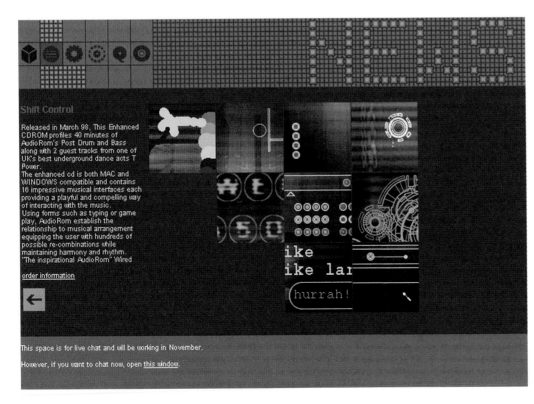

RICHARD ROGERS PARTNERSHIP
The Millennium Dome under construction, Greenwich,
London, 1997–99

1999

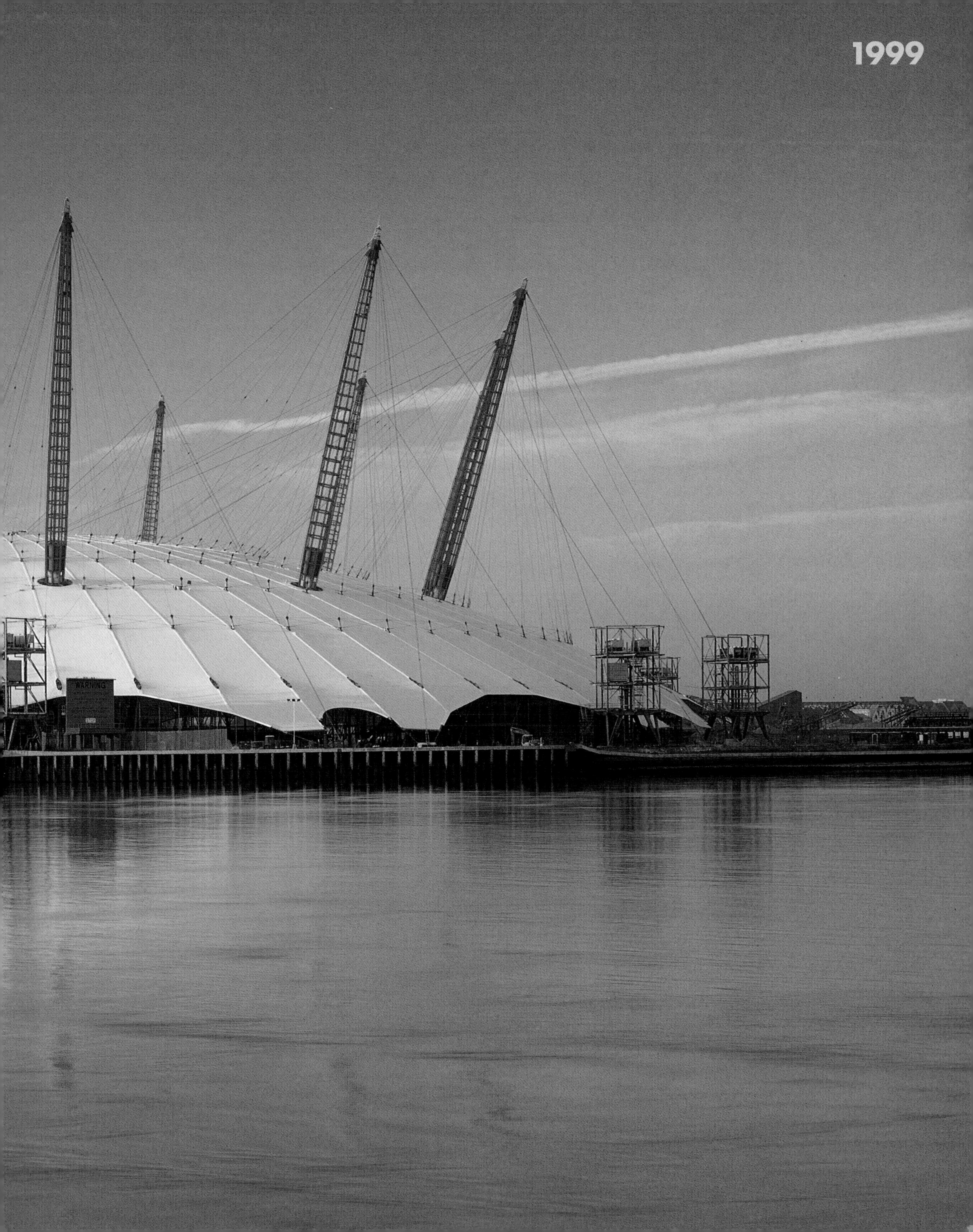

BIOGRAPHIES

AGIS, MAURICE   1966
b. 1931, sculptor

He studied at St Martin's and later taught there and at Goldsmiths. From the mid-1960s to the late 1970s he collaborated with **PETER JONES** on *Space Place* and *Colourspace* (in which they started using pneumatic structures), projects that explored the impact of colour on the perception of space in an environment open to the audience. Since 1980 he has worked independently as a sculptor – though collaborating with musicians, including Stephen Montague, to provide an electro-acoustic dimension to his environmental pieces – increasing the size of the *Colourspace* installations and moving on to the even larger *Dreamspace* works, the first of which was commissioned in 1996 for Copenhagen's year as European City of Culture.

AITCHISON, CRAIGIE   1989
b. 1926, painter

Born into a distinguished Edinburgh legal family, Aitchison trained as a lawyer, but having come to London in 1948 found that he preferred paintings to the law. After his discovery of Piero della Francesca and other artists at the National Gallery he enrolled at the Slade. He was given his first exhibition in 1959 at the Beaux Arts Gallery. Since 1987 he has worked on an important group of paintings of the Crucifixion.

ALDRIDGE, ALAN   1969
b. 1938, graphic artist

He studied at Romford Technical College and has been a freelance designer since 1963. He did much to introduce Pop styles to British book design in his work for Penguin and to advertising art with works such as his 1969 poster for Warhol's *Chelsea Girls*, for which he was threatened with prosecution. He has also collaborated on prizewinning children's books.

ALLINGTON, EDWARD   1984
b. 1951, sculptor

He studied at Lancaster College of Art (1968–71) and the Central (1971–74) and is associated with the sculptural movement that sought a renewal in a return to the 'poetic object'. He has been associated with the Lisson Gallery since 1983.

ANDERSON, LINDSAY   1973
1923–94, film and theatre director

Films he directed include *This Sporting Life* (1963); *If...* (1968), which won the Grand Prix at Cannes; and *O Lucky Man* (1973). He was artistic director of the Royal Court Theatre from 1969 to 1975.

ANDREWS, MICHAEL   1979
b. 1928, painter

He studied under William Coldstream at the Slade, a school where the students were more committed to traditional techniques of painting than at the RCA, and he had his first one-man exhibition at the Beaux Arts Gallery in 1958. Both **FREUD** and **BACON** influenced and encouraged his early work, and he painted them in their milieu in London with friends and models in Muriel Belcher's Colony Room in 1962. Later in the 1960s, in his *Good and Bad at Games* triptych, he was to paint other artist friends, **PAULA REGO**, **CRAIGIE AITCHISON** and Victor Willing. His figure paintings led to his inclusion in the 'School of London', but he is also an imaginative painter of landscape subjects.

ANNESLEY, DAVID   1964
b. 1936, sculptor

A pupil of **CARO** and **KING** at St Martin's, 1958–62, he returned to teach there and at the Central soon after his graduation. His work of this period is in the St Martin's 'New British Sculpture' mould, though more strongly influenced by Pop than that of his colleagues. He visited the USA in 1966, working with Kenneth Noland, and in 1969 gave up sculpture for a period to work on painting.

ARAD, RON   1988
b. 1951, furniture and interior designer

Born in Tel Aviv, he studied at Jerusalem Academy of Art and at the AA, founding One Off Ltd with Dennis Groves and Caroline Thorman in 1981. In 1989 he founded Ron Arad Associates in London. His work as an interior designer includes the shop for Bazaar (1985–86) and the Tel Aviv Opera House (1990).

ARCHIGRAM   1965
architectural group

The group, named after their polemical broadsheet, eight issues of which were published, was founded by Peter Cook (b. 1936) in 1963 as a 'loose gathering of architects bored with the then current architecture'. The other members were Warren Chalk (b. 1927), **RON HERRON**, Dennis Crompton (b. 1935), David Greene (b. 1937) and Michael Webb (b. 1937). *Archigram*, which was strongly influenced by Buckminster Fuller, promoted the ideal of 'adaptable and flexible architecture which could be plugged in when needed and thrown away when not needed, a continuous cycle of change and metamorphosis'.

ARMITAGE, KENNETH   1959
b. 1916, sculptor

He studied at Leeds College of Art and the Slade and resumed work as a sculptor after war service. However, he destroyed most of his prewar carvings, turning to work in plaster, cast in bronze. He taught for ten years, from 1946, at Bath Academy of Art. The human figure has remained his principal subject and bronze his favoured medium, although he has experimented with a variety of materials, including aluminium, wax, resins and paint.

ARNOLD, TOM   1955
b. 1928, ceramic designer

He studied industrial ceramic design at the RCA and joined the Ridgway group in 1953. He designed many revolutionary shapes for the company, partly inspired by a visit to the USA in 1956, including the 'Metro' pattern, used for the 'Homemaker' design, which won a Design of the Year award in 1958. He left Ridgway in 1960 to take up teaching at Wolverhampton College of Art, and was later Principal of both Guildford School of Art (during the 1968 student sit-in) and of West Surrey College of Art at Farnham. He later worked in Australia, New Zealand and back in England in art education.

ARROWSMITH, CLIVE   1972
b. 1947, photographer

He studied painting at Queensferry and Kingston-upon-Thames art schools. He took the photographs used on many of Paul McCartney's solo albums and from 1970 worked for *Vogue* as a fashion photographer. He was the photographer for two Pirelli calendars (1991, 1992), continues to do fashion and advertising photography and is an official photographer to both the Dalai Lama and the Prince of Wales.

ART & LANGUAGE   1985
conceptual art group

The group, based on Marxist principles and always signing its work collectively, was founded in Coventry in 1968 by Terry Atkinson (b. 1939), David Bainbridge (b. 1941), **MICHAEL BALDWIN**, a graduate of Coventry College of Art, and Harold Hurrell (b. 1940); their journal, *Art-Language*, was first published in 1969. In the 1970s membership of the group reached thirty, but Atkinson left to work independently in 1975, and by 1977 the group comprised Baldwin and two members who had joined in 1971, **MEL RAMSDEN** (who had studied at Nottingham College of Art and began contributing to *Art-Language* while living in New York) and the critic and editor Charles Harrison. The group, whose conceptual work has taken many different forms, was shortlisted for the Turner Prize in 1986.

AUDIOROM   1998
multi-media art group

A London collective of musicians, artists, programmers and designers. Their *Shift Control* won the 1998 BAFTA Interactive Design Award.

AUERBACH, FRANK   1973
b. 1931, painter

Born in Berlin, he came to Britain in 1939. He attended **BOMBERG**'s evening classes at the Borough Polytechnic and went on to St Martin's and the RCA. His first one-man show was at the Beaux Arts Gallery in 1956. His boldly executed paintings, with heavy impasto, have been confined to urban views near his Camden Town studio and figure paintings of close friends. He is a leading member of the 'School of London' defined by **R.B. KITAJ**. In 1986, representing Britain at the Venice Biennale, he won the Golden Lion award.

AYRES, GILLIAN   1966
b. 1930, painter

She studied at Camberwell and came to the fore in the late 1950s as the most painterly of the British artists who absorbed the influence of American Abstract Expressionism. She taught at Bath Academy of Art from 1959 to 1966 and then at St Martin's. She had her first one-person show at Gallery One in 1956 and took part in the 'Situation' exhibitions in 1960 and 1961. She has continued to develop her abstract idiom, often on a large scale, building up extremely heavy textures on the canvas with brilliant colours. She was shortlisted for the Turner Prize in 1989.

BACON, FRANCIS   1953, 1975
1909–92, painter

Born in Dublin of English parents, Bacon had no formal art training. During the 1920s and 1930s he worked principally as a furniture designer and interior decorator, and his painting at that time met with no commercial success. However, he made a strong impact immediately after the war with his *Three Figures at the Base of a Crucifixion* (Tate), and his work since that time was almost entirely devoted to the human figure. Although his models are readily identifiable, portraiture is as absent from his work as narrative, and the constant theme of his work is the individual human condition, with all the isolation, suffering and cruelty that this implies.

BAIER, FRED 1992
b. 1949, furniture designer

He studied at Birmingham College of Art and the RCA, and he has been a teacher and lecturer as well as a furniture maker at the forefront of the new craft revival.

BAILEY, BRIDGET 1987
b. 1960, textile artist, milliner

She studied at the West Surrey College of Art and has specialized in steam-moulded and pleated fabrics, in which carefully placed screenprinted stripes emphasize the forms created. She has provided fabrics for many designers and, with Anne Tomlin, founded the hat company Bailey Tomlin in 1987.

BAILEY, DAVID 1965
b. 1938, photographer, film director

After working for John French for a year, he started his career as a fashion photographer in 1960 and was responsible for many of the most striking images of the fashion and music worlds in that decade. From the mid-1960s he broadened the scope of his work, directing commercials and documentary films as well as producing many books of photographs.

BALDWIN, MICHAEL 1985
b. 1945, conceptual artist
See **ART & LANGUAGE**

BAWDEN, EDWARD 1950
1903–89, painter, printmaker, illustrator

He studied at Cambridge School of Art and the RCA Design School, returning to teach at the RCA for many years. He was an exceptional book illustrator, but also a fine poster artist and wallpaper designer. He worked on a large scale in murals such as those for Morley College (1928–30), done with Eric Ravilious and Cyril Mahoney, and for the Festival of Britain.

BAXTER, GEOFFREY P. 1966
1926–95, glass designer

He studied at Guildford School of Art and the RCA, immediately joining Whitefriars Glassworks as resident designer. He remained there from 1954 to 1980, influencing the development of British glass by his introduction of styles and techniques derived from Scandinavian glassmaking.

BEATON, SIR CECIL 1953
1904–80, photographer, theatrical and film designer

His prewar work included both designs for the theatre and photography in the worlds of society, fashion and the cinema, including several visits to Hollywood. During the war, his photographs of war leaders and of action both in the East and on the Home Front were widely published. His best known costume designs were for the film version of *My Fair Lady* (1963), starring Audrey Hepburn, and his subjects as a photographer in the 1950s and 1960s extended from members of the royal family sitting for official portraits to icons of fashion, music and show business.

BERRY, IAN 1977
b. 1934, photographer

Until 1958 he was working as a photographic assistant and press photographer. From 1959 to 1962 he worked in South Africa, where he was the only photographer to record the Sharpeville massacre. He was in Paris between 1962 and 1967, since when he has worked in London. He joined Magnum in 1963 and has received many awards for his work.

BIRDSALL, DEREK 1969
b. 1934, graphic designer

He studied at Wakefield College of Art and the Central and has been a prolific designer and art director for corporate clients as well as designing books, exhibition catalogues and gallery guides. He has taught at the LCP, the Central and the RCA.

BLAHNIK, MANOLO 1977
b. 1943, shoe designer

Born in the Canaries, he studied in Geneva and Paris before moving to New York. In 1971 he settled in London and opened his boutique, Zapata, in 1973.

BLAKE, PETER 1961
b. 1932, painter

He studied at Gravesend School of Art and, after national service, at the RCA, where he developed a style based on his fascination for the unsophisticated imagery of popular culture. He was close to the Pop generation of artists, but never really one of their group. He returned to teach at the RCA from 1964 to 1976. He designed album covers (*Sergeant Pepper's Lonely Hearts Club Band*) and advertisements and in 1975 was a founder member of the Brotherhood of Ruralists, when Victoriana and fairies became the dominant theme in his work. In his more recent work he has returned to urban popular themes.

BOMBERG, DAVID 1955
1890–1957, painter

Originally a lithographer's apprentice, Bomberg determined from the age of eighteen to become an artist, and the Jewish Educational Aid Society made it possible for him to study at the Slade from 1911 to 1913. He was associated with the Vorticists, but rejection by the art establishment during and after World War I led him to pursue an independent path, travelling extensively and painting landscape, still life and figure compositions with a broadly gestural technique. His work as war artist in 1942 again found no favour with the establishment, although his *Underground Bomb Store* (Imperial War Museum) is one of the masterpieces of the period. From 1945 to 1953 he taught evening classes at the Borough Polytechnic: through the work of pupils such as **AUERBACH**, **KOSSOFF** and Gustav Metzger, he became one of the father figures of British figurative painting in the second half of the century.

BOSHIER, DEREK 1961
b. 1937, painter, sculptor

He studied at Yeovil School of Art and the RCA, where he was one of the first Pop generation, and he later taught at the Central and at Hornsey from 1963; his work was included in the 'New Generation' show at Whitechapel in 1964 and he had his first one-man show at the Robert Fraser Gallery in 1965. His work moved to abstraction, then to minimalism and conceptual art before returning to figuration in the 1980s. He moved to the USA in the early 1980s.

BOWIE, DAVID 1980
b. 1947 (David Robert Jones), musician, actor, art collector

He made his debut in the age of Mod in the 1960s: his first hit was 'Space Oddity' in 1969, and he has progressed through several transformations – from Ziggy Stardust (1972) to Thin White Duke. His keen interest in the visual arts has led to collaborations with film directors and artists (**BOSHIER** designed the album cover for 'Lodger'), and he is an art publisher and an eclectic and discriminating collector.

BOYLE, MARK 1967
b. 1934, sculptor, multi-media artist

He studied law at Glasgow University in 1955–56, then moved to London with the painter **JOAN HILLS**. He was self-taught as an artist and exhibited assembled junk sculptures in 1963, while his first joint exhibition with Hills was at the Indica Gallery in 1966. Through the 1960s they collaborated on light-environments, both in their Sensual Laboratory and for rock music performances. Their work since then has combined aleatoric techniques with ecological concerns in such projects as *Journey to the Surface of the Earth*.

BRANDT, BILL 1953
1904–83, photographer

Born in London, he was educated in Germany and Switzerland and worked in Man Ray's photographic studio in Paris. During the 1930s he worked as a documentary photographer in Britain, later also specializing in portraits of writers and artists, landscapes and nudes.

BRATBY, JOHN 1958
1928–92, painter

He attended Kingston-upon-Thames School of Art and the RCA, having his first one-man show at the Beaux Arts Gallery in 1954 while still a student. He was the leader of the New Realists (with **GREAVES**, Middleditch and **JACK SMITH**), and his many paintings of domestic interiors (often with his wife Jean) led to their being called the 'Cornflakes' or 'Kitchen Sink' school. He represented Britain at the 1956 Venice Biennale, and in 1958 he became widely known for the group of large paintings used as the works of the fictional Gully Jimson in the film of *The Horse's Mouth*.

BRISLEY, STUART 1968
b. 1933, sculptor, performance artist

He studied at Guildford School of Art, the RCA, the Munich Akademie and Florida State University. After working as a sculptor (using both movement and light), he became a prominent performance artist in the late 1960s, undergoing rituals of endurance intended to draw attention to the political issues of power, authority and consumption. He was a member of the Artist Placement Group from 1967 to 1971 and has often worked in collaboration with other artists.

BROADHEAD, CAROLINE 1992
b. 1950, textile artist, jewelry designer

She studied at Leicester School of Art and the Central (under **RAMSHAW**). During the 1970s she started making jewelry from textiles – soft jewelry or 'wearable sculpture'. She moved on to 'conceptual clothing' and performance, which she financed by her commercial work (producing buttons and acrylic jewelry through the company C&N, which she founded in 1978 with Nuala Jamison). Her work has been widely exhibited internationally, and from 1987 she taught at Middlesex Polytechnic.

BRODY, NEVILLE 1984, 1991
b. 1957, typographer, graphic designer

He studied at Hornsey and the LCP and made his reputation producing record covers. He was art director for *The Face* from 1981 to 1986, winning several awards, and he subsequently designed *City Limits* and *Arena*. He started his own studio in the late 1980s to develop the expressive possibilities of digital forms of type, undertaking work for many international organizations, including Greenpeace and Amnesty International. He also set up the interactive magazine *Fuse* with FontShop International in 1991.

BROWN, DON 1998
b. 1962, sculptor

He studied at the Central and RCA. From 1994, in addition to his own sculpture, he collaborated with Stephen Murphy on photographic works that derive from a process of model-making and digital imaging.

BUCKLEY, STEPHEN 1972
b. 1944, painter

After studying at Newcastle-upon-Tyne (with **HAMILTON**) and Reading, he developed a method of working in which the processes his materials undergo are as important as the images of the abstract compositions. He taught for many years and was twice winner of a John Moores prize (1974, 1985).

BURGIN, VICTOR 1975
b. 1941, painter, conceptual artist

He studied at the RCA and at Yale, where the student radicalism of the 1960s led him to approach art as a form of political statement, in which technique, media and aesthetics are subordinated to the conceptual impact of images and words. He was shortlisted for the Turner Prize in 1986.

CAMPBELL, STEVEN 1988
b. 1953, painter

Born in Glasgow, he studied there and was a performance artist before concentrating on painting. He worked for five years in New York (1982–87), and his work was included in the 1989 'New British Painting' exhibition which toured the USA.

CARO, SIR ANTHONY 1962
b. 1924, sculptor

He studied engineering at Cambridge and after war service in the navy studied sculpture at the Regent Street Polytechnic, then at the RA Schools. From 1951 to 1953 he worked as an assistant to **MOORE**. He began teaching at St Martin's (reorganizing the department with Frank Martin, head of sculpture) in 1953, but changed his sculptural practice after a visit to the USA in 1959, turning from modelling to welded metal construction. Through his teaching he was a formative influence both on those who followed his own aesthetic practice (**ANNESLEY, KING, TUCKER** etc.) and those who reacted against it (**FLANAGAN, LONG, GILBERT AND GEORGE, McLEAN**). According to Clement Greenberg, 'Caro led the exodus from the bondage of the Anglo-Saxon space-frame'.

CAULFIELD, PATRICK 1971
b. 1936, painter, printmaker

He studied at Chelsea School of Art and the RCA, where he developed his characteristic style, related to Pop but with echoes of cubism (Léger and Gris) and Purism. He was included in the 1961 'Young Contemporaries' and in the 'New Generation' show

at the Whitechapel in 1964, and Robert Fraser gave him his first one-man show the following year. He was shortlisted for the Turner Prize in 1987.

CAVANAGH, JOHN 1955
b. 1914, fashion designer

Born in Ireland, Cavanagh's early career was spent in Paris, first with the (Irish-born) couturier Edward Molyneux and then with Pierre Balmain. He opened his own shop in London in 1952 and his designs are noted for their youthful elegance. The wedding dress he designed for Katherine Worsley for her marriage to the Duke of York in 1961 is now in the V&A.

CHADWICK, HELEN 1986
1953–96, sculptor, photographic, video and performance artist

She studied at Brighton Polytechnic and Chelsea School of Art, and her interest in the body as the subject of art already appeared in her student work. Later she worked with organic materials, making assemblages (sometimes cast) or photographs of arrangements of flowers, animal parts, melted chocolate, human body fluids and her own body in deceptively decorative form. She was shortlisted for the Turner Prize in 1987.

CHADWICK, LYNN 1955
b. 1914, sculptor

He worked as an architectural draughtsman from 1933 to 1939, before his war service as a pilot. He began making metal mobiles in the 1940s and also designed exhibition and light fittings. The first one-man exhibition of his sculpture was at Gimpel Fils in 1950, and he was commissioned to make three works for the Festival of Britain. He was one of the group of eight British sculptors in the 1952 Venice Biennale, and at the 1956 Biennale he won the international sculpture prize. The winged figure is his most characteristic form, which he has continued to develop throughout his career.

CHANG, PETER 1992
b. 1944, jewelry and furniture maker

He studied sculpture and graphic design at Liverpool College of Art and the Slade, but was self-taught as a jeweller. He is known for his massive, sculptural bracelets made from recycled plastic; Rifat Ozbek is among the fashion designers to use Chang jewelry in his collections.

CHAPMAN, JAKE AND DINOS 1996
b. 1966; 1962, sculptors

The Chapman brothers studied at the RCA and have been working together since the early 1990s. Their first solo installation, 'We Are Artists' (1992), was followed in 1993 by a diorama of remodelled plastic toy soldiers enacting eighty-three tableaux from Goya's *Disasters of War*. Their principal works since then have comprised groups of sexually mutated and joined figures of children in the form of shop-window dummies.

CLENDINNING, MAX 1964
b. 1924, architect

He studied at the AA and designed Oxford Road Station, Manchester, in 1955. He came to prominence in the sixties for his interiors, of which the demountable Maxima furniture he designed (manufactured by **RACE**) was an integral part. In his own dining room the painted stripes on the walls are related to the forms of the furniture and serve to dissolve and enlarge the space of the restored Victorian room.

COATES, NIGEL 1988
b. 1949, architect

He studied at Nottingham University and the AA, where he taught from 1975. He was the leader of the group of former AA students who founded NATO (Narrative Architecture Today) in 1983. In 1985 he founded Branson Coates with Doug Branson. Their work includes shops (for Jasper Conran and **KATHARINE HAMNETT**), restaurants and nightclubs, and their most ambitious projects have been in Japan, where Coates first gained a reputation when the theatrical designs for his own flat (1981) were published in the Japanese magazine *Brutus*. He was appointed Professor of Architecture at the RCA in 1995.

COHEN, HAROLD 1959
b. 1928, painter

He studied at the Slade and travelled in the USA (where he was eventually to settle) in 1959–61. He taught at a number of London art schools, including St Martin's, the Slade and Ealing School of Art, where his brother Bernard helped redesign the course; among their pupils there was **MICHAEL ENGLISH**. He was included in the 'Situation' exhibitions in 1960 and 1961 and represented Britain in the 1966 Venice Biennale. Since that time he has continued to develop his abstract idiom.

COLLETT DICKENSON PEARCE & PARTNERS 1980
advertising agency

The agency's 'Pure Gold' campaign for Benson & Hedges – which has won many awards – began in 1962, masterminded by CDP's first creative director Colin Millwood and carried on by John Salmon, now president of the agency.

COLLISHAW, MAT 1995
b. 1966, photographer, installation artist

Born in Nottingham, he studied at the Trent Polytechnic and Goldsmiths. His *Bullet Hole* – based on an enlargement of a photograph from a medical textbook – inspired the title of **HIRST**'s exhibition 'Freeze' (1988) and since then he has based his art on a technique of appropriation from artists and photographers of the past.

COLVIN, CALUM 1986
b. 1961, artist-photographer

Born in Glasgow, he studied sculpture in Dundee and photography at the RCA. He has developed a method of 'constructed photography', for which he assembles a tableau of objects, frequently based on an old master composition, which he then paints so that the tableau will appear two-dimensional when seen by the camera; the finished 'work' is in the form of a Cibachrome.

CONRAN, SIR TERENCE 1964, 1993
b. 1931, designer, restaurateur

He trained in textile design at the Central and worked as a textile and interior designer. He founded the Conran Design Group in 1955 and two years later opened a shop in London with **MARY QUANT**. He opened the first of his own Habitat furniture shops in Fulham Road in 1964. He expanded his business throughout the 1970s, though he eventually left the company he had founded. He has written many books on design and decoration and since the 1950s has developed a series of restaurants embodying the principles he has applied to the design of furniture and household objects.

CONROY, STEPHEN 1989

b. 1964, painter

Born in Helensburgh, he studied at Glasgow School of Art. He is one of the practitioners of 'New Figuration', and in 1989 he was given his first one-man show by the Marlborough Gallery, London, and was also youngest painter included in the touring exhibition 'New British Painting' (1989).

COPER, HANS 1972

1920–81, potter

Trained in Germany as an engineer, Coper came to England as a refugee and after the war began a collaboration with **LUCIE RIE**, working with her on a range of domestic ware. From 1959 he began to develop the architectural application of ceramics, producing two large murals composed of ceramic discs, and from the early 1960s he developed his distinctive sculptural pots. The composite forms he created in stoneware from thrown elements have a monumentality – whatever their size – and a sensuality of form and texture that justify his reputation as the greatest potter-sculptor of the twentieth century.

CRAGG, TONY 1981

b. 1949, sculptor

Born in Liverpool, he studied at Wimbledon School of Art and the RCA. In 1977 he moved to Germany, where he was able to exhibit some huge floor pieces composed of scraps of coloured plastic, establishing an international reputation. In 1985 he was shortlisted for the Turner Prize, which he was awarded in 1988, the year in which he was the featured artist in the British pavilion at the Venice Biennale. The same year he became co-director of the Düsseldorf Kunstakademie.

CRAIG-MARTIN, MICHAEL 1970, 1998

b. 1941, sculptor, painter, installation artist

Born in Dublin, he was raised in the USA, studying at Yale. In 1966 he moved to London, where he has been active as a conceptual artist, teacher and administrator. As Millard Professor of Fine Art at Goldsmiths he has been a guiding spirit to the generation of young artists who emerged from the college at the end of the 1980s.

CROSBIE, NICK 1996

b. 1971, product designer
See **INFLATE**

DAVENPORT, IAN 1998

b. 1966, painter

He was a student at Goldsmiths and first exhibited in the group show 'Freeze' (1988) curated by **HIRST**. His work has been particularly concerned with process and he has described his activity as 'dealing with the material rather than doing or dictating to it', allowing chance and the qualities of the industrial and household paints and varnishes he uses to contribute to the eventual image. He was shortlisted for the Turner Prize in 1991.

DAVIE, ALAN 1960

b. 1920, painter, poet, musician

Born in Scotland into an artistic family, Davie studied at Edinburgh College of Art. After the war he travelled in Europe and he was the first British artist to reflect the influence of American Abstract Expressionism, which he encountered at the 1948 Venice Biennale. With a broad range of interests – on which Zen philosophy and the symbolic psychology of Carl Jung have exerted strong influence – he has been a jeweller, poet and jazz musician as well as an artist whose aspiration has been to suppress his own individuality in order to 'evoke the inexpressible'.

DAVIES, JOHN 1975

b. 1946, sculptor

He studied painting at Hull and Manchester Colleges of Art and sculpture at the Slade and Gloucester College of Art. In his earlier work he cast heads and figures from life and then added clothing and the structures of wood, string and other objects with which they are often surrounded; more recently he has modelled his works from the outset. His first one-man show was at the Whitechapel in 1972 and he represented Britain at the 1976 Venice Biennale.

DAY, LUCIENNE 1951

b. 1917, textile designer

She trained at Croydon School of Art and the RCA, where she met **ROBIN DAY**. They married in 1942 and worked in close collaboration. The clients for her textile designs included Alistair Morton's Edinburgh Weavers, which commissioned designs from many leading artists, and Heal's. Her *Calyx* pattern was designed to complement Robin Day's furniture in the Homes and Gardens Pavilion he designed for the Festival of Britain. She and Robin Day were consultants to the John Lewis Partnership from 1962 to 1987.

DAY, ROBIN 1963

b. 1915, furniture and industrial designer

After training at High Wycombe School of Art and the RCA Day opened his own design office with **LUCIENNE DAY** in 1948. In addition to furniture, he designed radios and TVs, aircraft interiors and fittings and exhibition stands. He was an important influence in the 1950s, and the Days' house was featured in *Ideal Home*, 1953–54. Day's Polyprop chair made for Hille (to whom he was a consultant from 1948), still in current production, was designed to take advantage of the qualities of the new material polypropylene.

DEACON, RICHARD 1983

b. 1949, sculptor

Born in Bangor, Wales, he studied at Somerset College, St Martin's and the RCA. His concern for materials and the way they are assembled is like that of a craftsman – significantly he made pottery during the year he spent in New York after leaving the RCA, accompanied by his wife, the potter Jacqueline Poncelet – and he likens the process of assembling his raw materials to that of a lyric poet working with words. He was shortlisted for the Turner Prize in 1984, and won it in 1987.

DENNY, ROBYN 1959

b. 1930, painter

Denny was a student at St Martin's and the RCA and later taught at Hammersmith College of Art, Bath Academy of Art (1959–65) and the Slade. He was a prominent rebel at the RCA in the late 1950s and had his first one-man show at Gallery One in 1957. He was one of the instigators of the 'Situation' exhibitions. His later work has developed the hard-edged abstraction of this period.

DESIGNERS REPUBLIC 1996

design group

The group was founded in 1986 in Sheffield by Ian Anderson, who had begun his career in music management, and Nick Philips. Anderson's partners now include Vanessa Swetman, Michael Place and Nick Bax. With their slogans 'Think – Design or Die – Create', they appropriate existing graphic icons (some derived from Japanese *manga*) to create new typographic images. In their own words, 'compared to Tomato's "grunge aesthetic", Designers Republic's work could be called aesthetic'. Anderson has also designed a typeface for the *Fuse* project.

DIXON, TOM 1988

b. 1959, furniture designer

Born in Tunisia, he studied at Chelsea School of Art. In the early 1980s he was a nightclub performer in London before becoming a maker of metal furniture-sculpture. As an artist in bent, welded metal, he was one of the archetypal creators of 1980s 'designer' furniture.

DOIG, PETER 1991

b. 1959, painter

Born in Edinburgh, he grew up in Canada, where he returned after studying in London (at Wimbledon School of Art and St Martin's) in the early 1980s. His landscapes, generally snow-covered, painted from photographs, postcards or film-stills, are in a realist figurative style and reflect the land of his upbringing. He was awarded the John Moores prize in 1993 and was shortlisted for the Turner Prize in 1994.

DYSON, JAMES 1997

b. 1947, industrial designer, inventor

He studied at the RCA, and his first product, the Sea Truck, was launched while he was still at college. This was followed by the Ballbarrow, which has been widely adopted, and then – as a consequence of overcoming production problems with the Ballbarrow – the Dual Cyclone bagless vacuum cleaner, which applies a fundamental new approach to the vacuum cleaner. The success of these products enabled Dyson to open his own research centre and factory in Wiltshire in 1993.

EGLIN, PHILIP 1996

b. 1959, ceramic sculptor

Born in Gibraltar, he studied in Harlow New Town and Stoke-on-Trent and at the RCA. He has specialized in freestanding figures, following in the tradition of Staffordshire flatback figures, though generally on a much larger scale, often half lifesize. As with the work of many potters who have turned to sculpture in recent decades, the fired surface, emphasized by Eglin's method of procedure, becomes a focus for the spectator.

ENGLISH, MICHAEL 1967

b. 1941, painter, designer

He studied at Ealing College of Art. From 1967 he started designing psychedelic posters and storefronts, often in collaboration with **NIGEL WAYMOUTH** (working as 'Haphash and the Coloured Coat' or for Osiris posters). From the late 1970s he achieved a synthesis of minimalism and photorealism in his paintings of details of locomotives. More recently he has returned to his mystical roots in visionary art.

EPSTEIN, SIR JACOB 1959

1880–1959, sculptor

Born in New York, Epstein came to London after completing his studies in Paris. A combative figure, he created strong opposition with the primitivism of his carved public sculpture, but from the 1920s he was much sought after as a portraitist in bronze.

After the war he executed a number of monumental bronze groups for ecclesiastical sites, including *Christ in Majesty* (1954) for Llandaff Cathedral and the Coventry *St Michael and Lucifer*.

ERSKINE, RALPH
1974
b. 1914, architect

After studies at the Regent Street Polytechnic Erskine moved to Sweden in 1939, where he designed the Tibro housing scheme (1959). In addition to the Byker Wall in Newcastle-upon-Tyne, he has worked at Milton Keynes and designed the University of Stockholm Library (1983) as well as other factories and housing schemes in Sweden and the design of a new town at Resolute Bay, Canada.

FARRELL, TERRY
1982
b. 1938, architect

He studied at Durham University and the University of Pennsylvania, and from 1965 to 1980 was in partnership with Nicholas Grimshaw (b. 1939), designing buildings in the prevailing High-Tech idiom. Since the establishment of the Terry Farrell Partnership his work has been at the forefront of postmodern architecture in Britain, particularly in London: he endows his buildings with symbolic and iconographic gestures relating to their use rather than to the technical processes employed to construct them.

FARTHING, STEPHEN
1983
b. 1950, painter

He studied at St Martin's and the RCA. Throughout his career he has remained committed to figuration and he has combined painting with teaching – first at the RCA, then as Head of Painting at West Surrey College of Art (1985–90), and since that time as Ruskin Master of Drawing at Oxford. He was artist-in-residence at the Hayward Gallery in spring 1989.

FINLAY, IAN HAMILTON
1983
b. 1925, environmental artist, poet

Born in Nassau, Bahamas, he studied briefly at Glasgow School of Art before his war service. In 1961 he founded Wild Hawthorn Press in Edinburgh and he moved in 1967 to a remote farmhouse in the Pentland Hills. His principal work, undertaken with his wife Susan and a number of other collaborators, has been the transformation, since the 1970s, of his garden into 'Little Sparta'. He was shortlisted for the Turner Prize in 1985.

FLANAGAN, BARRY
1983
b. 1941, sculptor

Born in Prestatyn, Wales, he studied architecture and sculpture at Birmingham College of Art and, from 1964, sculpture at St Martin's under **KING**. He was one of the generation that challenged **CARO**'s influence, but his earlier 'process' sculptures were superseded at the end of the 1970s by bronze works, mainly based on the leaping hare. In 1982 he represented Britain at the Venice Biennale.

FLAVELL, RAY
1991
b. 1944, glass artist

He studied ceramics and lithography at Wolverhampton College of Art, turning to glass after attending a summer school at the RCA and training at the Orrefors Glass School in Sweden. He is a leading member of the studio glass movement and has taught at West Surrey and Edinburgh Colleges of Art. His constructed vessel sculptures are particularly characteristic works.

FLETCHER/FORBES/GILL
1962
design partnership

Alan Fletcher (b. 1931) studied at the Central, the RCA and Yale, where he was much influenced by Joseph Albers. He worked as a graphic designer in New York, returning to London in 1959. Colin Forbes (b. 1928) studied at the Central, where he was later Head of Graphic Design (1958–61), between spells of art direction in advertising. Fletcher and Forbes were co-founders of Fletcher/Forbes/Gill in 1962, of Crosby/Fletcher/Forbes in 1965 and of Pentagram in 1972. Bob Gill (b. 1931) was born and studied in the USA. He worked as a designer, filmmaker and teacher in London from 1960 to 1975.

FLUCK, PETER
1990
b. 1941, designer, sculptor, illustrator

He studied at Cambridge School of Art and worked as an artist-reporter, illustrator and cartoonist in the 1960s and 1970s. He co-founded Spitting Image Productions with **ROGER LAW** in 1982, winning many awards for the television series in which their caricature puppets appeared.

FOSTER, SIR NORMAN
1975
b. 1935, architect

He studied at Manchester University and at Yale, then formed Team 4 with fellow Yale student **RICHARD ROGERS**, Wendy Cheesman and Su Rogers. He set up Foster Associates with Cheesman (now Foster) in 1967. Notable buildings in Britain by the partnership include the Sainsbury Centre at the University of East Anglia (1977), the Renault distribution centre at Swindon (1983), and Stanstead Airport (1981–91). Foster has also worked extensively in Europe and Hong Kong.

FREUD, LUCIAN
1952, 1992
b. 1922, painter

Born in Berlin, Freud came to England at the age of nine. He briefly attended various art schools, but began to practice as a painter soon after being invalided out of the Merchant Navy in 1942. His early work, painted with a very fine brush, combined an intensity of observation with a polished realist technique, and while thicker brushes, used since the late 1950s, have given more physicality to his paintings of flesh, his subject-matter has remained consistent – principally figure-paintings and occasional still lifes. His merciless vision has contributed much to the controversy his art has always aroused and to his undoubted greatness. He was shortlisted for the Turner Prize in 1989.

FRINK, DAME ELISABETH
1960
1930–93, sculptor

She studied at Guildford School of Art and Chelsea and in 1953 won the student prize in the *Unknown Political Prisoner* competition. She had already been included among the sculptors who represented Britain at the 1952 Venice Biennale. Her work, in which the build-up of layers of plaster is faithfully reproduced in bronze, has been devoted principally to the male nude and to male horses, and she received many commissions for public sculptures. She taught at Chelsea, St Martin's and the RCA.

FRITSCH, ELIZABETH
1981
b. 1940, potter

Born in Wales, she studied at the Royal Academy of Music, then went on to the RCA, where her teachers included **HANS COPER** and **LUCIE RIE**. Illusionism, both in the forms and the decoration of her pots, has given her work a distinctive character.

FROST, SIR TERRY
1965
b. 1915, painter

He went to Cornwall in 1946, having spent much of the war in concentration camps, and studied at St Ives School of Painting, and then at Camberwell. He settled in St Ives in 1950, where he worked for a time as an assistant to **HEPWORTH** on her sculptures for the Festival of Britain. His work, which since 1949 has been characterized by an organically based abstraction, was first exhibited in 1952 at the Leicester Galleries. He taught at Reading University, where he was Professor of Painting 1977–81.

FULLARD, GEORGE
1960
1923–73, sculptor

He studied at Sheffield College of Art, then, after war service, at the RCA. In his assembled sculptures he made constant ironic reference to his wartime experiences, when he was severely wounded at the Battle of Cassino.

GALLIANO, JOHN
1997
b. 1960, fashion designer

Born in Gibraltar, he settled in England as a child. He studied fashion at St Martin's, and his degree show in 1984 made a remarkable impact and enabled him to start his own label immediately. After winning the British Designer of the Year Award for the third time in 1995, he was appointed chief designer for Givenchy, moving to Dior in 1997.

GAMES, ABRAM
1951
1914–96, graphic designer

Self-taught, he began his career as a designer in the early 1930s. During the war he was the first official poster designer for the War Office, and in the postwar period he was a prolific designer of posters, stamps, emblems and logotypes embodying his maxim 'maximum meaning, minimum means'.

GARRETT, MALCOLM
1984
b. 1956, graphic designer

He studied typography and psychology at Reading University and graphic design at Manchester Polytechnic. He founded the studio Assorted Images, working closely with groups such as Duran Duran, to produce a constantly developing promotional identity: 'In this way we could explore the freshness of each new release without risking alienating or confusing an existing audience'. 'The Reflex' was Duran Duran's second number one record and Garrett has described the sleeve as exploring an aspect of his trademark 'pop constructivist' style, 'by deliberately suggesting that the drawings are roughs for an unfinished piece'.

GIBB, BILL
1972
1943–88, fashion designer

He studied at St Martin's and the RCA, though he left before completing his course, having sold a collection to a store in New York. He founded his own business in 1972, establishing a notable collaboration in knitwear with Kaffe Fassett, and opened a shop in Bond Street in 1975. However, the recession forced him to close down before the end of the decade, and he continued to work as a freelance designer until his death.

GILBERT AND GEORGE
1970, 1982
b. 1943 (Gilbert Proesch) and 1942 (George Pasmore)
multi-media and performance artists

They met at St Martin's, where both studied 1967–70, and as students began their performances as 'living sculptures'. Later work includes large photo collages and prints, in which their artistic subversion is conveyed by the crudely offensive words or the decorative turds in their *Naked Shit Pictures* (1994), by which they aim to 'de-shock' the spurious taboos of taste. They made the film *The World of Gilbert & George* in 1981 and were shortlisted in 1984 for the Turner Prize, which they won in 1986.

GILLIAM, TERRY   1969
b. 1940, cartoonist, animator, film director
Born in Minnesota, his family moved to California when he was a child. He worked for magazines until moving to London in 1967, where he began to work in television, joining the team of *Monty Python's Flying Circus* (Graham Chapman, John Cleese, Eric Idle, Terry Jones and Michael Palin) as resident cartoonist. More recent credits as film director include *Time Bandits* (1981), *Brazil* (1985), *Twelve Monkeys* (1995) and *Fear and Loathing in Las Vegas* (1998).

GODFREY, NEIL   1980
art director, photographer
One of several art directors to work on **COLLETT DICKENSON PEARCE**'s long-running campaign for Gallahers.

GODLEY, GEORGINA   1989
b. 1955, textile and fashion designer
She studied at Wimbledon School of Art, Brighton Polytechnic and Chelsea School of Art. In the early 1980s she focused on fashion design in partnership with Scott Crolla, and in 1986 she started her own label. She experimented by altering the body shapes of Barbie dolls before designing her biomorphic dresses in the mid-1980s, and her clothes – which are more collectable than wearable – have emphasized womanliness at a time when androgyny was the fashion.

GOLDSWORTHY, ANDY   1988
b. 1956, environmental sculptor
Born in Cheshire, he studied in Bradford and Preston and now lives and works in Dumfriesshire, although he has realized projects in many countries of the world. His work is a collaboration with the forms he finds in the natural outdoor environment, and he records their ephemerality in colour photographs. In 1987 he was artist-in-residence at the Yorkshire Sculpture Park.

GORDON, DOUGLAS   1993
b. 1966, multi-media artist
Born in Glasgow, he studied at the School of Art there and was later a student of **BRUCE McLEAN** at the Slade. He works in Glasgow, where he is a noted member of the 'Scotia Nostra' group. Much of his work has involved the manipulation of well-known films, and he won the 1996 Turner Prize for his *Confessions of a Justified Sinner*, in which film clips of *Dr Jekyll and Mr Hyde* are grafted onto the theme of Hogg's romantic ghost story. He was awarded the Turner Prize in 1996 and the Premio 2000 at the 1997 Venice Biennale.

GORMLEY, ANTONY   1993
b. 1950, sculptor
He studied anthropology at Cambridge, then art at the Central, Goldsmiths and the Slade. His concern as a sculptor has been almost exclusively with the human body. Many of his works have been made by an elaborate process of making lead casts from his own body: all individual characteristics are erased in the finished work, since his intention is to create an interior portrait

within the cast shell, 'making a sculpture from the inside by using my body as the instrument and the material'. He won the Turner Prize in 1994.

GREAVES, DERRICK   1953
b. 1927, painter
Born in Sheffield, he enrolled at the RCA in 1948 having spent five years as a signwriter. He was one of the New Realists (known as the 'Kitchen Sink' painters) exhibited by the Beaux Arts Gallery in the 1950s. His later work tended towards a simplified linear style of representation.

GREENAWAY, PETER   1988
b. 1942, film director, painter, exhibition curator
After studying at Walthamstow College of Art, he joined the Central Office of Information as a film editor. He began making short films in 1966, and documentaries he made for the COI included films on Women Artists, on **ZANDRA RHODES** and on **TERENCE CONRAN**. His feature films, starting with *The Draughtsman's Contract* in 1982, and also including *The Belly of an Architect* (1987) and *The Cook, The Thief, His Wife and Her Lover* (1989), constitute the chief British contribution to postmodern film.

HADID, ZAHA   1991
b. 1950, architect
She was a student of Rem Koolhaas and Elia Zenghelis and in 1977–78 joined their Office for Metropolitan Architecture (OMA), which aimed to respond to pluralist and modern mass culture by reinvestigating the early phases of modernist architecture, specifically the work of the Suprematists. Her works include the remodelling of the Irish ambassador's residence in Eaton Place (1980–82) and the abandoned project for a Cardiff Opera House. She has been commissioned to design the Mind Zone in the Millennium Dome.

HAMILTON, RICHARD   1956, 1969
b. 1922, painter, printmaker
His art studies (at the RA Schools and the Slade) were interrupted by work as an industrial designer during the war. With **PASMORE** in Newcastle-upon-Tyne he was one of the pioneers of teaching Basic Design to art students in Britain. He was a member of the Independent Group at the ICA, and his exploration of the erotic possibilities of the automobile and other aspects of American mass culture made him one of the founders of British Pop. With his deep interest in the work of Marcel Duchamp (he reconstructed Duchamp's *Large Glass* in 1965–66), Hamilton has been extremely influential on subsequent generations of British artists. He was joint winner of the John Moores prize in 1969.

HAMNETT, KATHARINE   1984
b. 1947, fashion designer
She studied at St Martin's, and in 1979 established her own fashion house. She has always actively supported environmental and peace causes and launched her 'Choose Life' range of T-shirts in 1983. The following year, in which she was named Fashion Designer of the Year, the T-shirts carried anti-war slogans. In contrast to many of her contemporaries, she designs clothes not as icons of fantasy but to be worn by real people.

HATOUM, MONA   1994
b. 1952, video, performance and installation artist
Born in Beirut, she moved to London in 1975 and studied at the Byam Shaw School of Art and the Slade. While many of her sculp-

tures are minimalist works created in unusual materials, her most provocative pieces have been created with her own body as the medium. She was shortlisted for the Turner Prize in 1995.

HAYTER, SIR STANLEY WILLIAM   1952
1901–88, printmaker
The most influential British printmaker of the period, Hayter spent much of his early career in Paris, where his print workshop, Atelier 17, was frequented by many of the Surrealists as well as Picasso. During the 1940s he worked in New York and experimented with a technique of producing colour prints from a single plate etched in relief, which he continued to develop through the 1950s. Although he returned to Paris and reopened Atelier 17 in the 1950s, Hayter's work was frequently exhibited in London, and his techniques were widely adopted.

HEAD, TIM   1976
b. 1946, painter, photographer, sculptor, multi-media artist
He studied fine art under **HAMILTON** in Newcastle-upon-Tyne and sculpture at St Martin's. In 1968 he worked for Claes Oldenburg in New York. His first one-man show was at the Museum of Modern Art, Oxford, in 1972; he represented Britain at the 1980 Venice Biennale; and in 1987 was awarded the John Moores prize. He taught at Goldsmiths throughout the seventies. His work has been concerned with spatial dislocations and illusions and, more recently, with the imagery of food.

HENRION, FREDERICK HENRI KAY   1975
1914–90, graphic and industrial designer
Born in Nuremberg, he studied in Paris with Paul Colin, moving to England in 1936. He was a prolific exhibition designer during and after the war, with notable work for the GPO, and he did much through teaching (at the Central, the RCA and LCP) and example to pioneer the concept of corporate identity in Britain. He designed the Countryside Pavilion at the Festival of Britain.

HEPWORTH, DAME BARBARA   1955
1903–75, sculptor
She studied at Leeds School of Art and the RCA. In 1932–33 she travelled to Paris with **BEN NICHOLSON**, who became her second husband, joining the group Abstraction-Création. They moved from London to St Ives in 1939, forming, with Naum Gabo, the nucleus of the artistic colony there. She died in a fire in her studio, which was later turned into a museum. She represented Britain at the 1950 Venice Biennale.

HERBERT, JOCELYN   1973
b. 1917, stage and film designer
She studied painting in the Atelier Lhote in Paris and at the Slade and trained as a stage designer at the London Theatre Studio. She was particularly noted for her collaborations with Peter Brook for the English Stage Co. at the Royal Court Theatre (Wesker's *Roots*, 1959, Osborne's *Luther*, 1961) as well as acting as production designer for films by **LINDSAY ANDERSON** (*If*, 1969, *O Lucky Man*, 1973) and Tony Richardson. Her operatic work includes the designs for Birtwistle's opera *The Mask of Orpheus* at the Coliseum (1986).

HERITAGE, ROBERT   1954
b. 1927, furniture designer
He trained at Birmingham College of Art and the RCA, where he later returned as Professor of Furniture Design (1974–85). In addition to working in wood, he experimented in the use of new

materials for furniture, including plastics, polyurethane foam, aluminium alloys and special adhesives. His chairs for the liner QEII, manufactured by **RACE**, were designed in 1968–69. He has won more Design Council awards than any other designer.

HERON, PATRICK   1969
1920–99, painter

He studied at the Slade and during the war worked on a farm and as an assistant to **BERNARD LEACH** at St Ives. After the war he was an influential art critic, with a special interest in Matisse and Braque, who were also powerful influences on his own painting. Although impressed by American abstraction, his own abstract work always retains a figurative basis, and he has been a strong defender of British primacy in the Pop Art movement. He moved to Cornwall in 1956 and was awarded the John Moores prize in 1959.

HERON, SUSANNA   1971
b. 1949, jeweller, sculptor, photographer

The daughter of **PATRICK HERON**, she studied at Falmouth School of Art and the Central, where she specialized in jewelry. Later she developed soft 'wearables' made of plastics, for which the body served merely as the vehicle to display the objects; finally she became a sculptor.

HERRON, RON   1965
1930–94, architect

He studied at the Brixton School of Building and the Regent Street Polytechnic. He worked in the GLC Architects' Department, 1954–61, and with Warren Chalk designed plans for the South Bank Development (art gallery and concert hall), 1961–63, although their conception of this as a half-buried building covered with vegetation was never realized. He was a co-founder of **ARCHIGRAM** in 1960 and was a partner in Pentagram (1977–80) and in Imagination (1989–93). His work includes several urban plans, public buildings and airport terminals and he taught at the AA for twenty years.

HEYNES, WILLIAM   1961
1903–89, engineer

He began his career at Humber in the 1920s and was hired by William Lyons to head the engineering department at Jaguar in 1934. He became the most influential figure after Lyons at the company, and among his many achievements was the design of the great XK engine, planned before the war and first produced in 1948. He retired in 1969.

HILLER, SUSAN   1980
b. 1940, multi-media artist

Born and educated in the USA, she trained and worked as an anthropologist in Latin America before moving to London in 1973 and devoting herself to art. In this she constantly challenges the concepts and assumptions that are the basis for normal lives, exploring dream imagery and other supernatural phenomena. She undertook a major installation at the Freud Museum, Hampstead, in 1992–94.

HILLIARD, JOHN   1984
b. 1945, sculptor, artist photographer

He studied at Lancaster College of Art and St Martin's and began by photographing his own sculptures. Since 1970 his work has largely been based on photography, in which paired images have often played an important role.

HILLS, JOAN   1967
b. 1936, painter

She has worked together with **MARK BOYLE** throughout his artistic career, and more recently their collaboration has been prolonged by the participation of their children in works by the 'Boyle Family'.

HILTON, ROGER   1963
1911–75, painter

He studied at the Slade and in Paris but worked as a teacher after his war service. He became an abstract painter in 1950 and started to visit St Ives in 1956. He settled in Cornwall in 1965. He was awarded John Moores prizes in 1959 and 1963 and the UNESCO prize at the 1964 Venice Biennale.

HIM, GEORGE   1955
1900–82, painter, designer

Born in Łódź, he studied at the universities of Moscow, Bonn and Leipzig. In Poland he formed a partnership with Jan Le Witt (1907–91), which continued after both had come to England in the late 1930s, producing posters and books for children. He is best known for the series of Schweppes ads done in the 1950s and 1960s in collaboration with the humourist Stephen Potter and for his *Giant Alexander* books written by Frank Herrmann.

HIRST, DAMIEN   1994
b. 1965, painter, sculptor, installation artist

He studied at Leeds College of Art and Goldsmiths and made his first major impression with the three-part exhibition 'Freeze' that he curated in August–September 1988 with work by sixteen artists, including **COLLISHAW**, **DAVENPORT**, **RAE**, **HUME**, Sarah Lucas, Richard Patterson, Anya Gallaccio and Hirst himself. His work, which includes paintings, glass tank pieces and 'cabinet sculptures', has taken Duchamp to extremes, particularly in his use of the museum vitrine to present the most surprising or shocking content. He wants to 'make art that everybody can believe in'. He was shortlisted in 1992 for the Turner Prize, which he won in 1995.

HITCHENS, IVON   1950
1893–1979, painter

He studied intermittently at the RA Schools before, during and after World War I and in 1920 was a founder member of the Seven and Five Society. He was influenced by French abstract art, particularly that of Braque, and from the late thirties most of his paintings, generally in an exaggeratedly landscape format, were devoted to abstracted landscapes. He has been grouped with the Neo-Romantics, but his work is more personal and more abstract than that of other Neo-Romantics and was untouched by Surrealism. He represented Britain at the 1956 Venice Biennale.

HOCKNEY, DAVID   1962, 1970
b. 1937, painter, printmaker, stage designer

Born in Bradford, he studied at the local art school, then at the RCA, where he was one of the leading figures in the Pop generation. He moved to California in 1963, where he still lives, though he has worked in London at various times during this period. Like his revered hero Picasso, Hockney has always had to struggle against an extraordinary facility, particularly in drawing. During the 1980s his collages of Polaroid photographs, equivalents of cubist portraits, initiated a genre which has been widely imitated. Since the 1970s he has also worked extensively for the stage. He was awarded the John Moores prize in 1967.

HODGKIN, SIR HOWARD   1962, 1984
b. 1932, painter

He studied at Camberwell and Bath Academy of Art, and his paintings have always shown a strong individuality which sets him apart from the succession of art movements that swept over Britain during this period. Two particular influences have been the painting of India (which he first visited in the 1960s) and the art of Matisse. He represented Britain at the 1984 Venice Biennale. He won the Turner Prize in 1985, having been shortlisted the previous year.

HOPKINS, MICHAEL   1977, 1985
b. 1935, architect

He studied at the AA and worked with a number of firms, including Norman Foster (1969–75), collaborating on the IBM Pilot Head Office in Portsmouth (1970). His own house in Hampstead, which established his High-Tech credentials, was his first independent work and he formed Michael Hopkins & Partners in 1976. Their work includes the Schlumberger Cambridge Research Centre (1985), the Mound Stand at Lords Cricket Ground (1987), a cutlery factory for **DAVID MELLOR** in Derbyshire (1988), and the new Glyndebourne Opera House (1987–94).

HOUSE, GORDON   1960
b. 1932, painter, printmaker, graphic designer

He studied at Luton and St Albans Schools of Art, worked as a sculptor's assistant, and until 1959 was a graphic designer for the chemical industry. In that year he had his first one-man show at the New Vision Centre, London. He contributed as a painter to the 'Situation' exhibitions as well as designing the logos and printed materials for them, but his principal career has been as a distinguished graphic artist.

HOUSHIARY, SHIRAZEH   1992
b. 1955, sculptor

Born in Iran, she studied at Chelsea and Cardiff Schools of Art. Her early sculpture employed natural materials for the creation of sensuous forms, sometimes on a monumental scale, while more recent work has exploited the mystical and poetic values of geometry and of the substance and appearance of metals. She was shortlisted for the Turner Prize in 1994.

HOYLAND, JOHN   1966
b. 1934, painter, printmaker

He studied at Sheffield College of Art and the RA Schools and has taught at Hornsey, Chelsea, St Martin's and the Slade. He exhibited in the 'Situation' exhibitions and was included in the 'New Generation' show at the Whitechapel in 1964. Later in the 1960s his abstraction was strongly influenced by American art, particularly by the painter and teacher Hans Hofmann, and colour has remained the fundamental element in his work. He was awarded the John Moores prize in 1982.

HUME, GARY   1992
b. 1962, painter

He studied at Chelsea, Liverpool Polytechnic and Goldsmiths College and participated in **HIRST**'s 'Freeze' (1988). His early work consisted of paintings of doors, which were taken to symbolize human rites of passage. More recently this self-proclaimed 'beauty terrorist' has produced abstract paintings, like brightly coloured Rorschach images, whose simplicity and lack of explanation have a disturbing power. He was shortlisted for the Turner Prize in 1996.

HUNTER, TOM 1998
b. 1965, photographic and video artist

He studied at the LCP and RCA, and his work attracted considerable attention during his student years. He draws on the language of old master art to focus on the dignity and beauty of communities that are marginalized by society.

INFLATE 1996
design partnership

After studying at the RCA **NICK CROSBIE** formed the partnership in 1995 with the brothers Mark and Michael Soudeau, one of them an engineer, the other a product designer. They apply the technique of inflatability to products of all kinds, from furniture to lights to egg cups, fruit bowls and ashtrays.

ISSIGONIS, SIR ALEC 1959
1906–88, industrial designer

Born in Smyrna, he studied engineering at Battersea Polytechnic before entering the motor industry in 1933. He worked for Morris Motors (later BMC) from 1936 to 1972, where his most innovative designs were the Morris Minor (1948), Mini Minor (1959) and Morris 1100 (1962).

IVE, JONATHAN 1998
b. 1967, industrial designer

Born in London, he joined the design group Tangerine in 1989, working on ceramic bathroom ware and many other products. In 1992 he joined Apple and moved to California, but it was not until August 1997 that he was able to embark on the radical new design – both in form and colours – for the iMac computer, which was launched worldwide in autumn 1998.

JARAY, TESS 1964
b. 1937, painter, printmaker

Born in Vienna, she studied at St Martin's and the Slade. After graduation she travelled in Italy and France, where she worked in **HAYTER**'s Atelier 17. Committed to abstraction, she executed a mural for the British pavilion at the Montreal 1967 Expo and more recently has designed a number of architectural projects to be executed in patterned brickwork, including the forecourt of Victoria Station and Jubilee Square outside Leeds General Infirmary (1998). She began teaching at Hornsey in the 1960s and is now head of postgraduate studies at the Slade.

JARMAN, DEREK 1995
1942–94, painter, filmmaker

He studied at King's College, London, and the Slade and designed for opera, ballet and films (for Ken Russell) in the late 1960s and 1970s. His own films, which explore the themes of homosexuality and, finally, AIDS, include *Sebastiane* (1976), *Jubilee* (1978), a Punk *Tempest* (1979), *Caravaggio* (1986) – for which he was shortlisted for the Turner Prize that year – *The Garden* (1990), *Wittgenstein* (1993) and *Blue* (1993).

JIRIČNA, EVA 1987
b. 1939, architect

Born in Prague, she studied at the university there, coming to London in 1968. She designed schools for the GLC and worked for the Louis de Soissons Partnership before forming a partnership with David Hodges in 1980. Two years later she set up her own practice. She is best known for her restaurants, shops and apartment interiors in which High-Tech is transformed into a decorative style.

JONES, ALLEN 1969
b. 1937, painter, printmaker, sculptor

He studied at Hornsey and, until his expulsion, at the RCA. He was a leading member of the Pop generation (secretary of the 1961 'Young Contemporaries' exhibition), with a strong interest in philosophical and psychological theory. The fetishistic subject-matter for which he is best known entered his work in the mid-1960s. He designed the sets and costumes for Kenneth Tynan's erotic revue *Oh! Calcutta!* in 1970.

JONES, PETER 1966
sculptor

He studied at St Martin's and collaborated for a number of years with **MAURICE AGIS** on his experiments in the activation of space. Since 1980 he has worked independently, developing his own *Colourscape* installations.

JONES, TERRY 1982
b. 1945, graphic designer

He worked for numerous magazines, starting with *Vanity Fair*, in the 1970s and founded *i-D* in 1980. In 1976 he planned to document Punk fashion on the King's Road, Chelsea, which led to *Not Another Punk Book*, published in 1978.

KAPOOR, ANISH 1990
b. 1954, sculptor

Born in Bombay, he has lived in England since 1973 and studied at Chelsea and Hornsey. He was given his first solo exhibition in 1982 at the Lisson Gallery. His interest in mysticism, derived both from oriental religion and the psychological theories of Carl Jung, has led him to seek archetypal imagery, in which the polarities of male–female, interior–exterior, light–dark, solid–void and the transformative power of intensely saturated colours play key roles. He won the Turner Prize in 1991.

KELLY, MARY 1979
b. 1941, conceptual artist

Born in the USA, she studied in Florence and at St Martin's. She taught at Goldsmiths and was an active member of the Women's Movement in London. *Post-Partum Document* was followed by her monumental *Interim* (1984–89), which relates to the crisis of identity in the post-maternal woman. She returned to New York in 1989.

KING, PHILLIP 1963
b. 1934, sculptor

Born in Tunisia, he came to England at the age of twelve. After university he studied for a year (1957–58) with **CARO** at St Martin's, where he returned to teach from 1959 to 1978. In the late 1950s he worked as an assistant to **MOORE**, but in 1962 he changed his sculptural practice, working in fibreglass and incorporating colour as a substantive element. With **RILEY** he represented Britain at the 1968 Venice Biennale. He taught at the Slade and was appointed Professor of Sculpture at the RCA in 1980.

KINSMAN, RODNEY 1971
b. 1943, furniture designer

With Jerzy Olejnik and Bryan Morrison, fellow students at the Central, he set up OMK Design in 1966. Their T5 chair (1969), with chromium-plated or nylon-coated tubular steel frame was one of their earliest successes, and they have consistently designed items that can be manufactured inexpensively.

KITAJ, R.B. 1964
b. 1932, painter, printmaker

Born in Cleveland, Ohio, he had worked as a seaman and studied art in New York, Vienna and Oxford before enrolling at the RCA in 1959. There he became the mentor of the Pop generation, while developing a deceptively appealing style heavily loaded with social and political content. His first one-man show was at the Marlborough New London Gallery in 1963. In 1976 he selected 'The Human Clay' exhibition at the Hayward Gallery, identifying a group of leading figurative painters as the 'School of London'. His later work became more expressionistic in form, while the content was often concerned with Jewish issues. The hostile response to his outstanding retrospective at the Tate in 1994 drove him into voluntary exile from his adoptive country.

KNIGHT, NICK 1997
b. 1958, photographer

He studied photography at Bournemouth and Poole College of Art and from the outset has been interested in the graphic possibilities of his medium. He worked on record covers and in 1985 did a series of one hundred portraits for *i-D* magazine, which introduced him to fashion photography. He is now considered Britain's leading fashion photographer.

KOSSOFF, LEON 1973
b. 1926, painter

After national service he studied at St Martin's (while attending Bomberg's evening classes at the Borough Polytechnic) and then the RCA. A leading member of the 'School of London', he has restricted his paintings to urban landscapes, often with many figures – as in his swimming-pool paintings – and figures painted in his studio.

LAMBIE-NAIRN, MARTIN 1982
b. 1945, designer, art director
See **ROBINSON LAMBIE-NAIRN**

LANE, DANNY 1988
b. 1955, glassmaker

Born in the USA, he came to Britain in 1975, working with **PATRICK REYNTIENS**. He then studied painting at the Central, setting up his studio in 1981 and founding Glassworks in 1983. His association with **ARAD**'s One Off showroom started the following year. He designed the glass staircase and balustrade for the glass gallery at the V&A in 1993.

LANYON, PETER 1952
1918–64, painter

Born in Cornwall, he studied with **BEN NICHOLSON** and Naum Gabo. He was particularly interested in spatial relationships in the landscape, and during the early 1950s he would sometimes construct three-dimensional models to help transfer these relationships to his canvases. He was one of the first British painters to learn from American Abstract Expressionism and he exhibited successfully in New York, where he became friendly with Mark Rothko and other New York painters. In 1959, in order to pursue his spatial investigations further, he took up gliding, and his death was the result of a gliding accident.

LASDUN, SIR DENYS 1960
b. 1914, architect

He studied at the AA and from 1935 to 1959 – with an interruption for war service – he worked successively with leading modernists Wells Coates, Lubetkin and Tecton, and Lindsey Drake. He started his own practice in 1960, and among his best-known buildings are the new University of East Anglia (1962–68), the Royal College of Physicians (1964) and the National Theatre (1967–76) on the South Bank.

LATHAM, JOHN   1963
b. 1921, artist

He studied at Regent Street Polytechnic and Chelsea School of Art after war service in the Royal Navy, sharing his first exhibition, in 1948, with John Berger. During the mid-1950s his application of paint with a spray-gun and his association with the scientists C.C.L. Gregory and Anita Kohsen led him to develop a time- or event-based theory of art. He began using books as sculptural material in 1958 and in 1964 began his 'Skoob tower' ceremonial happenings, in which book-sculptures were burnt. One of these took place during the Destruction in Art Symposium (1966). He set up the Artist Placement Group in 1967.

LAW, BOB   1970
b. 1934, painter, sculptor

Self-taught, he went to St Ives in 1957, where he painted, made pots and worked as a carpenter for three years. He made his first 'field' paintings in 1959 and his first black paintings the following year, when he also began working as a sculptor. His work was included in the 'Situation' shows. While much impressed by American Abstract Expressionism, his own paintings derive from his personal metaphysical philosophy and are characterized by the build-up of many coats of paint to produce an immaculate surface.

LAW, ROGER   1990
b. 1941, caricaturist, illustrator

With **PETER FLUCK** he designed the Spitting Image puppets.

LEACH, BERNARD   1957
1897–1979, potter

Born in Hong Kong, he studied pottery in Japan and Korea, 1909–20. He formed the Leach Pottery in St Ives in 1920 in collaboration with Shoji Hamada and became the leading figure in British studio pottery for more than half a century, combining the oriental sensibility to forms, glazes and decoration with the vigorous tradition of English earthenware.

LIJN, LILIANE   1969
b. 1939, kinetic sculptor

Born in New York, she studied in Paris and had worked and exhibited in New York, Paris and Athens before moving to London in 1965. Her sculpture is concerned with light, reflection and movement.

LONDON COUNTY COUNCIL ARCHITECTS   1955

The superintending architects at the LCC before it was succeeded by the GLC in 1965, when much of the responsibility for planning and housing was handed over to the individual London boroughs, were Sir Robert Matthew (1946–53), Sir Leslie Martin (1953–56) and Sir Hubert Bennett (from 1956). The architects' department had to implement plans for the rebuilding of London after the war and deal with the acute problems of housing and schools, and its development team pioneered new systems of design and construction. Their most notable achievements were on the South Bank site (the Royal Festival Hall,

National Film Theatre, Hayward Gallery and smaller concert halls) and on the Alton Estate at Roehampton, where the teams for the two stages were led by R. Stjernstedt and Colin Lucas.

LONG, RICHARD   1984
b. 1945, environmental sculptor

He studied in Bristol and, from 1966, at St Martin's, where his fellow-students included **McLEAN** and **FLANAGAN**. From his earliest work in 1964, he has been concerned with the geometry of nature (including the dimension of time), and his own intervention in it, and he has remained closer to the English landscape tradition than any of his contemporaries. He represented Britain at the 1976 Venice Biennale and was shortlisted in 1984 and 1987 for the Turner Prize, which he won in 1989.

LOWRY, LAWRENCE STEPHEN   1953
1887–1976, painter

Born in Manchester, he studied art in evening classes, although he continued to work as a clerk until he retired at the age of sixty-five. His scenes of urban life are outside any contemporary trends, but by the 1950s he had established a considerable reputation and he was for many years Britain's most popular artist.

MAAZ-DESIGN   1997
design group

The group was formed in 1992 by Louis Nixon (a sculpture graduate of Chelsea School of Art and the Slade) and Georgia Vaux (who had studied painting and site-specific sculpture at Chelsea and Wimbledon Schools of Art) for the production of furniture and accessories and interior objects by embedding items in polished cast resin.

McCONNELL, JOHN   1972
b. 1939, graphic designer

He studied at Maidstone College of Art and worked in advertising before starting his own design practice in 1963. In 1967 he co-founded Face Photosetting and since 1974 he has been a principal of Pentagram.

MACH, DAVID   1986
b. 1956, sculptor, installation artist, collagist

Born in Fife, he studied in Dundee and at the RCA. He first became known for his gallery installations, including 101 Dalmatians at the Tate in 1988. In his more recent work he has applied the principles of collage and the multiplication of standard units to portraits and monumental sculpture in both two and three dimensions. He was shortlisted for the Turner Prize in 1988.

MACKENDRICK, ALEXANDER   1951
1912–93, film director

Born in Boston and brought up in Glasgow, Mackendrick worked in advertising and documentary film before joining Ealing Studios. His first film was Whisky Galore (1948), and he directed The Man in the White Suit (1951) and The Ladykillers (1955) for Ealing. His later films included Sweet Smell of Success (1957) and A High Wind in Jamaica (1965).

McLEAN, BRUCE   1971
b. 1944, painter, sculptor, performance artist

He studied at Glasgow School of Art and St Martin's, where he responded to the 'New British Sculpture' led by **CARO** with satirical irreverence. In 1971 he formed the performance group Nice Style, 'The World's First Pose Band', with events at the Garage

such as High up on a Baroque Palazzo (1974). His subsequent work has included painting, sculpture, ceramics, carpets and, more recently, video – all of which are characterized by a seriousness of purpose tempered by a gleeful wit. He was awarded the John Moores prize in 1985 and has taught at the Slade.

McQUEEN, ALEXANDER   1997
b. 1969, fashion designer

He worked in tailoring in London, Tokyo and Milan before taking a fashion course at Central St Martin's. His final-year collection in 1992 was an immediate commercial success. After becoming the youngest ever winner of the Designer of the Year Award in 1997, he succeeded **GALLIANO** as chief designer at Givenchy.

MALLET, DAVID   1980
b. 1945, film and video director

He has made a speciality of pop videos, having worked with Queen, AC/DC, Tina Turner and the Boomtown Rats, and collaborated with **BOWIE** on 'Dancing in the Streets' (with Mick Jagger) and 'China Girl' as well as 'Ashes to Ashes'. In the 1990s he has continued to work in pop music, making TV specials with Madonna, Janet Jackson, Diana Ross and others.

MARTIN, KENNETH   1976
1905–84, sculptor, painter

He first studied at Sheffield College of Art and, after working as a graphic designer, enrolled at the RCA in 1929. During the 1940s his painting became increasingly abstract, and after 1951 he also turned to sculpture. He took part in 'This is Tomorrow' (1956) in a group with Mary Martin and John Weeks and was a leading member of the Constructionist movement in the 1960s.

MAYHEW, MICHAEL   1967
b. 1947, graphic designer, art director

He collaborated with **WAYMOUTH** on the design and execution of the shopfront of 'Granny Takes a Trip' in the King's Road, Chelsea. Since 1976 he has been art director for the National Theatre.

MEADOWS, BERNARD   1952
b. 1915, sculptor

After attending Norwich School of Art he worked as assistant to **MOORE** from 1936 to 1940. His studies at the RCA, which he entered in 1938, were interrupted by service in the RAF and he completed his course in 1948. He was one of the eight British sculptors at the 1952 Venice Biennale whose work gave rise to Herbert Read's epithet the 'Geometry of Fear'. He returned to the RCA as Professor of Sculpture from 1960 to 1980.

MELLOR, DAVID   1957
b. 1930, silversmith, industrial designer

He studied at Sheffield College of Art and the RCA, and set up as a silversmith and industrial designer in Sheffield in 1954. He specialized in cutlery and opened his first London shop, selling well-designed kitchenware, in 1969, but his work embraces all aspects of design in metal, from sterling silver cutlery for British embassies to traffic signals.

MILROY, LISA   1987
b. 1959, painter

Born in Vancouver, she studied at the Sorbonne, St Martin's and Goldsmiths. She was one of the principal still life painters included in the 1989 'New British Painting' exhibition that toured the USA. She was awarded the John Moores prize in 1989.

MOORE, SIR HENRY — 1956
1898–1986, sculptor

Born into a mining family, he studied at Leeds School of Art and the RCA after service in World War I. He was a co-founder with Paul Nash of the avant-garde group Unit One in 1933 and took part in the international Surrealist exhibitions in 1936 and 1938. He was an official war artist in World War II, producing his celebrated 'shelter' drawings. In 1948 he won the international sculpture prize at the Venice Biennale, and from that time he was widely considered to be Britain's greatest artist. Even when closest to abstraction, Moore's concern was always with the human figure.

MORLEY, LEWIS — 1963
b. 1925, graphic designer, photographer

Born in Hong Kong, Morley came to England after the war, studying at Twickenham College. He started as a painter and commercial artist but turned to photography in the late 1950s. He worked extensively in fashion and the theatre and was associated with the boom in satire during the 1960s. He emigrated to Australia at the end of the decade.

MORLEY, MALCOLM — 1979
b. 1931, painter

After a troubled youth, when he ran away to sea and took a correspondence course in art from prison, he studied at Camberwell and the RCA. Impressed by the Abstract Expressionist art exhibited in London in 1956, he moved to New York in 1958. His work went through Abstract Expressionist and 'super-realist' phases before settling into a witty, narrative postmodernism. In 1984 he was the first winner of the Turner Prize.

NICHOLSON, BEN — 1955
1894–1982, painter

The son of two painters, he had little formal artistic training and did not begin painting seriously until 1920. In 1932, with his second wife **BARBARA HEPWORTH**, he went to Paris, and the joint influence of Arp, Brancusi, Picasso and Braque led them to join Abstraction-Création; in 1934 he met Mondrian and made his first geometric reliefs. At the start of the war he and Hepworth moved to St Ives, and their studios became centres for the group of painters who congregated there. He painted murals for the Festival of Britain and won many international prizes during the 1950s. He separated from Hepworth in 1951 and moved to Switzerland in 1958.

OFILI, CHRIS — 1996
b. 1968, painter

He studied at Chelsea School of Art and the RCA, and in 1992, having already won several prizes, was awarded a travel scholarship to Zimbabwe. His use of elephant dung on his canvases dates from this time as does his technique of using tiny repeated images in the form of dots – inspired by cave paintings in the Matapos Hills. He is a bold colourist, and has used layers of transparent resins to enhance his pigments. He was awarded the Turner Prize in 1998.

OPIE, JULIAN — 1993
b. 1958, sculptor, painter

He studied at Goldsmiths. He exhibited sculptures constructed of welded steel, painted with Pop imagery, at the Lisson Gallery in 1982 and had his first one-man show there the following year. Later he created brightly coloured minimalist works from synthetic and industrial materials and processes, while in other pieces the car and the motorway have been recurrent images.

PAOLOZZI, SIR EDUARDO — 1958, 1965
b. 1924, sculptor, printmaker

He studied at Edinburgh College of Art and the Slade and worked in Paris from 1947 to 1950. He has taught textile design, ceramics and sculpture at several art schools including the RCA. He was an influential member of the Independent Group, and exhibited in 'This is Tomorrow' (1956) together with the photographic artist Nigel Henderson and the **SMITHSONS**, with whom he had collaborated at the ICA in 1953 on the exhibition 'Parallel of Life and Art'. The principle of collage – starting with the scrapbooks he made in Paris from American magazines given to him by GIs – has always been central to his work, which has shown a strong consistency of purpose in the many forms it has taken.

PARK, NICK — 1993
b. 1958, animator

The creator of the animated plasticine figures (claymations) Wallace & Gromit had his first animated film, *Archie's Concrete Nightmare*, shown by the BBC in 1975. He joined Aardman Animation in 1985. He has won Oscars for both *Creature Comforts* (1989) and *The Wrong Trousers* (1993).

PARKER, CORNELIA — 1991
b. 1956, environmental sculptor

She studied at Gloucester, Wolverhampton and Reading. Among her best-known installations was *The Maybe* (1995) at the Serpentine Gallery, in which the actress Tilda Swinton slept beside a selection of objects said to have been associated with famous people. She was shortlisted for the Turner Prize in 1997.

PARKINSON, NORMAN — 1955
1913–90, fashion photographer

He began his photographic career in 1931, opening his own London studio in 1933, but his success as a fashion photographer came after the war, when he worked with Norman Hartnell and other leaders of British fashion.

PARR, MARTIN — 1986
b. 1952, photographer

He studied at Manchester Polytechnic and has worked as a freelance photographer since 1974, when he was co-founder of the Albert Street Workshop. He moved to Ireland in 1980 and joined Magnum in 1994.

PASMORE, VICTOR — 1951
1908–98, painter

Although he had only taken evening classes at the Central, Pasmore was elected a member of the London Group in 1934 and became interested in abstraction. However, in 1937 he helped form the 'Euston Road School', a realist group led by Claude Rogers and William Coldstream, painting delicate urban landscapes. In 1947–48 he returned to abstraction and also became concerned to broaden the basis of art school training in Britain, founding the 'Developing Process' course at Newcastle-upon-Tyne with **HAMILTON**. In the mid-1950s he worked on a number of geometric reliefs, sometimes in conjunction with architectural projects, such as Peter Moro's Fairlawn School in Forest Hill, but returned to painting in 1960, when he was featured at the Venice Biennale, continuing to develop a more organic abstraction in the succeeding decades.

PAWSON, JOHN — 1995
b. 1949, architect

He studied at Nagoya University of Commerce and the AA and formed a partnership with Claudio Silvestrin in 1983 principally devoted to the design of commercial and domestic interiors. Pawson's own projects include the Jigsaw shop in Bond Street and the new Young Vic theatre. His philosophy, in which decoration and colour are as far as possible excluded, was enshrined in his book *Minimum* (1996).

PEAKE, BRIAN — 1951
b. 1912, architect

He studied at the AA and collaborated with the Design Research Unit on the design of the Festival of Britain Science Exhibition. His London architectural practice handled domestic and exhibition work as well as shop design. He retired to Jersey in 1968.

PECCINOTTI, HARRI — 1967, 1969
b. 1935, art director, photographer

After working as a commercial artist, musician and advertising art director, he combined a growing interest in his own photography with the art direction of *Flair* and *Vanity Fair*. Most notably he was the first art director of *Nova*, founded in 1965. He settled in Paris during the 1970s.

PHILLIPS, PETER — 1961
b. 1939, painter

He studied at Birmingham College of Art and the RCA, where he was a member of the first Pop generation, finishing his course in the Television School after disagreements with his painting tutors. He taught at Coventry and Birmingham Colleges of Art and travelled to the USA in 1964 and (with **ALLEN JONES**) in 1965. In 1966 he settled in Zurich.

PHILLIPS, TOM — 1971
b. 1937, painter, writer, composer

After studies at Oxford University and Camberwell School of Art, Phillips embarked on a career as a painter, although he is also active as a writer, composer and exhibition organizer. His work has achieved a remarkable fusion between Pop elements and conceptualism. He was a John Moores prizewinner in 1969.

PIPER, JOHN — 1959
1903–92, painter, printmaker, stage designer, stained glass designer

He first studied law, then art at Richmond College of Art and the RCA. His earliest work was in an abstract Constructivist style, but from the late 1930s he turned to evocative landscapes, becoming one of the principal exponents of English Neo-Romanticism. He worked in a wide variety of media, and his landscape prints, stained-glass windows and stage designs are especially notable.

POWELL & MOYA — 1951
architectural partnership

The partnership between Sir Philip Powell (b. 1921) and John Hidalgo Moya (1920–94), both graduates from the AA, was formed in 1946. Projects they designed include Churchill Gardens, Pimlico (1948–62), heated by waste hot water from Battersea Power Station and one of finest postwar integrated high-rise developments; Chichester Festival Theatre (1961–62); the Museum of London (1976); and many new university buildings in Oxford.

PYE, WILLIAM 1971
b. 1938, sculptor

He studied at Wimbledon School of Art and the RCA and had his first one-man show at the Redfern Gallery in 1966. He has worked mainly with fabricated steel and cast bronze and has incorporated running water into many of his public works, including *Slipstream* and *Jetstream* at Gatwick Airport and the *Water Wall* in the British Pavilion at Expo '92 in Seville, designed in collaboration with the architect Nicholas Grimshaw

QUANT, MARY 1966
b. 1934, fashion designer

Trained at Goldsmiths College, she opened a boutique, Bazaar, in Chelsea in 1955, for which she started designing herself the following year. Her clothes designed specifically for the young had a hugely liberating influence and she earned the accolade of 'cheerleader of swinging London'. The exhibition 'Mary Quant's London' at the London Museum in 1974 was the first museum retrospective of the work of a British fashion designer.

RACE, ERNEST 1951
1913–64, furniture designer and manufacturer

He studied interior design at University College, London, and founded Race Fabrics in 1937 and Race Furniture, in partnership with Noel Jordan, in 1945. His BA chair, designed that year for use in public spaces and first shown at 'Britain Can Make It' in 1946, was the first British mass-produced item of furniture, over 250,000 eventually being manufactured. His firm manufactured the work of many designers, including **ROBERT HERITAGE**.

RAE, FIONA 1997
b. 1963, painter

Born in Hong Kong, she studied at Croydon College of Art and Goldsmiths. She participated in 'Freeze' (1988) and was short-listed for the Turner Prize in 1991. She has used the postmodern technique of appropriation, so that the abstraction of her paintings is made accessible not only by the brilliant colour (often reminiscent of postmodern architecture) but also by the shock of recognition.

RAMSDEN, MEL 1985
b. 1944, conceptual artist
See **ART & LANGUAGE**

RAMSHAW, WENDY 1972
b. 1939, jewelry designer

She trained in illustration and fabric design at Newcastle-upon-Tyne College of Art and Reading University before turning to jewelry in the late 1960s, studying for a year at the RCA in 1969. Unlike many of her contemporaries, she continues to use precious metals and precious and semi-precious stones in her work.

RANKIN 1996
b. 1966, photographer, creative director

He is best known for his portrait photography and for his magazine cover stories in *Q* magazine and *Dazed and Confused*, which he founded with Jefferson Hack in 1991.

RAY-JONES, TONY 1968
1941–72, photographer

He studied commercial design and photography at the LCP and design at Yale, going on to work with Alexey Brodovitch and Richard Avedon in New York. He returned to London in 1966, and devoted much of the next three years to capturing images of the British at work and relaxation.

REGO, PAULA 1987
b. 1935, painter, printmaker

Born in Lisbon, she studied at the Slade. She moved between London and Portugal before settling in London in 1976. She was married to the visionary painter Victor Willing (1928–88). She was shortlisted for the Turner Prize in 1989 and in 1990 was made the first Associate Artist at the National Gallery, where her large painting, *Crivelli's Garden*, decorates the restaurant in the new Sainsbury Wing.

REID, JAMIE 1977
b. 1947, graphic designer

He was a fellow-student of Malcolm McLaren at Croydon College of Art, which they occupied in 1968. He was associated with McLaren in his Punk designs for the Sex Pistols, using the assembled typographic style that inspired designers of the 1980s and beyond. Now a Druid, he has continued to use his design techniques to communicate his anarcho-political messages.

REYNTIENS, PATRICK 1959
b. 1925, stained glass maker

He studied at Edinburgh College of Art and, after war service, at Marylebone School of Art and again in Edinburgh. Churches for which he made stained glass, often in collaboration with other artists (**PIPER**, **RICHARDS**, Cecil Collins etc.), include Coventry, Liverpool RC Cathedral, Derby Cathedral and Eton College. With his wife, the painter Anne Bruce, he founded the art school Burleighfield, where stained glass and other decorative arts were taught. He was Head of Fine Art at the Central, 1976–86.

RHODES, ZANDRA 1977
b. 1940, fashion designer

She studied at Medway College of Art and the RCA and worked as a textile designer. In 1967, since her designs were too outrageous for established fashion outlets, she opened her own shop on the Fulham Road. After building up her business in the USA she set up her own fashion company in 1975 and the following year started licensing the Zandra Rhodes name. She opened a new factory in Hammersmith in 1984, where her business has been concentrated since 1991.

RICHARDS, CERI 1949
1903–71, painter

Born into a Welsh-speaking family, Richards studied at Swansea School of Art and the RCA and during the 1930s flirted with both abstraction and Surrealism. During the war he was Head of Painting at Cardiff School of Art, while also working as a war artist. He was an exceptional draughtsman and did many illustrations for the work of Dylan Thomas, but he also executed several large commissions both for the theatre and for churches, including Liverpool RC Cathedral.

RIE, DAME LUCIE 1978
1902–95, potter

Born Lucie Gomperz in Vienna, Rie came to London as a refugee in 1938. Although she made exceptional pots before the war, it was the combination of her Viennese training, the influence of **BERNARD LEACH** and her close collaboration from 1946 with **HANS COPER** which led her to develop her uniquely sensitive range of thrown bowls and vases.

RILEY, BRIDGET 1964, 1981
b. 1931, painter

She studied at Goldsmiths and the RCA, and her interest in Seurat and Divisionism as well as American Abstract Expressionism led to the development of her Op Art technique, at first largely monochromatic, later using colour. She had her first solo exhibition at Gallery One in 1962 and was included in the 'New Generation' show at the Whitechapel in 1964. She represented Britain at the 1968 Venice Biennale, winning the international painting prize. Her work has continued to explore the visual qualities of space in nature.

ROBINSON LAMBIE-NAIRN 1982
design group

Founded in 1976 by **MARTIN LAMBIE-NAIRN** and Colin Robinson, the group (now Lambie-Nairn) specializes in corporate identities and, in particular, the branding of television stations. It has been responsible both for the original Channel Four animated logo and for the identities introduced during the 1990s for BBC1 and BBC2.

RODD, PETER 1958
industrial designer

He was a member of Richard Steven's design team at Atlas Lighting.

ROGERS, LORD (RICHARD) 1986, 1999
b. 1933, architect

He studied at the AA and at Yale and was a member of Team 4 with **FOSTER**. He collaborated with Renzo Piano on the Pompidou Centre (1975) and a number of other buildings. His major British projects include the Lloyd's Building and the Millennium Dome. He believes firmly in the 'need to research and partake in a system which offers the have-nots shelter, food, education and the quality of life, whilst reducing the stress, strain, and other anxieties of the haves ... by using our productive capacity and tremendous supply of technical innovation to develop suitable types of technology to answer the real needs of the world.'

ROWE, MICHAEL 1988
b. 1948, silversmith

After studies at High Wycombe and the RCA, he set up his own silversmith's workshop in 1972. Working with Richard Hughes, he has made a special study of the colouring and patination of metals, and he combines traditional craftsmanship with modern techniques of metallurgy. He has developed a concept of craftwork that goes beyond the utilitarian and decorative function of the 'applied arts' to give it a semiological basis, allowing it to stand beside architecture and the 'fine arts'. He has been Course Leader of metalwork and jewelry at the RCA since 1984.

ROWLANDS, MARTYN 1964
b. 1923, industrial designer

Born in Wales, his studies at the Central were interrupted by war service. After working for Ekco Plastics, he started his own design consultancy in 1959, and the products he has designed range from telephones and water taps to airline servicewares in moulded plastic.

SAMUELY, FELIX J. 1951
1902–59, structural engineer

Born in Vienna and educated in Berlin, he settled in England in 1932 and was associated with many of the modernist projects built in Britain before the war. His lectures at the AA from 1938 introduced many young architects to the principles of economy in structure as well as to new materials and structural techniques. One of his greatest contributions was in the application of space frames to buildings, and at the time of the Festival of Britain (where he worked on the Transport and Communications Pavilion as well as the Skylon) he wrote that the period would be remembered as the time which 'saw the birth of a new architecture ... when construction changed over from "plane" to "space"'. Samuely's successor was Frank Newby (b. 1926), whose contribution can be seen in projects from Cedric Price's Fun Palace and **STIRLING** and Gowan's Leicester Engineering Laboratory to Stirling's Clore Gallery and the Milton Keynes shopping centre.

SAVILLE, JENNY   1996
b. 1970, painter

She studied at Glasgow School of Art, and in 1990, while she was still a student, her work was exhibited at the RCA. Her female nudes, executed in a painterly realist style on a large scale, have made her one of the most prominent artists of her generation.

SAVILLE, PETER   1983
b. 1955, graphic designer

He studied at Manchester Polytechnic and established his reputation with his designs for album covers and posters for the music industry. He helped Tony Wilson set up Factory Records, whose groups included New Order and Joy Division. His practice, Peter Saville Associates (1983–90), created many award-winning advertising campaigns, and from 1990 to 1993 he was a partner in Pentagram, after which he went into partnership with the German advertising company Meiré und Meiré.

SAYER, MALCOLM   1961
1916–70, industrial designer

A former aircraft engineer, he became Jaguar's aerodynamicist in their racing heyday in the 1950s, starting with the C-type. His finest achievement was the XJ13 (1965–67). Rather than use models he would work out details theoretically and then make full-scale drawings of the cars on the wall.

SCHLESINGER, JOHN   1961
b. 1926, film director

He studied at Oxford after war service and began to make films during the 1940s. From 1958 he made documentaries for the BBC's *Tonight* and *Monitor* programmes, including *Terminus* (1961). His feature films include *A Kind of Loving* (1962), *Billy Liar* (1963), *Darling* (1965), *Midnight Cowboy* (1969), *Sunday Bloody Sunday* (1971), *Day of the Locust* (1975), *Marathon Man* (1976), and he has also directed theatre and opera.

SCOTT, WILLIAM   1957
1913–89, painter

Born in Scotland, he studied in Belfast, at the RA Schools and in France (1937–39). He taught at the Bath Academy of Art from 1942 to 1956, and represented Britain at the 1958 Venice Biennale. He won a John Moores prize in 1959. He was a frequent visitor to St Ives from 1952 and, after he had visited America in 1953, was one of the first British painters to absorb the lessons of Abstract Expressionism. His still lifes, nudes and other figures are painted to draw attention to the surface of the canvas, on which the abstract outlines and shapes set up strong rhythmic patterns.

SCULLY, SEAN   1993
b. 1945, painter

Born in Dublin, he moved with his family to London in 1949. He studied at Croydon College of Art, Newcastle-upon-Tyne University and Harvard, after which he taught for two years at Chelsea School of Art and Goldsmiths. He has lived in the USA since 1975, and with their focus on the qualities of both paint and surfaces, his works belong to the school of American abstraction. He was shortlisted for the Turner Prize in 1989 and 1993.

SEENEY, ENID   1955
b. 1932, ceramic designer

She studied at Burslem School of Art and was the first woman to train in the design studio at Spode Copeland. She joined the Ridgway group in 1953, working with **ARNOLD** on various designs including a chess set and a coronation figure of the Queen, though neither of these went into production. She took a year off to study at the RCA (1954–55), and designed both 'English Garden' and 'Homemaker' for Arnold's 'Metro' pattern. She left Ridgway on her marriage in 1957.

SLOAN, NICHOLAS   1983
b. 1951, letter-cutter, printer

Having studied art history, he served his apprenticeship with David Holgate in Norfolk. The majority of his larger works have been done in collaboration with **IAN HAMILTON FINLAY**, with whom he has worked since the late 1970s.

SMITH, JACK   1957
b. 1928, painter

Born in Sheffield, he studied at the local College of Art and then at St Martin's and the RCA. He was one of the 'Kitchen Sink' New Realists, having his first one-man show at the Beaux Arts Gallery in 1952. In the late 1950s he abandoned realism for an abstraction based on musical rhythms, which he has continued to develop.

SMITH, RICHARD   1965
b. 1931, painter

He studied at Luton and St Albans Schools of Art, with an interruption for national service, and then at the RCA. He took part in the 'Situation' exhibitions and was close to several of the Pop artists, making a ten-minute film incorporating Pop imagery, *Trailer*, with the photographer Robert Freeman in 1963. From the late 1950s he spent much of his time in New York, eventually settling there in 1976. He developed the ideal of abstract paintings as strong living presences in themselves, rather than representations of aspects of reality. His work was chosen for the British pavilion at the 1966 Venice Biennale.

SMITHSON, ALISON AND PETER   1953
1928–93 and b. 1923, architects

Husband and wife, both studied at Newcastle-upon-Tyne University and worked briefly in the **LCC ARCHITECTS** Department. Although only a small number of their projects were realized – the Economist Building (1959–64) in St James's is their finest work – they had a great influence through their theoretical writings, their collaboration with artists such as **PAOLOZZI**, and Peter Smithson's teaching at the AA. Their 'new brutalism' combined the architectural principles of Le Corbusier and Mies van der Rohe with Dubuffet's *art brut*, while their 1958 House of the Future was seen by Reyner Banham as a serious attempt to create an architectural parallel to Pop Art.

SNOWDON, LORD (ANTHONY ARMSTRONG-JONES)   1971
b. 1930, photographer, designer

One of the principal photo-journalists of the colour supplement era, he was an artistic adviser to the *Sunday Times* from 1962 to 1990. The Snowdon Aviary at London Zoo (1961), which he designed with Cedric Price and Frank Newby, has become a favourite London landmark. He has also made award-winning films for television.

SOOLEY, HOWARD   1995
b. 1963, photographer

Born in Doncaster, he studied photography and filmmaking at the Polytechnic of Central London. Since then he has worked as a freelance photographer for a range of magazines, concentrating on portraits and gardens. Through his friendship with **DEREK JARMAN** he came to create the remarkable photographic record of the artist's garden in Dungeness published as *Derek Jarman's Garden* in 1995.

SPENCE, SIR BASIL   1959
1907–76, architect

Born in India, he studied at London and Edinburgh Universities and worked for a time for Sir Edwin Lutyens. He designed a number of large private houses before the war, and in 1951 his Sea and Ships Pavilion was one of the outstanding structures built for the Festival of Britain. The same year he won the competition for the rebuilding of Coventry Cathedral (for which his consulting engineer was Ove Arup), which remains the finest architectural expression of the Neo-Romantic school. His later buildings, which share a strong sense of monumentality, included Sussex University (1961–64), the British Pavilion at Montreal Expo (1967), the British Embassy in Rome (1968) and Knightsbridge Barracks overlooking Hyde Park.

SPENCER, STANLEY   1952
1891–1959, painter

He studied at the Slade and exhibited in Roger Fry's second Post-Impressionist exhibition in 1912. His paintings after World War I reflected his own war experiences; his devotion to Christ, whose life he depicted among the villagers of Cookham where he lived; and his belief in the unity of sex and heavenly love. The body of his work prolonged the British tradition of visionary realism.

STEVENS, RICHARD   1958
1924–97, industrial designer

He studied at the Regent Street Polytechnic and was chief designer for Atlas Lighting (1954–63), and later design manager for British Telecom (1969–83). He founded his own design group in 1987.

STIRLING, JAMES   1986
1926–92, architect

He studied at Liverpool University School of Architecture and in his early partnership with James Gowan designed the Engineering Laboratory at Leicester University (1959–63), a building in which, for the first time in Britain, the forms of a modernist building reflected the engineered structure in a representational way. His shift from a revolutionary to an evolutionary attitude to architecture was confirmed by his Stuttgart Staatsgalerie (1977–84), in which the site and the typological context strongly affected the design – as was also the case with his other museum projects in Germany, Britain and the USA.

SUTHERLAND, GRAHAM 1949, 1959
1903–80, painter
Sutherland's early career, after study at Goldsmiths College, was as an etcher, and he turned to painting only in 1931, having spent two years as a commercial designer. His printmaking influenced a whole generation of British artists who emulated the work of Samuel Palmer and Edward Calvert, laying the foundations of the Neo-Romantic school. His painting retained strong reminiscences of the earlier English landscape tradition, although after the war it took on an expressionistic quality – in both landscapes and religious paintings – in part a reflection of the horrific scenes he had painted as a war artist. From 1955 he lived mainly in the south of France.

TAYLOR-WOOD, SAM 1996
b. 1967, video artist, photographer
She studied at Goldsmiths and began exhibiting in the early 1990s. Her work has often been self-referential, while the theme of social and sexual alienation runs through the ambiguity of her fragmented video presentations. She won an award for most promising young artist at the 1997 Venice Biennale.

TILSON, JAKE 1983
b. 1958, sculptor, painter, audio-visual artist
He studied painting at Chelsea School of Art and the RCA. In addition to his own artistic work, he has produced artist's books and magazines conceived as collaborative artwork, including *Atlas*. He has also made fashion designs for Warehouse. More recently he has composed audio works and has designed websites both for himself (www.thecooker.com) and for the Ruskin School of Drawing, where he was artist-in-residence at The Laboratory, 1994–96.

TILSON, JOE 1969
b. 1928, painter, sculptor, printmaker
After service in the RAF he attended St Martin's and the RCA, working in Spain and Italy in 1955–59. He was later closely associated with the Pop generation at the RCA, making compartmented paintings and extremely inventive prints and multiples. He represented Britain at the 1964 Venice Biennale.

TIMNEY-FOWLER 1985
textile designers
The partnership was set up in 1979 by Susan Timney (b. 1950) and Grahame Fowler (b. 1956), both of whom had studied at the RCA. For several years they developed print designs for Japanese companies, including Issey Miyake, then produced their first product range for the UK in 1984–85. During the 1980s they expanded from interior fabrics to fashion fabrics for major couture houses in Paris, Milan, New York and Los Angeles, and more recently they have developed a wide range of interior and fashion accessories, including designs developed together with Linda McCartney.

TOMATO 1996
design group
The group was started in 1991 by Steve Baker, Dirk van Dooren, Karl Hyde, Richard Smith, Simon Taylor, John Warwicker and Graham Wood, who were later joined by Greg Rood, Jason Kedgley and Dylan Kendle. Their activities include filmmaking, typography, and all areas of design, but also embrace music (two of the members form the group Underworld), painting, sculpture, writing and new media: they adopt a holistic approach to all artistic media and see their highly successful commercial work as a means of funding the experimental activity of the group's members individually and collectively.

TREVELYAN, JULIAN 1959
1910–88, painter, printmaker
After Cambridge he went to Paris, studying painting at the Académie Moderne and printmaking at **HAYTER**'s Atelier 17. He exhibited Surrealist work in 1934 and 1936 and was later one of the artists to take part in the Mass Observation project. During and after the war the element of Surrealist fantasy was absorbed into the Neo-Romantic idiom within which he executed many landscapes and riverscapes, in both paintings and prints.

TUCKER, WILLIAM 1966
b. 1935, sculptor
Born in Cairo, he studied sculpture at the Central and St Martin's. He was a leading figure in the early 1960s, when his friendship with **HOYLAND** brought him into contact with the 'Situation' painters. Like them, he wanted the work of art to have an independent existence, seeing it as part of a 'non-world, as yet unexplored between human beings and the world of recognizable, useful, conditioning things in which they live'. He taught at Goldsmiths, St Martin's and Leeds University and later worked in the USA.

TURNBULL, WILLIAM 1963
b. 1922, sculptor, painter
Born in Dundee, he worked as an illustrator for comics before serving in the war with the RAF. He then studied at the Slade and lived in Paris for two years from 1948. On his return, he exhibited with **PAOLOZZI**, a friend from the Slade, and became a regular member of the Independent Group at the ICA. He was one of the British sculptors featured in the 1952 Venice Biennale and played an important role in 'This is Tomorrow' (1956). His painting was much influenced by his first experience of American Abstract Expressionism in 1956, and he took part in the 'Situation' exhibitions, while his sculpture owes much to the ritualistic functions of primitive carvings. As a teacher of experimental design and, later, sculpture at the Central during the 1950s and 1960s he was a key figure in motivating the postwar generation of artists.

VAUGHAN, KEITH 1956
1912–77, painter
The only art training he received was at school, and during the 1930s he worked in advertising, taking up painting as war approached. After the war he shared a flat for several years with John Minton, working in a similar Neo-Romantic style. In 1951 he executed a mural for the Dome of Discovery and the following year he did his first *Assembly of Figures* composition. His paintings thereafter, largely devoted to male figures, are in a bold abstract idiom overshadowed by a strong sense of menace. His remarkable published diaries portray the inner turmoil which led to his eventual suicide.

VON ETZDORF, GEORGINA 1989
b. 1955, textile designer
Born in Lima, Peru, she studied at Goldsmiths, setting up the company that bears her name in 1981 in partnership with two other designers, Martin Simcock (b. 1954) and Jonathan Docherty (b. 1955), who had both graduated in 1977 – Simcock from Camberwell, Docherty from St Martin's. They specialize in handprinted textiles, accessories and clothes.

WALKER, JOHN 1976
b. 1939, painter, printmaker
After Birmingham College of Art he studied in Paris, and he taught at the RCA for four years, before moving to Australia in 1979. Although he learned the lessons of Abstract Expressionism, his work has always remained 'just this side of abstraction' and is executed with great sensitivity to the textures of the media – often used in highly original ways. He represented Britain at the 1972 Venice Biennale, was awarded the John Moores prize in 1976 and was shortlisted for the Turner Prize in 1985.

WALLINGER, MARK 1994
b. 1959, painter, multi-media and installation artist
He studied at Loughton, Chelsea and Goldsmiths. He uses his art to explore issues of social, cultural, political and personal identity. Football and horseracing have been important themes in his work, and he has taken part in numerous solo and group exhibitions since 1981: in 1994 he presented his own racehorse *A Real Work of Art* as a work of art. He was shortlisted for the Turner Prize in 1995.

WATKINS, DAVID 1984
b. 1940, artist-jeweller
After training as a sculptor at Reading University, he turned to jewelry-making in the mid-1960s, initially using acrylic or stainless steel, but later preferring colourcore or neoprene. He describes his work as 'rather ideal or utopian, belonging more to a world of imagination and metaphor than to that of everyday life'. He was appointed Professor of Gold and Metalsmithing at the RCA in 1984.

WAYMOUTH, NIGEL 1967
b. 1941, designer
Born in India, he worked as an illustrator and decorator in the late 1960s and did graphic work for *IT* and *Oz* magazines. Shopfronts he designed included his own shop 'Granny Takes a Trip' and the Indica Bookshop. He collaborated in 1967 with **MICHAEL ENGLISH** on Osiris posters and as 'Haphash and the Coloured Coat'. More recently he has become a fashionable portrait painter.

WEARING, GILLIAN 1996
b. 1963, photographic and video artist
She studied at Goldsmiths. Her work aims to document the underlying natural responses of ordinary people by confronting them with extreme situations – in contrast to the stock reactions elicited in conventional documentary photographs or films: in one of her projects, *Signs that say what you want them to say not signs that say what someone else wants you to say* (1992–93), she photographed passers-by holding just such signs, which she had encouraged them to write. She won the Turner Prize in 1997.

WEBB, BOYD 1990
b. 1947, sculptor, photographic artist
Born in New Zealand, he studied at Ilam School of Art and the RCA. While at college he worked with fibreglass casts of the human body, but from using photography as a means of documenting his work he went on to assemble tableaux to be photographed, where the photographs are themselves the final form of the work of art. The medium of a large Cibachrome print allows him to combine fantasy and subversion in documenting a world where the familiar laws of nature appear to be suspended. He was shortlisted for the Turner Prize in 1988.

WEIGHT, CAREL 1950
1908–97, painter
He studied at Hammersmith School of Art and Goldsmiths, and, after the war, taught at the RCA, where he was Professor of Painting from 1957 to 1973. His paintings convey a sense of menace in quite ordinary surroundings, emphasized by the disarming realism with which they are executed.

WEIL, DANIEL 1981
b. 1953, designer
He studied in Buenos Aires and, after moving to England in 1978, at the RCA. Initially he carried out furniture and interior projects for a number of companies, while marketing his own products – digital clocks, radios and lights sealed in screen-printed clear plastic envelopes – through Parenthesis. In 1992 he joined Pentagram and he has taught at the AA and the RCA.

WELCH, ROBERT 1962
b. 1929, designer, silversmith
He studied at Malvern and Birmingham art schools and at the RCA. He started his own workshop in the Cotswolds in 1955, and became a consultant designer to Old Hall Tableware the same year. He has worked in silver, stainless steel and enamel steel, designing kitchen utensils and many domestic fittings.

WENTWORTH, RICHARD 1984
b. 1947, sculptor
After studies at Hornsey and the RCA he was associated with **CRAGG**, **DEACON** and **WOODROW** in the 1980s 'New British Sculpture' movement, using discarded objects and junk materials as his media. He was tutor at Goldsmiths for sixteen years to 1987.

WESTWOOD, VIVIENNE 1990
b. 1941, fashion designer
Her early career was spent designing for the shop at 430 King's Road, Chelsea, that she ran with her partner Malcolm McLaren; it began as 'Let it Rock' and changed its name as each new collection was introduced, finally becoming 'World's End'. From the mid-1980s she concentrated on fashion design for both women and men, catering to the concept of power dressing. She was named British Designer of the Year in both 1990 and 1991. Recently she has designed costumes for opera, theatre and movies, including *Leaving Las Vegas* (1995).

WHITEREAD, RACHEL 1993
b. 1963, sculptor
Having studied at the Slade, Whiteread made her first sculptures by taking casts of everyday objects. She soon moved on to make casts of the space surrounding or enclosed by objects, investing the image with personal or collective memories and associations in such works as *Ghost* (1990) and *House* (1993). She was shortlisted in 1991 for the Turner Prize, which she was awarded in 1993. In 1996 she won the commission to design and make the Austrian Holocaust Memorial in Vienna (a concrete cast of a library), and the following year she became the first woman to represent Britain in a solo exhibition at the Venice Biennale.

WHY NOT ASSOCIATES 1997
design group
The group was formed in 1987 by Andy Altman and David Ellis (with Howard Greenhalgh, who remained in the partnership until 1993). Credits for Why Not include pop videos, stamps for the Queen's fortieth anniversary, stationery for **NIGEL COATES**, an exhibition of erotica, party political broadcasts and a book on the culture of football.

WILDING, ALISON 1983
b. 1948, sculptor
She studied at Ravensbourne College of Art and the RCA. Part of the 'New British Sculpture' movement of the early 1980s, her work is characteristically made up of two contrasting parts, whose relationship is often ambiguous; the duality is achieved by contrasts of materials, textures, colours and forms and can be understood to represent many of the elemental polarities. She was shortlisted for the Turner Prize in 1992.

WILFORD, MICHAEL 1986
b. 1938, architect
He studied at the Northern Polytechnic School of Architecture and the Regent Street Polytechnic. He worked with **STIRLING** and Gowan from 1960 and was Stirling's partner from 1964, collaborating with him on all his major projects in Britain and overseas. On Stirling's death in 1992 he founded Michael Wilford Associates.

WILSON, COLIN ST JOHN 1998
b. 1922, architect
After war service he studied at the School of Architecture, London University, and then worked in the **LCC ARCHITECTS** Department (1950–55). In 1955 he began teaching at Cambridge, while practising with Sir Leslie Martin, undertaking a number of university commissions in Cambridge and elsewhere. He took part in 'This is Tomorrow' (1956) in a group with Robert Adams, Peter Carter and Frank Newby. The British Library, which began construction in 1982, is the outstanding building designed by his own practice. He was Professor of Architecture in Cambridge from 1975 to 1989.

WILSON, RICHARD 1987
b. 1953, sculptor, performance artist
He studied at the LCP, Hornsey and Reading University, and during the 1980s was a member of a performance art group. His installation work, which involves the radical disruption and transformation of specific architectural spaces, is in many ways a continuation of his performances – with the active role transferred to his audience. He was shortlisted for the Turner Prize in 1989.

WOLFF OLINS 1996
design group
The group was founded in Camden Town in 1965 by Wally Olins (b. 1930) and Michael Wolff (b. 1933), and they were pioneers in the field of corporate identity design, focusing on the image and culture of the concerns they work for and becoming 'brand guardians' for their clients.

WOMERSLEY, PETER 1955
1923–93, architect
He studied at the AA after his war service and from 1953 practised architecture in Scotland. The main influences on his work were Mies van der Rohe and the 'International Style' architects, and he preferred to work without partners, taking a close personal involvement in each of his projects. He founded a practice in Hong Kong in 1962 and moved there in 1978.

WOODROW, BILL 1988
1948, sculptor
He studied at Winchester College of Art, St Martin's and Chelsea and had his first solo exhibition at the Whitechapel Art Gallery in 1972, the year he left college. However, for the next seven years he worked as a teacher, making very little sculpture until he set up a studio in 1978. His early work was made from materials recovered from dumps and scrapyards, out of which he fabricated works with a strong narrative element, and this quality was retained in his later work, made from new materials. He was shortlisted for the Turner Prize in 1986.

WYLIE, DONOVAN 1995
b. 1971, photographer
Born in Belfast to a Catholic mother and a Protestant father, Wylie has followed in the tradition of the British photographers who have documented the lives of groups excluded from society. He is the youngest photographer ever to join the Magnum group.

BIBLIOGRAPHY AND SOURCES

The books, catalogues and other publications listed below contain useful information or good illustrations relating to various aspects of the period under review. Useful monographs, websites, solo exhibition catalogues and National Art Library information files exist for many of the individual artists, designers etc.; these are well referenced and are not included here.

Addressing the Century: 100 Years of Art & Fashion, exh. cat. London, Hayward Gallery, 1998

Lawrence Alloway. 'The Development of British Pop', in Lucy R. Lippard. **Pop Art**. London 1966

Arts Council Collection, cats. London 1979, 1984, 1989, 1998 (CDRom)

Austerity to Affluence: British art and design 1945–1962, exh. cat. London, Fine Art Society, 1997

Haig Beck (ed.). **The State of the Art: A Cultural History of British Architecture (UIA-International Architect 5)**. London 1984

Louisa Buck. **Moving Targets: A User's Guide to British Art Now**. London 1997

Virginia Button. **The Turner Prize**. London 1997

Joann Cerritto. **Contemporary Artists**. Detroit 1996

Bridget Cherry and Nikolaus Pevsner. **London 2: South (The Buildings of England)**. Harmondsworth 1983

The British Neo-Romantics 1935–1950, exh. cat. London, Fischer Fine Art, 1983

Chloe Colchester. **The New Textiles: Trends and Traditions**. London 1991

Matthew Collings. **Blimey! From Bohemia to Britpop: The London Artworld from Francis Bacon to Damien Hirst**. London 1997

Susan Compton (ed.). **British Art in the 20th Century: The Modern Movement**, exh. cat. London, Royal Academy of Arts, 1987

Helen Drutt English and Peter Dormer. **Jewelry of Our Time**. London 1995

Anton Ehrenzweig. **The Hidden Order of Art**. London 1967

Charlotte and Peter Fiell. **Modern Furniture Classics since 1945**. London 1991

Lyn FitzGerald. **The History of Mod**. www.geocities.com/Fashion Avenue/5362/history.html

Adrian Forty. 'Le Corbusier's British reputation', in **Le Corbusier: Architect of the Century**, exh. cat. London, Hayward Gallery, 1987

Kenneth Frampton. **Modern Architecture: A Critical History**. London 1980

Jonathan Glancey. **New British Architecture**. London 1989

Calouste Gulbenkian Foundation. **The Economic Situation of the Visual Artist**. London 1985

Alistair Hicks. **New British Art in the Saatchi Collection**. London 1989

Paul Huxley (ed.). **Exhibition Road: Painters at the Royal College of Art**, exh. cat. London, Royal College of Art, 1988

Christopher Johnstone. **Fifty 20th Century Artists in the Scottish National Gallery of Modern Art**. Edinburgh n.d. [c. 1984]

Nicola Kearton (ed.). **British Art: Defining the Nineties**. London 1995

G.E. Kidder Smith. **The New Architecture of Europe**. Harmondsworth 1962

R.B. Kitaj. 'Introduction', in **The Human Clay**, exh. cat. London, Hayward Gallery, 1976

Udo Kultermann. **Art-Events and Happenings**. London 1971

Alan and Isabella Livingston. **Dictionary of Graphic Design and Designers**. London 1992

Gabriele Lueg and Karin-Beate Phillips. **Highlights: Design aus Grossbritannien**, exh. cat. Cologne, Museum für Angewandte Kunst, 1997

Fiona McCarthy and Patrick Nuttgens. **Eye for Industry: Royal Designers for Industry 1936–1986**. London 1986

Charles McKean. 'The Twentieth Century', in Michael Raeburn (ed.). **Architecture of the Western World**. London 1980

Anne Massey. **Interior Design of the Twentieth Century**. London 1990

David Mellor. **The Sixties Art Scene in London**, exh. cat. London, Barbican Art Gallery, 1993

National Art Collections Fund Reviews, 1990–98

Terry A. Neff. **A Quiet Revolution: British Sculpture Since 1965**, exh. cat. Chicago, Museum of Contemporary Art, 1987

George Orwell. **The English People**. London 1947

Ted Owen and Denise Dickson. **High Art: A History of the Psychedelic Poster**. London 1999

Dr Andreas C. Papadakis (ed.). **40 Under 40: The New Generation in Britain**. London 1989

Nikolaus Pevsner. **The Englishness of English Art**. London 1956

David Robbins (ed.). **The Independent Group: Postwar Britain and the Aesthetics of Plenty**. Cambridge, MA, and London 1990

Sensation: Young British Artists from the Saatchi Collection, exh. cat. London, Royal Academy of Arts, 1997

Frances Spalding. **British Art Since 1900**. London 1986

Frances Spalding. **20th Century Painters and Sculptors**. Woodbridge 1990

The Tate Gallery: an illustrated companion. London 1984

Andrew Tucker. **The London Fashion Book**. London 1998

John A. Walker. **Glossary of Art, Architecture and Design since 1945**. Hamden, CT, 1973

Art journals and periodicals are invaluable in documenting the critical reception of artists' new work and the contemporary cultural environment. Many journals that were at the cutting edge were shortlived; of those in the mainstream – covering a very wide range of critical standpoints – the following are especially informative:

Art and Artists (1966–86)

Art and Design (1985–)

Art Monthly (1976–)

Art News and Review/Arts Review (1949–)

Flash Art (1981–)

Frieze (1991–)

Modern Painters (1988–)

Studio (to 1964)

Studio International (1965–87)

LIST OF ILLUSTRATIONS

Measurements are given in centimetres followed by inches, height before width before depth.

p. 14: **GRAHAM SUTHERLAND**
Somerset Maugham, 1949
Oil on canvas 137.2 x 63.5 (54 x 25).
Tate Gallery, London 1998

p. 15: **CERI RICHARDS**
Saudade, 1949
Oil on canvas 112.5 x 142.5 (44 $^1/_2$ x 56 $^1/_8$).
Pallant House Gallery, Chichester. Hussey Bequest 1985. By consent of Rhiannon Gooding. Estate of Ceri Richards 1999.
All rights reserved DACS

p. 22 above: **IVON HITCHENS**
Woodland and Blue Distance, c. 1950
Oil on canvas 40.6 x 74.3 (16 x 29 $^1/_4$). Private collection, London. Courtesy Waddington Galleries, London. © The Estate of Ivon Hitchens

p. 22 below: **EDWARD BAWDEN**
The English Pub, 1949–51
Oil on panel 176 x 506 (69 $^1/_4$ x 200).
Courtesy Peter Nahum Ltd at The Leicester Galleries, London. © Estate of Edward Bawden 1999. All rights reserved DACS

pp. 22–23: **CAREL WEIGHT**
Going Home, 1950
Oil on canvas 91.5 x 152.5 (36 x 54). Private collection. Photo courtesy Sotheby's Picture Library, London

p. 24 left: **ERNEST RACE**
Antelope chairs, 1951
Photo Hulton Getty

p. 24 right: **LUCIENNE DAY**
Calyx, 1951
Textile design for Heal's Wholesale & Export, Heal & Son Ltd
Screen-printed linen 63.5 x 76.2 (25 x 30).
V&A Picture Library, London

p. 25 left: **POWELL & MOYA WITH FELIX SAMUELY**
Skylon, 1951
British Architectural Library, RIBA, London

p. 25 inset: **ABRAM GAMES**
Festival of Britain logo, 1951
© Abram Games

p. 25 above right: **BRIAN PEAKE**
Science Exhibition at the Science Museum, London 1951
Photo The General Electric Company Plc, courtesy Design Council

p. 25 below right: **ALEXANDER MACKENDRICK**
The Man in the White Suit, 1951
Poster designed by S. John Woods and A.R. Thompson
Photo BFI Stills, Posters & Designs, London

pp. 26–27: **VICTOR PASMORE**
At work on a mural for the Regatta Restaurant, South Bank, 1951
Photo Hulton Getty

p. 28: **STANLEY SPENCER**
The Glen, Port Glasgow, 1952
Oil on canvas 76.2 x 50.9 (30 x 20).
Glasgow Museums: Art Gallery & Museum, Kelvingrove. © Estate of Stanley Spencer 1999. All Rights Reserved DACS

p. 29: **LUCIAN FREUD**
Girl With a White Dog, 1951–52
Oil on canvas 76.2 x 101.6 (30 x 40).
Tate Gallery, London 1998

pp. 30–31: **PETER LANYON**
Bojewyan Farms, 1951–52
Oil on masonite 121.9 x 243.9 (48 x 96).
Collection British Council, London

p. 30 below: **STANLEY WILLIAM HAYTER**
Night and Day, 1951–54
Engraving, soft-ground etching and scorper 60.3 x 45.2 (23 $^3/_4$ x 17 $^7/_8$). Copyright British Museum. © ADAGP, Paris and DACS, London 1999

p. 31 right: **BERNARD MEADOWS**
Black Crab, 1952
Bronze, height 43.2 (17). Gimpel Fils Gallery, London

p.32 above: **CECIL BEATON**
The Queen after her Coronation, 1953
Photo © Cecil Beaton/Camera Press

p. 32 below: **BILL BRANDT**
Untitled Nude, 1953
© Bill Brandt Archive Ltd

p. 33: **FRANCIS BACON**
Study after Velázquez's Portrait of Pope Innocent X, 1953
Oil on canvas 153 x 118 (60 $^1/_4$ x 46 $^1/_2$).
Purchased with funds from the Coffin Fine Arts Trust; Nathan Emory Coffin Collection of the Des Moines Art Center, 1980.1. Photo Michel Tropea, Chicago/© 1997 by the Des Moines Art Center. © Estate of Francis Bacon/ARS, NY and DACS, London 1999

p. 34 above: **DERRICK GREAVES**
Sheffield, 1953
Oil on canvas 86.2 x 203.3 (34 x 80).

Sheffield Galleries and Museum Trust/City Art Gallery

p. 34 below: **L.S. LOWRY**
Industrial Landscape, 1953
Oil on canvas 118 x 156 (46.5 x 61.5). Salford Museum & Art Gallery, Salford. Courtesy Mrs Carol Ann Danes

p. 35: **ALISON AND PETER SMITHSON**
Secondary School, Hunstanton, 1949–54
Photo courtesy Architects Journal

pp. 36–37: **ROBERT HERITAGE**
Sideboard made for G.W. Evans, c. 1954
Courtesy Fiell International Ltd, London.
Photo P. Hodsoll

pp. 38–39: **LCC ARCHITECTS**
Cadnam Point, Alton East Estate, Roehampton, 1951–55
Reproduced courtesy of the Architectural Review

p. 39 below: **PETER WOMERSLEY**
House at Farnley Hey, Yorkshire, 1953–55
Reproduced courtesy of the Architectural Review. Photo de Burgh Galwey

p. 40 above: **LYNN CHADWICK**
Winged Figures, 1955
Bronze, height 55.9 (22). Tate Gallery, London 1998

p. 40 below: **DAVID BOMBERG**
The Vigilante, 1955
Oil on canvas 61 x 50.7 (24 x 20). Scottish National Gallery of Modern Art, Edinburgh

p. 40 right: **BARBARA HEPWORTH**
Curved Form (Delphi), 1955
Scented guarea, height 106.7 (42). Ulster Museum, Belfast. © Alan Bowness, Hepworth Estate

p. 41: **BEN NICHOLSON**
December 1955 (Night Façade), 1955
Oil on board 108 x 116.2 (42 $^1/_2$ x 45 $^3/_4$).
Solomon R. Guggenheim Museum, New York. Photo by Carmelo Guadagno © The Solomon R. Guggenheim Foundation, New York (FN 57.1461). © Angela Verren-Taunt 1999. All Rights Reserved DACS

p. 42 above: **GEORGE HIM**
Schweppes advertisement, 1955–56
Courtesy Cadbury Schweppes Ltd

p. 42 below: **ENID SEENEY AND TOM ARNOLD**
'Homemaker' plate for Ridgway Potteries, 1955
© Manchester City Art Galleries

p. 43: **JOHN CAVANAGH**
Slink suit, 1955
Photo by Norman Parkinson. Courtesy Hamiltons Photographers Ltd, London

p. 44: **RICHARD HAMILTON**
Just What is it that Makes Today's Homes so Different, so Appealing?, 1956
Collage 26 x 25 (10 $^1/_4$ x 9 $^3/_4$). Kunsthalle, Tübingen. © Richard Hamilton 1999. All rights reserved DACS

p. 44 above: **KEITH VAUGHAN**
Fourth Assembly of Figures, 1956
Oil on canvas 45 x 48 (114.3 x 121.9). Castle Museum, Nottingham

p. 44 below: **HENRY MOORE**
The Fallen Warrior, 1956–57
Bronze, length 147 (57 $^7/_8$). Clare College, Cambridge. Photo James Austin

p. 46 above: **BERNARD LEACH**
Stoneware Pilgrim Bottle, c. 1957
Height 30.5 (12). Private collection. Photo Bonhams Auctioneers, London

p. 46 below: **WILLIAM SCOTT**
Orange Still Life with Figure, 1957
Oil on canvas 122 x 152 (48 x 60). Courtesy William Scott Foundation

p. 47 above: **JACK SMITH**
Creation and Crucifixion, 1957
Oil on board 243.8 x 304.3 (96 x 119 $^7/_8$).
Board of Trustees of the National Galleries on Merseyside, Walker Art Gallery, Liverpool

p. 47 below: **DAVID MELLOR**
'Pride' cutlery, 1954
Silver plate with white xylonite knife handle, designed for Walker & Hall Ltd. Winner of a Council of Industrial Design award in 1957
Courtesy David Mellor

p. 48 above: **RICHARD STEVENS AND PETER RODD**
Pendant light fitting from the 'Chelsea' range, 1958
Glass fittings by James Powell & Sons Ltd., Whitefriars Glass Company
Courtesy Target Gallery, London

pp. 48–49: **JOHN BRATBY**
Four Lambrettas and Three Portraits of Janet Churchman, 1958
Oil on canvas 182.9 x 365.8 (72 x 144).
© Granada Television

p. 49 above: **EDUARDO PAOLOZZI**
Japanese War God, 1958
Bronze, height 153 (60). Albright Knox Art Gallery, Buffalo. Photo David Farrell.

© Eduardo Paolozzi 1999. All Rights Reserved DACS

p. 50 above: ALEC ISSIGONIS
Austin Seven Mini, 1959
The National Motor Museum, Beaulieu

pp. 50–51: KENNETH ARMITAGE
Figure Lying on its Side, 5th Version, 1958–59
Bronze, length 81.3 (32). Collection British Council, London

p. 51 above: JULIAN TREVELYAN
Portrait of the Bird that Doesn't Exist, 1959
Ink and watercolour 24 x 31 (9 ¹/₂ x 12 ¹/₈). Musée National d'Art Moderne, Centre Georges Pompidou, Paris

p. 51 below: HAROLD COHEN
Vineyard, 1959
Textile design for Heal Fabrics Ltd, Heal & Son Ltd
Printed cotton, length 54.5 (21 ¹/₂). The Whitworth Art Gallery, University of Manchester

p. 52: BASIL SPENCE
Exterior of Coventry Cathedral, 1954–62, with **JACOB EPSTEIN**'s sculpture **St Michael and Lucifer**
Photo Collections/McQuillan & Brown

p. 53 above: GRAHAM SUTHERLAND
Christ in Glory in the Tetramorph, 1955–61
Tapestry woven by Marie Cuttoli
Photo Collections/McQuillan & Brown

p. 53 below: JOHN PIPER AND PATRICK REYNTIENS
Stained-glass windows, 1958–62, in the baptistery of Coventry Cathedral, with the font in the foreground
Photo Collections/McQuillan & Brown

pp. 54–55: ROBYN DENNY
Great Big London
Mural for the Austin Reed store, Regent Street, London, 1959
Oil on board 190 x 305 (74 ⁷/₈ x 120). Courtesy Autsin Reed Group Plc

p. 62: GORDON HOUSE
Diagonal, 1960
Casein on canvas, height 239 (94). Courtesy the artist

p. 63 above: DENYS LASDUN AND PARTNERS
Keeling House, Claredale Road, London, 1955–60
Photo Architectural Association, London/© Edmund Cooney

p. 63 below: DENYS LASDUN AND PARTNERS
Luxury flats, 26 St James's Place, 1959–60
Photo Robert P. Hymers

p. 64: GEORGE FULLARD
The Patriot, 1959–60
Painted wood 177.5 x 214.5 (70 x 84 ¹/₂). Southampton City Art Gallery Hampshire. Photo Bridgeman Art Library, London/New York

p. 65 above: ALAN DAVIE
Cornucopia, 1960
Oil on canvas 213 x 173 (83 ⁷/₈ x 68 ¹/₈). Glasgow Museums: Gallery of Modern Art

p. 65 below: ELISABETH FRINK
Harbinger Bird III, 1960
Bronze, height 43.5 (17). Private collection. Photo courtesy Waddington Galleries, London

p. 66: PETER BLAKE
Self-Portrait with Badges, 1961 (detail)
Oil on board 174.3 x 121.9 68 ⁵/₈ x 48). Tate Gallery, London 1998. © Peter Blake 1999. All Rights Reserved DACS

p. 67 left: MALCOLM SAYER AND WILLIAM HEYNES
E-Type Jaguar, 1961
Courtesy Jaguar & Daimler Heritage Trust, Coventry

p. 67 above: PETER PHILLIPS
For Men Only, Starring MM and BB, 1961
Oil and collage on canvas 274.5 x 152.5 (107 ⁷/₈ x 60). Centro de Arte Moderna – Fundaçion Calouste Gulbenkian, Lisbon

p. 67 below: DEREK BOSHIER
Airmail Letter, 1961
Oil on canvas 152.4 x 152.4 (60 x 60). Private collection

p. 68: HOWARD HODGKIN
Portrait of Mr and Mrs James Tower, 1962
Oil on canvas 91.5 x 121.5 (36 x 47 ⁷/₈). The Saatchi Gallery, London

p. 69: DAVID HOCKNEY
The Cruel Elephant, 1962
Oil on canvas 19 x 23 ⁵/₈ (48 x 60). Private collection. © David Hockney

pp. 70–71: FLETCHER/FORBES/GILL
Bus poster for Pirelli slippers, 1962
Courtesy Pentagram Design Ltd, London

pp. 72–73: ANTHONY CARO
Hopscotch, 1962
Aluminium 250 x 475 x 213 (98 ¹/₂ x 187 x 83 ⁷/₈). Collection of the artist. Courtesy Annely Juda Fine Art. Photo John Riddy

p. 73: ROBERT WELCH
Vase from the 'Alveston' range designed for Old Hall, J. & J. Wiggin Ltd, 1962
Stainless steel, height 25 (10). Courtesy Target Gallery, London

p. 74: PHILLIP KING
Genghis Khan, 1963
Plastic and painted steel 274.3 x 426.7 (108 x 168). Collection Neuberger Museum of Art, Purchase College, State University of New York. Purchased by the Purchase College Foundation with funds provided by Roy R. Neuberger. Photo Jim Frank

p. 75 left: LEWIS MORLEY
Christine Keeler, 1963
© Lewis Morley/Akehurst Bureau, London

p. 75 right: ROGER HILTON
Dancing Woman, 1963
Oil and charcoal on canvas 123 x 101.5 (48 ³/₈ x 40). Scottish National Gallery of Modern Art, Edinburgh. © Estate of Roger Hilton 1999. All Rights Reserved DACS

p. 76: ROBIN DAY
Polyprop chairs, 1963
Polypropylene sheet moulded in one piece with black nylon coated steel bases 73.7 x 53.5 x 41.9 (29 x 21 x 16 ¹/₂). V&A Picture Library, London

pp. 76–77: JOHN LATHAM
Untitled Relief Painting, 1963
Books, metal, wire, plaster, emulsion on hardboard 91.4 x 122 x 9 (36 x 48 x 3 ⁵/₈). Courtesy Lisson Gallery, London

pp. 78–79: WILLIAM TURNBULL
Spring Totem 2, 1963
Bronze, rosewood and stone 101.6 x 44.5 x 155 (40 x 10¹/₂ x 61). Private collection, courtesy Waddingon Galleries, London. Photo Richard Thomas

p. 80: BRIDGET RILEY
Crest, 1963
Oil on canvas 166 x 166 (65 ³/₈ x 65 ³/₈). Collection British Council, London

p. 81 above: TESS JARAY
Minuet, 1963
Oil on canvas 183 x 229 (72 x 90). Private collection

p. 81 below: MARTYN ROWLANDS
Delta telephone, 1963
© Design Council/DHRC, University of Brighton

p. 82 above: TERENCE CONRAN
The first Habitat carrier bag, 1964

RIBA Photographs Collection, London. Photo John Maltby

p. 82 below: DAVID ANNESLEY
Swing Low, 1964
Painted steel 128.3 x 175.9 x 36.8 (50 ¹/₂ x 69 ¹/₄ x 14 ¹/₂). Tate Gallery, London 1998

p. 82 right: MAX CLENDINNING
The designer's dining room, c. 1964
Photo Elizabeth Whiting & Associates, London

p. 83: R.B. KITAJ
The Ohio Gang, 1964
Oil and graphite on canvas 183.1 x 183.5 (72 ¹/₈ x 72 ¹/₄). The Museum of Modern Art, New York. Philip Johnson Fund. Photograph © 1998 The Museum of Modern Art, New York

p. 84: EDUARDO PAOLOZZI
Wittgenstein at the Cinema Admires Betty Grable, 1965, plate 12 from the **As is When** series
Screenprint 83 x 55 (32 ⁵/₈ x 21 ⁵/₈). Copyright British Museum. © Eduardo Paolozzi 1999. All Rights Reserved DACS

p. 85 above: ARCHIGRAM
Seaside Bubbles, 1965
Drawing by Ron Herron. Architectural Association, London/© Archigram

p. 85 below: RICHARD SMITH
Tailspan, 1965
Acrylic on wood 120 x 212.7 x 90.2 (47 ¹/₄ x 83 ³/₄). Tate Gallery, London 1998

p. 86 left: JOHN SCHLESINGER
Darling, 1965
Poster. Photo BFI Stills, Posters & Designs

p. 86 right: TERRY FROST
June, Red and Black, 1965
Oil on canvas 244.5 x 183.5 (96 ¹/₄ x 72 ¹/₄). Tate Gallery, London 1998

p. 87: DAVID BAILEY
Jane Birkin, 1965
© David Bailey

p. 88 above: MAURICE AGIS AND PETER JONES
Poster for **Space Place**, 1966

p. 88 below: GEOFFREY BAXTER
Drunken Bricklayers, 1966
Vases designed for Whitefriars Glass
Photo courtesy Richard Dennis Publications

pp. 88–89: JOHN HOYLAND
21.2.66, 1966

Oil on cotton duck 198 x 365 (78 x 144).
Private collection

p. 89: **GILLIAN AYRES**
Umbria, 1966
Oil on canvas 152.4 x 152.4 (60 x 60). Arts
Council Collection, Hayward Gallery, London.
Photo Bridgeman Art Library, London/New
York

p. 90 above: **MARY QUANT**
Miniskirt, c. 1966
Courtesy Mary Quant. Photo William Claxtom

p. 90 below: **WILLIAM TUCKER**
Memphis, 1966
Plywood and fibreglass 76.2 x 142.3 x 165.1 (30
x 56 x 65). Collection British Council, London

p. 92 above: **NIGEL WAYMOUTH AND
MICHAEL MAYHEW**
'Granny Takes a Trip' shopfront in King's
Road, Chelsea, featured in **Nova** magazine,
April 1967
Photography and design by Harri Peccinotti.
Courtesy of IPC Magazines, London

p. 92 below: **MARK BOYLE AND JOAN HILLS**
Sensual Laboratory Lightshow, c. 1967–68
© Mark Boyle and Joan Hills

pp. 92–93: Collection of posters, many by
MICHAEL ENGLISH, including his **UFO Love
Festival** poster, 1967
From Observer Magazine. Topham Picture
Library

p. 94: **TONY RAY-JONES**
Chatham May Queen, 1968
NMPFT/Science & Society Picture Library

p. 95: **STUART BRISLEY**
Ritual Murder Nodnol, 1968
Photo Peter Kuttner

p. 96: **PATRICK HERON**
Orange in Deep Cadmium with Venetian,
1969
Oil on canvas 208.3 x 335.3 (82 x 132). Private
collection. © Patrick Heron 1999. All Rights
Reserved DACS

p. 97 above: **TERRY GILLIAM**
Animation still from the **Monty Python's
Flying Circus** television series, 1969
Courtesy Python (Monty) Pictures Ltd,
London

p. 97 below: **LILIANE LIJN**
See Thru Koan, 1969
Fibreglass, perspex and motor 112 x 41.5 x 41.5
(44 x 16 3/8 x 16 3/8). Arts Council Collection.
Photo Bridgeman Art Library, London

p. 98: **DEREK BIRDSALL**
Pirelli Calendar, 1969
Photos © by Harri Peccinotti

p. 99 above: **ALAN ALDRIDGE**
Cover design for **The Beatles Illustrated
Lyrics**, 1969
Illustrations © 1969 Alan Aldridge Associates
Ltd, London

p. 99 below: **ALLEN JONES**
Table, 1969
Mixed media with metal flake on fibreglass
60.9 x 83.8 x 144.8 (24 x 57). Courtesy the
artist. Photo Erik Hesmerg TBC

p. 100: **JOE TILSON**
Transparency, The Five Senses, 1969
Plastic and colour print 147.3 x 147.3 x 5.1 (58 x
58 x 2). Tate Gallery, London 1998. © Joe
Tilson 1999. All Rights Reserved DACS

pp. 100–01: **RICHARD HAMILTON**
Swingeing London '67, 1968–69
Acrylic and metal on board 67.3 x 85.1
(26 1/2 x 33 1/2). Tate Gallery, London 1998.
© Richard Hamilton 1999. All rights reserved
DACS

pp. 108–09: **DAVID HOCKNEY**
Mr and Mrs Clark and Percy, 1970–71
Acrylic on canvas 213.4 x 304.8 (84 x 120).
Tate Gallery, London 1998. © David Hockney

p. 110 above: **BOB LAW**
In front of his painting **Number 95 Mister
Paranoia IV**, 1970
Oil on canvas 243.8 x 421.6 (96 x 166). Photo
Tate Gallery Archive, London/Lisson Gallery,
London

p. 110 below: **MICHAEL CRAIG-MARTIN**
On the Table, 1970
Wood, metal, water, rope 122 x 122 (48 x 48).
Collection of the artist. Courtesy Waddington
Galleries, London. Photo Prudence Cuming
Associatiates Ltd

p. 111: **GILBERT AND GEORGE**
The Singing Sculpture, 1971
Photo © Lord Snowdon/Camera Press.
Courtesy Anthony d'Offay Gallery, London

p. 112 above: **SUSANNA HERON**
Bracelet, 1971
Silver and resin. © Susanna Heron/Crafts
Council, London

p. 112 below: **PATRICK CAULFIELD**
Interior with Room Divider, 1971
Oil on canvas. Courtesy Waddington
Galleries, London

pp. 112–13: **TOM PHILLIPS**
Benches, 1971
Acrylic on canvas 121.9 x 276.2 (48 x 108 3/4).
Tate Gallery, London 1998

pp. 114–15: **RODNEY KINSMAN**
Omkstak chair, 1971
Tubular steel frame with punched sheet-steel
seat and back 53.5 x 74 x 51 (21 x 29 1/8 x 20).
V&A Picture Library, London

p. 115: **BRUCE McLEAN**
Posework for Plinths 1, 1971
Photograph on board 74.6 x 68.6 (29 3/8 x 27).
Tate Gallery, London 1998

pp. 116–17: **WILLIAM PYE**
Zemran, 1972
Stainless steel 518.2 x 548.6 x 274.3 (17 x 18 x
9). South Bank, London. Photo © Grant
Smith

p. 118 above: **BILL GIBB**
White-splashed brown fake ponyskin tight-
bodiced jacket with plum frill, tight-hipped
skirt flaring into scallops from the knee, from
Vogue magazine August 1972
Photo by Clive Arrowsmith@British
Vogue/The Condé Nast Publications Ltd

p. 118 below: **JOHN McCONNELL**
Biba logo, designed in 1969

p. 119: **WENDY RAMSHAW**
Ring Set, five turned pillar rings, 1971
Winner of Council of Industrial Design award
in 1972
Silver with amethyst, cornelian and
chrysoprase sphere. Private collection. Photo
David Watkins

p. 120: **HANS COPER**
Stoneware thistle form pot, c. 1972
Height 26.5 (10 1/2). Private
collection/Bonhams, London. Photo
Bridgeman Art Library, London/New York

pp. 120–21: **STEPHEN BUCKLEY**
Chestnuts, 1972
Mixed media on four panels 183 x 488 (72 x
192). Collection of the artist

p. 122 above: **LINDSAY ANDERSON**
Still from the film **O Lucky Man**, 1973.
Production design by Jocelyn Herbert
Photo BFI Stills, Posters & Designs, London

p. 122 below: **LEON KOSSOFF**
**Dalston Junction Ridley Road Street Market,
Stormy Morning**, 1973
Oil on board 139.7 x 183 (55 x 72). Private
collection

p. 123: **FRANK AUERBACH**
**Looking Towards Mornington Crescent
Station – Night**, 1973
Oil on canvas 121.9 x 121.9 (48 x 48). Sheffield
Galleries and Museum Trust. Photo
Marlborough Fine Art (London) Ltd

pp. 124–25: **RALPH ERSKINE**
Byker Wall, Newcastle-upon-Tyne, 1969–80
Reproduced courtesy of the Architectural
Review. Photo Bill Toomey

pp. 126–27: **FOSTER ASSOCIATES**
Willis, Faber & Dumas head office, Ipswich,
1970–75
Photo Richard Bryant/Arcaid

p. 128 above: **VICTOR BURGIN**
Sensation, 1975
Photographic print on board 127. 5 x 249.5
(50 1/8 x 98 1/4). Courtesy Lisson Gallery,
London

p. 128 below left: **F.H.K. HENRION**
Logo for the National Theatre, 1975
© F.H.K. Henrion

p. 128 below right: **JOHN DAVIES**
Head with Shell Device, 1973–75
Mixed media, height 27.3 (10 3/4). Courtesy
Marlborough Fine Art (London) Ltd

p. 129: **FRANCIS BACON**
Three Figures and Portrait, 1975
Oil and pastel on canvas 198.1 x 147.3 (78 x
58). Tate Gallery, London 1998

p. 130 above: **KENNETH MARTIN**
Chance, Order, Change 2 (Ultramarine Blue),
1976
Oil on canvas 91.4 x 91.4 (36 x 36). Arts
Council Collection, Hayward Gallery, London.
Photo Bridgeman Art Library, London/New
York

p. 130 below: **TIM HEAD**
Equilibrium (Knife Edge), 1975–76
Black and white photograph 50.6 x 50.4
(20 x 19 7/8). Arts Council Collection, Hayward
Gallery, London. Photo Bridgeman Art Library,
London/New York

p. 131: **JOHN WALKER**
Ostraca V, 1975–78
Acrylic and oil on canvas 302 x 245.7
(119 x 96 3/4). Arts Council Collection,
Hayward Gallery, London. Photo Bridgeman
Art Library, London/New York

p. 132 above: Sex Pistols Jubilee badge and
royal Jubilee badge
Collection of Frank R. Setchfield

p. 132 below: **JAMIE REID**
Never Mind the Bollocks, 1977
Sex Pistols album cover
Courtesy the artist

p. 133: **IAN BERRY**
Fulham Jubilee Celebrations, 1977
Photo © Ian Berry/Magnum

p. 134: **ZANDRA RHODES**
Ripped and slashed jersey dress with blue
stitching from the **Conceptual Chic** collection,
Spring/Summer 1977, with gold sandals by
Manolo Blahnik from **Vogue** magazine
September 1977
Photo by Lothar Schmid@British Vogue/The
Condé Nast Publications Ltd

p. 135 left: **BRITISH AIRCRAFT CORPORATION
WITH SUD AVIATION**
Concorde, 1964–77
Courtesy Rolls Royce Plc

p. 135 right: **MICHAEL HOPKINS**
Staircase, Downshire Hill, Hampstead,
1975–77
Photo Architectural Association, London/
© C. Shields

pp. 136–37: **LUCIE RIE**
Stoneware bowl, c. 1978
Diameter 33.7 (13 $^1/_4$). Private
collection/Bonhams, London. Photo
Bridgeman Art Library, London/New York

p. 138 above: **MALCOLM MORLEY**
**Christmas Tree (The Lonely Ranger Lost in
the Jungle of Desires)**, 1979
Oil on canvas 183 x 274.5 (72 x 108). Private
collection

p. 138 below: **MICHAEL ANDREWS**
Melanie and Me Swimming, 1978–79
Acrylic on canvas 182.9 x 182.9 (72 x 72). Tate
Gallery, London 1998

p. 139: **MARY KELLY**
**Post-Partum Document, Documentation VI
(3.806c)**, 1978–79
Slate and resin 35.6 x 27.9 (14 $^1/_8$ x 11). Arts
Council Collection, Hayward Gallery, London

p. 246 left: **DAVID BOWIE AND DAVID
MALLET**
Stills from the video **Ashes to Ashes**, 1980
Courtesy EMI Records UK

p. 146 right: **COLLETT DICKENSON PEARCE
& PARTNERS LTD**
Benson & Hedges advertisement for Gallaher
Ltd, 1980
Art direction and photography by Neil Godfrey
The Advertising Archives, London

p. 147: **SUSAN HILLER**
**Sentimental Representations in Memory of
my Grandmothers (Part 1 for Rose Ehrich)**,
1980–81
Rose petals in acrylic medium, ink on paper,
photocopies 113.7 x 81 (44 $^3/_4$ x 32). Arts
Council Collection, Hayward Gallery, London

p. 148: **TONY CRAGG**
Postcard Union Jack, 1981
Blue and red found plastic objects 300 x 400
(118 x 157 $^1/_2$). Leeds City Art Gallery. Photo
Bridgeman Art Library, London/New York

p. 149: **TONY CRAGG**
Britain Seen From the North, 1981
Mixed media relief 369.6 x 698.5 (145 $^1/_2$ x
275). Tate Gallery, London 1998

p. 150: **BRIDGET RILEY**
Sea Cloud, 1981
Oil on linen 170.5 x 171.5 (67 $^1/_8$ x 67 $^1/_4$).
Mayor Rowan Gallery, London

p. 151 above: **ELIZABETH FRITSCH**
Optical Pot, 1981
Stoneware 31.1 x 23.2 (12 $^1/_4$ x 9 $^1/_8$). V&A
Picture Library, London

p. 151 below: **DANIEL WEIL**
Radio in a welded PVC envelope, 1981
Design Department, Museum Boijmans van
Beuningen, Rotterdam

p. 152: **GILBERT AND GEORGE**
Naked Faith, 1982
Photo-piece 241 x 401 (95 x 158). Courtesy
Anthony d'Offay Gallery, London

p. 153 left: **ROBINSON LAMBIE-NAIRN LTD**
Corporate identity for Channel Four, 1982
Courtesy Robinson Lambie-Nairn Ltd

p. 153 above right: **TERRY JONES**
Cover of **i-D** magazine, 1982
Courtesy **i-D** Magazine

p. 153 below right: **TERRY FARRELL AND
PARTNERS**
TV AM Building, London, 1981–82
Photo Richard Bryant/Arcaid

p. 154 left: **JAKE TILSON**
Bar, The Highstreet SW11, 1983
Mixed media diorama 251 x 76 x 61 (98 $^7/_8$ x
30 x 24). Private collection

p. 154 right: **ALISON WILDING**
Pond, 1983
Copper, portland roach, slate 27 x 183 x 183
(10 $^5/_8$ x 72 x 72). Private collection

p. 155: **STEPHEN FARTHING**
The Nightwatch, 1983
Oil paint, beeswax, damar varnish on cotton
duck 173 x 250 (68 x 98 $^3/_8$). Bradford Art
Gallery and Museums, courtesy
Contemporary Art Society

p. 156: **BARRY FLANAGAN**
Carving No. 1, 1983
Romano scuro marble 72 x 151.1 x 78 (28 $^1/_4$ x
59 $^1/_2$ x 30 $^3/_4$). Collection of the artist.
Courtesy Waddington Galleries, London

p. 157 above: **IAN HAMILTON FINLAY WITH
NICHOLAS SLOAN**
**The Present Order is the Disorder of the
Future**, 1983
Stonypath Garden, Little Sparta, Dunsyre.
Photo David Paterson

p. 157 below: **PETER SAVILLE**
Power, Corruption and Lies, 1983
New Order album cover
Courtesy the artist

pp. 158–59: **RICHARD DEACON**
Two Can Play, 1983
Galvanized steel 183 x 365.8 x 183 (72 x 144 x
72). Private collection

p. 160 left: **NEVILLE BRODY**
Cover of **The Face** magazine, issue No. 50,
June 1984, featuring T-shirts by Katharine
Hamnett
Photo © Mario Testino. Courtesy The Face

p. 160 right: **MALCOLM GARRETT**
The Reflex, 1984
Duran Duran single cover
Courtesy the artist

p. 161: **JOHN HILLIARD**
Dark Shadow, 1984
Acrylic and ink on canvas 221 x 300 (87 x 118).
Courtesy the artist

p. 162: **EDWARD ALLINGTON**
The Groan as a Wound Weeps, 1984
Wood, steel, plastic tomatoes, polystyrene,
plaster, paint 211 x 135 (83 x 53). Private
collection. Courtesy Lisson Gallery, London.
Photo Edward Woodman

pp. 162–63: **HOWARD HODGKIN**
Clean Sheets, 1982–84
Oil on wood 55.8 x 91.4 (22 x 36). Tate Gallery,
London 1998

p 164 above: **DAVID WATKINS**
Voyager, 1984
Neckpiece: neoprene-coated steel, wood, 5
sections 34.9 x 30.5 (13 $^3/_4$ x 12). Courtesy the
artist. Photo David Watkins

p 164 below: **RICHARD WENTWORTH**
Fin, 1983–84
Galvanized and tinned steel 32 x 63 x 41
(12 $^1/_2$ x 23 $^3/_4$ x 16 $^1/_8$). Private collection

p. 165: **RICHARD LONG**
Piemonte Stone Circle, 1984
Diameter 550 (215 $^1/_2$). Courtesy Castello di
Rivoli – Museo d'Arte Contemporanea, Rivoli,
Turin

pp. 166–67: **MICHAEL HOPKINS & PARTNERS**
Schlumberger Cambridge Research Centre,
Phase 1, 1982–85
Photo Dennis Gilbert/Arcaid

pp. 168–69: **ART & LANGUAGE**
Index: Incident in a Museum V, 1985
Oil and alogram on canvas 174 x 271 (68 $^1/_2$ x
106 $^3/_4$). Courtesy Lisson Gallery, London

p. 169: **TIMNEY-FOWLER**
Textile from the **Neoclassical** collection, 1985
Black and white cotton. Courtesy Timney-
Fowler Design Studio, London

pp. 170–71: **DAVID MACH**
Fuel for the Fire, August 1986
Riverside Studios, London. Photos Edward
Woodman

p. 172 left: **MARTIN PARR**
New Brighton
Photographed for **The Last Resort** project,
published 1985–86
Photo © Martin Parr/Magnum

p. 172 right: **CALUM COLVIN**
Death of Venus, 1986
Cibachrome print 76 x 51 (30 x 20). Private
collection

p. 173: **HELEN CHADWICK**
Vanity II, 1986
Cibachrome print, mounted in circular matt,
diameter 60.9 (24). © The Estate of Helen
Chadwick. Photo Edward Woodman

p. 174: **RICHARD ROGERS AND PARTNERS**
Lloyd's Building, London, 1978–86
Photo Richard Bryant/Arcaid

p. 175: **JAMES STIRLING AND MICHAEL
WILFORD**
Clore Gallery, Tate Gallery, London, 1980–86
Photo Richard Bryant/Arcaid

p. 176: **LISA MILROY**
Tyres, 1987
Oil on canvas 203.2 x 284.5 (80 x 112).
The Saatchi Gallery, London. Courtesy
Waddington Galleries, London. Photo Sue
Omerod

p. 177: **RICHARD WILSON**
20/50, 1987
Used sump oil, steel and wood, Matt's
Gallery, London 1987. Courtesy Matt's Gallery.
Photo Edward Woodman

p. 178: **BRIDGET BAILEY**
Hand-painted, steam-pleated silk organza,
1987
Courtesy the artist. Photo John Kaine

p. 179 left: **EVA JIRIČNA**
Interior of Legends nightclub, London, 1987
Photo Richard Bryant/Arcaid

p. 179 right: **PAULA REGO**
The Policeman's Daughter, 1987
Acrylic on paper on canvas 213.4 x 152.4
(84 x 60). Courtesy Marlborough Fine Art
(London) Ltd

p. 180: **MICHAEL ROWE**
Conditions for Ornament No. 6, 1988
Brass, copper, tinned finish 55 x 44 x 60
(21 $^5/_8$ x 17 3/8 x 23 $^5/_6$). Courtesy the artist.
Photo David Cripps

pp. 180–81: **ANDY GOLDSWORTHY**
Blades of grass
creased and arched
secured with thorns
Penpont, Dumfriesshire,
14 August 1988
Courtesy the artist

p. 182 above left: **DANNY LANE**
Solomon chair and table, 1988
Clear and sandblasted float glass with
stainless steel studding, table with etched
marble shelf, chair 117 x 62 x 42.5 (46 x 24 $^1/_2$
x 16 $^3/_4$); table 130 x 110 x 40 (51 x 43 $^3/_8$ x 15
$^3/_4$). Courtesy the artist

p. 182 below left: **NIGEL COATES**
Genie stool, 1988
Carved, sandblasted solid ash seat on twisted
mild steel legs 67 x 34 x 41 (26 $^3/_8$ x 13 $^3/_8$ x
16 $^1/_8$). Courtesy the artist

p. 182 above right: **STEVEN CAMPBELL**
**Painting Influenced by the Foot of a Chair and
the Top of a Building**, 1988
Oil on canvas 243.8 x 243.8 (96 x 96).
Courtesy Marlborough Fine Art (London) Ltd

p. 182 below right: **TOM DIXON**
'S' chairs, 1988
Bent mild steel frames with latex rubber, rush
and wicker coverings. Courtesy the artist

p. 183: **RON ARAD**
The Big Easy Volume 2, 1988
Hollow welded stainless steel with polished-

off welds 120 x 130 x 100 (47 x 51 x 39).
Courtesy the artist

p. 184: **PETER GREENAWAY**
Still from **Drowning by Numbers**, 1988,
showing the Bognor Brothers, Jonah (Kenny
Ireland) and Moses (Michael Percival)
Photo Ronald Grant Archive, London

pp. 184–85: **BILL WOODROW**
Let's Eat Fish, 1988
Steel, bronze, fabric, alkyd varnish 156 x 407 x
370 (61 $^3/_8$ x 160 $^1/_4$ x 120 $^7/_8$). Courtesy Lisson
Gallery, London

p. 186 above: **GEORGINA GODLEY**
Corrugated Strides, 1989
Silk taffeta trousers
Courtesy the artist

p. 186 right: **STEPHEN CONROY**
Che Gelida Manina, 1988–89
Oil on canvas 153 x 123.2 (60 $^1/_4$ x 48 $^1/_2$).
Courtesy Marlborough Fine Art (London) Ltd

p. 186 below: **GEORGINA VON ETZDORF**
Invitation to the **Rhythm & Blues** collection,
Autumn/Winter 1989
Courtesy the artist

p. 187: **CRAIGIE AITCHISON**
Portrait of Patrice Felix Tchicaya, 1989
Oil on canvas 30.5 x 25.5 (12 x 19). Private
collection. Courtesy Timothy Taylor Gallery,
London

pp. 194–95: **ANISH KAPOOR**
Untitled, 1990
Fibreglass and pigment, triptych, each 250 x
167 (98 $^3/_8$ x 65 $^3/_4$). Courtesy Lisson Gallery,
London. Photo Tom Haartsen, Otterlo

p. 196: **VIVIENNE WESTWOOD**
From the **Portrait** collection, Autumn/Winter
1990
Photo © Anthony Crickmay/Camera Press

p. 197 above: **PETER FLUCK AND ROGER LAW**
Spitting Image puppet of Margaret Thatcher,
1990
Spitting Image/Central TV

p. 197 below: **BOYD WEBB**
Mezzanine, 1990
Colour photograph 123 x 158 (48 $^3/_8$ x 62 $^1/_8$).
Courtesy the artist

p. 198 above: **RAY FLAVELL**
Greenpiece, 1991
Blown and flat glass construction, cut and
polished with sandblasting 30 x 40 x 12 (11 $^7/_8$
x 15 $^3/_4$ x 4 $^3/_4$). Victoria & Albert Museum,
London. Photo courtesy the artist

p. 198 below: **NEVILLE BRODY**
Poster for the typeface **F State**, from **Fuse 1**,
1991 published by FontShop International
Courtesy the artist

pp. 198–99: **CORNELIA PARKER**
Cold Dark Matter: An Exploded View, 1991
A garden shed and contents blown up for the
artist by the British army, the fragments
suspended around a lightbulb. Installation at
Chisenhale Gallery, London. Tate Gallery
Collection. Courtesy Frith Street Gallery. Photo
Max Glendinning

pp. 200–01: **ZAHA HADID**
London 2066, 1991
Painting for **Vogue** magazine (UK). Computer
modelling Daniel R. Oakley. Courtesy the
artist

p. 200: **PETER DOIG**
The Architect's Home in the Ravine, 1991
Oil on canvas 200 x 275 (78 $^3/_4$ x 108 $^1/_4$).
The Art Collection of Arthur Andersen & Co.,
London. Courtesy Victoria Miro Gallery,
London

p. 202 above: **PETER CHANG**
Bracelet, 1992
Acrylic, polyester, PVC found objects,
diameter 19.7 x 4.4 (7 $^3/_4$ x 1 $^3/_4$). Courtesy the
artist

p. 202 below: **GARY HUME**
Naturalist, 1992
Oil and collage on panel (3 parts) 243.8 x
355.6 (96 x 140). Courtesy Mathew Marks
Gallery, New York

p. 203: **LUCIAN FREUD**
Back View (Leigh Bowery), 1992
Oil on canvas 183 x 137.2 (72 x 54). Courtesy
Acquavella Galleries, New York

p. 204 left: **CAROLINE BROADHEAD**
Wobbly Dress II, 1992
Nylon 115 x 55 x 30 (43 $^1/_2$ x 21 $^5/_8$ x 11 $^7/_8$).
Courtesy Barratt Marsden Gallery, London.
Photo Peter Mackertich

p. 204 right: **FRED BAIER**
Steel chairs, 1992
Folded steel, plated with copper and zinc
90 x 50 x 45 (35 x 20 x 18). Courtesy the artist.
Photo © David Cripps

p. 205: **SHIRAZEH HOUSHIARY**
Bright Night in Dark Day, 1992
Copper and lead 13 x 96 x 96 (5 $^1/_8$ x 37 $^7/_8$ x
37 $^7/_8$). Courtesy Lisson Gallery, London.
Photo Sue Ormerod

p. 206: **RACHEL WHITEREAD**
House, 1993
Sprayed concrete. Commissioned by Artangel
Trust and Beck's, corner of Grove Road on
Roman Road, London E3, destroyed 1994.
Courtesy Anthony d'Offay Gallery, London.
Photo Sue Ormerod

p. 207: **SEAN SCULLY**
Vita Duplex, 1993
Oil on canvas 254 x 330.2 (100 x 130).
Courtesy Waddington Galleries, London

p. 208 above: **DOUGLAS GORDON**
Psycho, 1993
Black and white photograph, edition of 10,
46 x 59.9 (18 $^1/_8$ x 23 $^1/_2$). Produced in
collaboration with Tramway, Glasgow.
Courtesy Lisson Gallery, London. Photo John
Riddy

p. 208 below: **TERENCE CONRAN**
Quaglino's ashtray and salt and pepper pot,
1993
Courtesy the artist

p. 209: **JULIAN OPIE**
Imagine You are Driving, 1993
Acrylic on wood, glass and aluminium
93 x 123 x 3 (36 $^5/_8$ x 48 $^1/_2$ x 1 $^1/_8$). Courtesy
Lisson Gallery, London

p. 210: **NICK PARK**
Still from the animated film **The Wrong
Trousers**, 1993 produced by Aardman
Animations
™ © Aardman/Wallace & Gromit Ltd 1993.
Licensed by BBC Worldwide

pp. 210–11: **ANTONY GORMLEY**
Field for the British Isles, 1993
Installation Tate Gallery, Liverpool. Terracotta,
dimensions variable, each figure approx.
8–26 cm (3 $^1/_8$–10 $^1/_4$), approx. 40,000
figures. Courtesy Jay Jopling, London

p. 212 above: **MONA HATOUM**
Corps Etranger, 1994
Video installation 350 x 300 x 300 (137 $^7/_8$ x
118 $^1/_8$ x 118 $^1/_8$). Courtesy the artist

p. 212 below: **DAMIEN HIRST**
Away From the Flock, 1994
Steel, glass, lamb, formaldehyde solution
96.5 x 148.5 x 51 (38 x 58 $^1/_2$ x 20). The Saatchi
Gallery, London. Courtesy Jay Jopling, London

p. 213: **MARK WALLINGER**
**Half-Brother (Exit to
Nowhere/Machiavellian)**, 1994
Oil on canvas 230 x 300 (90 $^1/_2$ x 118 $^1/_8$).
Tate Gallery, London 1998. Courtesy Anthony
Reynolds Gallery, London

p. 214 above: **DONOVAN WYLIE**
Children from the A46 site playing in a nearby field, 1994
From the Losing Ground project, 1993–95
Photo © Donovan Wylie/Magnum

p. 214 below: **MAT COLLISHAW**
Leopardskin Lily, 1995
Transparency and lightbox, edition of 8,
50 x 76 (19 ⁵/₈ x 30). Courtesy Lisson Gallery,
London

p. 215: **DEREK JARMAN**
The artist's garden, Dungeness, Kent
Photo © Howard Sooley, 1995

pp. 216–17: **JOHN PAWSON**
Interior of the architect's house in Notting
Hill, 1992–95
Photo Richard Glover/Arcaid

p. 218 left: **DESIGNERS REPUBLIC**
Present, 1996
CD artwork for Sun Electric on R&S Records.
Designed and built by the Designers
Republic. Courtesy the artists

p. 218 right: **TOMATO**
Poster for the film **Trainspotting**, 1996
© Polygram/Pictorial Press

p. 218 below right: **WOLFF OLINS**
Corporate identity for Orange™, 1996
Designed by Doug Hamilton, Robbie
Laughton and Daren Cook
Courtesy Wolff Olins and Hutchison Microtel
Ltd, London

p. 219 above: **SAM TAYLOR-WOOD**
Pent-Up, 1996
Five screen laser disc projection with sound,

shot on 16mm, duration 10 minutes,
30 seconds. Courtesy Jay Jopling, London.
Photo Justin Westover

p. 219 below: **GILLIAN WEARING**
60 Minutes Silence, 1996
Video projection, duration 60 minutes.
Courtesy Maureen Paley/Interim Art, London

p. 220 above: **INFLATE**
UFO Light, designed by Nick Crosbie, 1996
PVC inflatable ceiling light 45 x 45 x 15
(17 ³/₄ x 17 ³/₄ x 6). Courtesy Inflate Ltd,
London

p. 220 below: **JAKE AND DINOS CHAPMAN**
Zygotic, 1996
Fibreglass, resin and paint 170 x 210 x 100
(67 x 82 ³/₄ x 39 ³/₈). Courtesy the artists

p. 221: **RANKIN**
Hungry, 1996
Photo © Rankin/Dazed & Confused

p. 222: **CHRIS OFILI**
The Holy Virgin Mary, 1996
Paper collage, oil paint, glitter, polyester resin,
map pins, elephant dung on linen 243.5 x
182.9 (95 ⁷/₈ x 72). The Saatchi Gallery,
London. Courtesy Victoria Miro Gallery,
London

p. 223 above: **JENNY SAVILLE**
Shift, 1996–97
Oil on canvas 365.8 x 365.8 (144 x 144).
The Saatchi Gallery, London

p. 224 below: **PHILIP EGLIN**
Seated Nude, 1996
Ceramic (earthenware) 70 x 38 x 26 (27 ¹/₂ x 15
x 10 ¹/₄). Private collection. Photo Ken Shelton

p. 224: **ALEXANDER McQUEEN**
From the **Bellmer la Poupée** collection,
Spring/Summer 1997
Photo © Nick Knight

p. 225: **JOHN GALLIANO**
Necklace for Christian Dior Autumn/Winter
1997–98
Photo © Nick Knight

p. 226 above left: **WHY NOT ASSOCIATES**
Poster for the 'Sensation' exhibition at the
Royal Academy of Arts, 1997
Cover Photography Rocco Redondo and
Photodisc

p. 226 below left: **MAAZ**
Doorknobs, 1997
Various objects in resin and aluminium 6.5 x
5.9 (2 ¹/₂ x 2 ³/₈). Courtesy Maaz Ltd, London

p. 226 right: **JAMES DYSON**
Dyson Dual Cyclone™ DC02, 1995
Winner of the Design Council Award for
European Design in 1997
Courtesy Dyson Ltd

p. 227: **FIONA RAE**
Untitled (Sky Shout), 1997
Acrylic on canvas 274.3 x 243.8 (108 x 96).
The Saatchi Gallery, London. Courtesy
Waddington Galleries, London. Photo
Prudence Cuming Associates Ltd

p. 228: **COLIN ST JOHN WILSON**
British Library, London, 1982–98
Photo Richard Bryant/Arcaid

p. 229: **TOM HUNTER**
Woman Reading Possession Order, 1998
Mounted photographic print 150 x 120

(59 x 47 ¹/₄). The Saatchi Gallery, London.
Photo © Tom Hunter

pp. 230–31: **MICHAEL CRAIG-MARTIN**
Room 3 from **Always Now**, a site-specific
project at the Kunstverein, Hanover, 1998.
Includes **Untitled**, 1989. Venetian blinds
243.8 x 243.8 x 3.2 (96 x 96 x 1 ¹/₄). Courtesy
Waddington Galleries, London. Photo Helge
Mundt, courtesy Kunstverein, Hannover

p. 232 above: **DON BROWN**
Don, 1998 (detail)
Aluminium 176 x 64 x 68 (69 ¹/₄ x 25 ¹/₈ x
26 ³/₄). Photo Martin Thompson

p. 232 below: **AUDIOROM LTD**
www.audiorom.com
News page from the AudioRom website, 1998
Courtesy AudioRom Ltd/André Ktori

p. 232 right: **JONATHAN IVE**
iMac, 1998
Courtesy Apple Computer UK Ltd

p. 233: **IAN DAVENPORT**
**Poured Painting: Lime Green, Pale Yellow,
Lime Green**, 1998
Household paint on medium density
fibreboard 182.9 x 182.9 (72 x 72). Collection
of the artist. Courtesy Waddington Galleries,
London. Photo Prudence Cuming
Associatiates Ltd

pp. 234–35: **RICHARD ROGERS PARTNERSHIP**
The Millennium Dome under construction,
Greenwich, London, 1997–99
Richard Rogers Partnership with engineers
Buro Happold
Photo Richard Bryant/Arcaid